DEFINING MUSIC THERAPY
SECOND EDITION

Kenneth E. Bruscia

Barcelona PUBLISHERS

Second Edition

ISBN 1-891278-07-X

2 4 6 8 9 7 5 3 1

Distributed throughout the world by

Barcelona Publishers
4 White Brook Road - Lower Village
Gilsum NH 03448
Tel: 603-357-0236 Fax: 603-357-2073
SAN 298-6299

Cover illustration and design: Frank McShane

Printed in the United States of America

This book is dedicated
to
my best friend

Daniel A. Pardo

Contents

FOREWORD

I did not write a foreword to the first edition, and as my mind is presently racing with things I want to say in introducing this version, I certainly wonder why I did not. Perhaps in 1989 I did not think it necessary or important for me to give my own perspective on writing such a technical book—well, now I do.

The first edition has been quoted, misquoted, plagiarized, criticized, praised, translated, overlooked, purposely ignored, and even angrily dismissed. This pleases me a lot! At the same time, I cannot help wonder why the book evokes such diverse reactions. Was it the definition? The questions I posed? Were the answers controversial? Was it the terminology I used? Was it that I drew boundaries and made fine distinctions? Or was it the complex issues that were raised in doing so?

Interestingly, I have noticed that philosophical orientation to the field is of very little value in predicting one's reaction to the book. Some therapists in the tight and right camp loved it, some hated it; some in the loose and fringy camp loved it, some hated it; and the same split was observed in the great majority of eclectics in the middle.

For some, the book was disturbing because it drew clear boundaries, and placed various practices within them. For them, such definitions place unnecessary limits on who we are and what we do, and though they provide a collective identity and thereby help others to understand what music therapy is, they also camouflage the many individual identities (and egos) that make up our field. Another disturbing thing about the book, for some, was that it put into boxes the many magical things we do as music therapists. Many feel that it is banal to put into words all the ineffable experiences that we share with clients through music.

On the other hand, many found the book a positive contribution. For some, it brought a brief respite to the continual soul-searching that seems part and parcel of being a music therapist. Maybe conceptual boxes provide the support we need to explore the boundless therapeutic potentials of music, and the daunting task of becoming a competent music therapist. For many, terms and definitions do provide clarity, legitimacy and validation; they give us a persona, and they also reassure us that we are not alone—or delusional in our beliefs about our work. Furthermore, words themselves, even for the most nonverbal musician, can bring incredible insights to one's own work as well as the work of others. We do need and want to communicate, and to do so, we have to find words for the ideas and experiences that we have, and certainly this book constitutes a search for the right words.

So what is it about this book that hits so many different nerves? My own opinion is that it exposes and attempts to work through the identity issues that seem to be at the core of our personality, both as individual music therapists and as a profession at large. This seems most obvious when interviewing high-school students applying for entrance into a music therapy degree program. They sum up our collective identity struggle quite articulately when they look you proudly in the eyes and say: "Well, I have always loved music, and I have always loved psychology (or medicine, or people), and I would really like to have a job where I can help others; and so when I discovered that there was such a thing as music therapy, which put all of these things together, I knew it was for me." I have never met a music therapist who has not uttered some version of this statement at one time or another during their career, and this seems quite incredible to me. It seems as if we are saying: I am this—but not entirely; I am that—but not entirely; and so I want to be and do both—but not entirely.

Of course, this kind of split is a basic human dilemma, and integration is a very healthy way of dealing with it; but in our case, we have built an entire discipline and profession by ignoring, crossing, bridging, or integrating the many boundaries within and between music and health care. This will become more obvious when we see the number of professional boundaries that music therapists negotiate within the everyday reality of their work, and the number of distinctions that we make within practice, theory and research. For this reason, I have always wondered whether what draws individuals into music therapy is a basic need to work around boundaries and splits. As a group, we seem to be most comfortable when boundaries are clearly confusing, or confusingly clear. We seem to enjoy dancing over cracks in the intersecting sidewalks of health care and the arts!

What else could explain the defensive polarities that we find among music therapists? At the one extreme are those who overcompensate for the boundary confusions, by insisting on adherence to one classification system and a single vocabulary to describe all of music therapy; and on the other extreme are those who overcompensate by insisting on diversity, no classification systems, and multiple vocabularies. Meanwhile, the middle sway back and forth, wondering which way the scale will eventually tilt.

From my earliest years as a music therapy educator, I had suspected that the field is built around boundary and identity struggles, but it was not until several years later that I began to realize it more fully. In 1982, I was asked to edit the first *International Newsletter of Music Therapy*, and not knowing where or how to begin, I decided to ask every association of music therapy around the world to send me their official definition of music therapy. The replies were astonishing to me, and I was both fascinated and overwhelmed by the fundamental differences I found in how they defined who they were and what they did. Each country seemed to be at different stages of identity formation, and each seemed to have its own unique focus.

As an outgrowth of this survey, I decided to give a presentation at a regional conference, entitled "Our Identity as *Music* Therapists." Unexpectedly, as I was to begin, the organizer of the conference asked if she could videotape the presentation. I was somewhat reluctant, because I did not think that the topic or my ideas were particularly tintillating, but I agreed anyway. Then, much to my surprise, the audience reacted quite excitedly. They seemed catalyzed, if not taunted, by the questions that I posed, and the enormous variations in definitions of music therapy. One year later, I was shocked to learn that the tape had traveled around the country and had worn out from use. I was flattered, but even more, I was intrigued. What questions were music therapists struggling to answer? And so, it was this reaction to that presentation that ultimately led to my writing of the first edition of *Defining Music Therapy*.

The first writing was terribly difficult. I had trouble sequencing the ideas without being repetitious, I had trouble making the distinctions I had set out to make, and I had trouble expressing myself in a way that was easy to read and understand. Fortunately however, the last nine years of using the book in my introductory course has taught me a lot, and though I may not have found all the remedies in this edition, I have certainly tried to accommodate the many suggestions and criticisms of my students. The main feedback from them has been that I raised more questions than I answered. I can certainly understand this perception, because when I was writing it, I was afraid that I would be perceived as giving *too many* answers, and so I purposely hedged, hid and ducked whenever I did give them. And for this same reason, many of my colleagues criticized the book because they felt that I had not revealed my own personal views. I do hope that perceptions of this edition will be different. I feel that I have taken a lot of stances in this book, and that I have tried to formulate answers to many of the questions that seem to bedevil music therapy.

I decided to do a second edition, not only because I wanted to improve the book, but also because my perspective has changed considerably in the last nine years. Readers do not always realize that authors move on. The first edition of this book was not my last word on the subject! I am not the same person that wrote the 1989 version: I do not think the same way, I do not feel the same way, and I have completely different questions and answers as a music therapist, and as a human being. I do not want to be cemented into the person or professional that I was then, at least, not without some recognition that I am still in process—and I can still change my mind. More important, I certainly do not have any final answers, nor do I expect to have any in the very near future!

Thus, the second edition is substantively different from the first. Given the space limitations here, I can only outline the main changes I have made, and I urge the reader to consider their implications carefully as they come across them in the text. The main changes are as follows:

- After the definition is presented in Chapter 3, one entire chapter is given to each word in the definition. This is a significant expansion of the ideas presented in the first edition.
- Only one word in the definition has been changed. I substituted "to *achieve* health with "to *promote* health." This signals a complete shift in my ideas about the nature of health; it is a continuum rather than an either-or state.
- Much more attention has been given to defining both health and music (See Chapters 10 and 11).
- Chapter 13 ("Types of Music Experience") is a new addition to the book. It defines the four main methods of music therapy, and the various ways in which they are implemented.

- Chapter 15 ("Dynamic Forces") presents a theory on the various ways that music experiences are conceived and utilized in music therapy. This is entirely new.
- The original areas of practice have been redefined, and several areas in the first edition have been subsumed under other areas. For example, the new area called "didactic" practices now includes several areas that were originally separate (viz., educational, instructional, and supervisory/training practices). Other previously separate areas, such as activity practices and creative arts therapy practices, have now been subsumed under other areas as merely different approaches.
- An entirely new area of practice has been identified and described. It is called "Ecological" (see Chapter 23).
- Three chapters have been added to define research and theory, and the various approaches therein.
- The Appendix has been updated to include new definitions of music therapy.
- The References have been updated, and more examples have been provided for many of the practices.

With all this said, I can now state the specific purposes of this edition:

- To articulate the questions that have endured in defining music therapy;
- To examine similarities and dissimilarities in how music therapy is conceived and practiced, and to sketch out internal and external boundaries for the field accordingly;
- To construct a vocabulary which reflects these boundaries, and which respects the many differentiations found in research, practice, and theory;
- To provide the necessary foundation for the development of "indigenous" theories of music therapy—which I define as theories that emerge from clinical practices in the field, rather than from theories of music or theories of therapy.

- To reduce the fallacies and exclusions that have impeded our growth as a discipline, and that have obstructed our understanding of one another within the profession.

Last but not least, I want to clarify my concept of this book, and what I hope it will accomplish. Please understand that I do not regard the definitions I give here as true or final—they are only my constructs, and as such, they are arguable, if not in some cases, completely arbitrary. In fact, in some cases, I have actually created words and phrases to describe the differences I have found in concept and practice. And similarly, the answers that I offer to the questions posed are strictly my own. I have made lots of decisions in offering all these definitions and constructing this vocabulary, and I want the reader to know that these are *my* decisions. My intent has not been to discover what is true or false, or to propose a vocabulary that is right for everyone. I am not trying to establish a dictionary for music therapy, I am merely trying to identify the main variables involved in making basic discriminations in our field. Thus, the names and definitions are not important; what really matters is the discriminatory acumen needed to understand how one concept or practice in music therapy is similar and dissimilar to another. Thus, defining is acknowledging and supporting individual identities within a collective context. For me, these definitions and discriminations are not only the very basis of all discovery and learning, they also provide the necessary context for mutual respect among professionals. If we take the time to study one another's work, and if we can recognize and respect the uniqueness of each approach, as well as what unites us, then we can marvel at the diversity of music therapy, and appreciate one another as contributors to that diversity.

Kenneth E. Bruscia, Ph.D. MT-BC
Professor of Music Therapy
Temple University
July 30, 1998

DEFINING MUSIC THERAPY
SECOND EDITION

Chapter One

THE NEED FOR
DEFINITIONS

Defining music therapy is an integral part of being a music therapist. Hardly a day goes by that a music therapist is not asked the inevitable "What is music therapy?" The question arises when meeting clients and their families for the first time, when starting a new job, upon being introduced to coworkers and administrators, upon meeting colleagues in other fields, when talking to prospective students, when recruiting subjects for research, when writing about the field, and in countless other professional situations. And if that were not enough, it is also the first topic of discussion in many social situations, such as when being introduced at a party or when meeting a new friend. It never fails: After the initial "What do you do?" and reply "I'm a music therapist," there will be a long, respectful silence, a dazed look, and then the inevitable: "Exactly what is music therapy?" Then, after receiving an initial response, most people will ask more detailed questions, and it is usually necessary to give a more complex and elaborate definition. And this is certainly not the last time these kinds of questions will arise! Family members and long-time friends who have already heard "the question" answered several times seem to linger in a continuing fog about exactly what music therapy is. In fact, they often need periodic reviews and more in-depth discussions.

People are curious about music therapy not only because it is still a relatively new field—certainly it is not yet in the mainstream of public awareness or widely understood by many professionals—but also because they are genuinely intrigued by the idea itself. It seems to make such good sense to use music therapeutically! Nearly everyone loves music, and because it is such an integral part of everyday life, most people develop a very personal relationship to it. It soothes and stimulates us; it accompanies us through joy and sadness; it plays with us and helps us to play; it moves us into and out of every human emotion. Most people recognize the power of music to comfort and heal, and many have already discovered its therapeutic benefits through their own personal experiences.

Nevertheless, providing a simple and accurate definition of music therapy to lay people, students, or other professionals is not always simple. Standard or textbook definitions are not always comprehensible or relevant to people outside the field, most often because they are too technical or abstract. As a result, it is often necessary to create a definition to meet the unique demands of each situation. When this happens, the music therapist has to be sensitive to what the questioner wants or needs to know, as well as how prepared he or she is for a detailed answer.

When creating a definition extemporaneously, it is important to consider which facet of music therapy or which clinical approach will be of greatest interest and relevance to the person inquiring. Usually, for example, trained musicians have different mind-sets towards music therapy than average listeners or persons who sing or play an instrument as an avocation. Average listeners have different mind-sets than those who have personally experienced the therapeutic powers of music. Administrators and legislators have different informational needs than clinicians in other fields, who have different questions than prospective students of music therapy. Clients and their families require different information than colleagues and personal friends.

Some questioners want to hear the philosophical rationale for music therapy, others need to validate their own personal experiences of the therapeutic power of music. Some want specific, technical information on how a music therapist works with different populations, while others want a broad overview of the field. Some want clinical examples, others want specific proof that it works in the form of research findings. Obviously the same pat answer cannot be given to everyone. Rather, each definition must be tailored to the specific background, interests, and informational needs of the questioner.

Aside from the challenge of meeting the demands of each situation, music therapists themselves often find it a soul-searching experience to define what they do. Kenny (1982) explains:

> Every time someone asks me the question . . . I have to absorb the silence, center myself and think "My God, here it is again. What am I going to say this time?" Every time it is a challenge, a task,

an invitation to increase my own understanding by assigning words to something which is indescribable by nature and has the additional aspect of being something different every time it happens (p. 1).

In the process of identifying the essence of music therapy and communicating it to others, music therapists often have to confront issues and questions that are at the core of the discipline itself. Every definition distills and delimits the field to its very essence, because within a few sentences, the definer sketches out what is music therapy and what is not, what belongs to it and what does not. Thus every definition of music therapy sets boundaries for the field. Having such boundaries is crucial, for without them, it is impossible to know which types of clients and problems are best served by music therapy, which goals and methods are legitimately part of clinical practice, which topics are relevant for theory and research, and what kinds of ethical standards must be upheld. Furthermore, without these boundaries, it is impossible to design curricula and field training programs for preparing music therapists, and to establish meaningful requirements for earning credentials in the field. In the end, boundaries protect clients by defining the limits of therapists! Thus, as brief or simple as they might sound, definitions have profound implications for outlining the overall purpose of the discipline as well as the limits of the profession.

Definitions are always more than factual statements or objective descriptions of music therapy; they also express the personal and professional beliefs of the definer. Whenever individuals or groups create their own definitions, they are not just quibbling over words or splitting academic hairs. They are usually trying to express their particular viewpoints on music therapy or emphasize something very specific about it. This becomes quite evident when the myriad and diverse definitions found in the field are compared. Fundamental differences in philosophies about music, therapy, health, illness, and even life are quite evident. Each definition of music therapy reflects a very specific viewpoint on what music is and what is therapeutic about it, what therapy is and how music relates to it, and why people need music and therapy to be healthy. And going even further, each definition also implies how the definer conceives and differentiates illness and health. Thus, every definition is more than a concise summary of what music therapy is, it presents a whole world of thought about the field and the professional identity of the person creating the definition.

Perhaps this is why music therapists often change their definitions as time passes and as they gain more experience—it's because their perspectives on the field are changing. As clinicians forge new approaches and serve new populations, and as researchers and theorists in the field gain more knowledge, new horizons of music therapy are discovered. And at the same time, as the health professions at large gain greater insight about illness and wellness, and as new concepts and models of therapy develop, fundamental notions about music therapy are bound to gain greater breadth and depth. As a result, definitions of music therapy continually need to be changed to reflect the state of the art. Thus, when definitions are compared over a period of time, one can actually see stages of individual and collective development in the field as well as in the health community at large.

Because definitions reflect personal philosophies and professional identities, music therapists frequently use them as the basis for communicating with others in the field. When used at the beginning of a lecture or workshop, or when used to introduce an article or book, a definition informs the audience of the presenter's perspective with regard to music therapy, and thereby sets the stage for an exchange or comparison of boundaries, philosophies, and clinical practices.

In summary, definitions serve several important functions: they provide an effective tool for educating others outside of the field and answering their specific questions; they raise fundamental issues and questions for professionals within the field; they provide boundaries for clinical practice, theory, and research; they specify the body of knowledge, skills, and abilities needed to be in the field; they project a professional identity; they reveal the definer's personal viewpoint; they reflect stages of individual and collective development; and they provide a context for communication among music therapists.

Chapter Two

THE CHALLENGES
OF DEFINING
MUSIC THERAPY

Music therapy has many different definitions. In the USA, the one most frequently used is the definition put forth several years ago by the National Association for Music Therapy (NAMT): "Music therapy is the use of music in the accomplishment of therapeutic aims: the restoration, maintenance, and improvement of mental and physical health" (NAMT 1980, p. 1). Though often quoted, this is certainly not a universal definition. Many individual therapists have constructed their own definitions, and nearly every foreign association for music therapy has created an official definition for its country which reflects concepts and practices of its members (Bruscia 1984a, 1985; Maranto, 1993). (See the Appendix for a comprehensive list of definitions found in the literature).

Music therapy is different things to different people for myriad reasons. Many of the differences can be attributed to the elusive nature of music therapy itself. Music therapy is very difficult to define, and many aspects make it so! As a body of knowledge and practice, it is a transdisciplinary hybrid of two main fields, music and therapy, both of which have unclear boundaries and are themselves difficult to define; as a fusion of music and therapy, it is at once an art, a science, and an interpersonal process; as a treatment modality, it is incredibly diverse in application, goal, method, and theoretical orientation; as a worldwide tradition, it is influenced by differences in culture; as a discipline and profession, it has a dual identity; and as a young field, it is still in the process of becoming.

TRANSDISCIPLINARY

The first challenge in defining music therapy is that it is transdisciplinary in nature. That is, music therapy is not a single, isolated discipline with clearly defined and unchanging boundaries. Rather it is a dynamic combination of many disciplines around two main subject areas: music and therapy. Figure 1 is a graphic representation of how music-related disciplines merge with therapy-related disciplines to form the hybrid called music therapy.

The transdisciplinary nature of music therapy makes it very difficult to establish clear boundaries between it and all of its related disciplines. Music often overlaps with the other arts, and therapy often overlaps with other human professions, thereby creating many fuzzy areas. For example, when is moving to music a purely artistic undertaking and when does it become a form of therapy? When it does become a therapy, what kind of therapy is it—music therapy, dance therapy, or physical therapy? Similarly, when does music learning become a form of therapy, and what kind of therapy is it?

PROBLEMS IN DEFINING MUSIC

Philosophers, psychologists, and musicologists have struggled for centuries with the elusiveness of music to definition. In the simplest of terms, music is the art of organizing sounds in time. But at what point does the organization of sound become an art? Certain sound combinations and sequences sound more like noise than music, even when they have been organized very carefully; on the other hand, certain sound combinations and sequences clearly sound like music, but some are more artistically organized than others. By what criteria do we judge what is organized and what is not, and what is art and what is not? What is aesthetically meaningful in music and what is not? What determines when a musical response can be considered an aesthetic or artistic endeavor? Can universal standards be applied to judgments of aesthetic or artistic merit?

Figure 1.

**DISCIPLINES RELATED
TO MUSIC AND THERAPY**

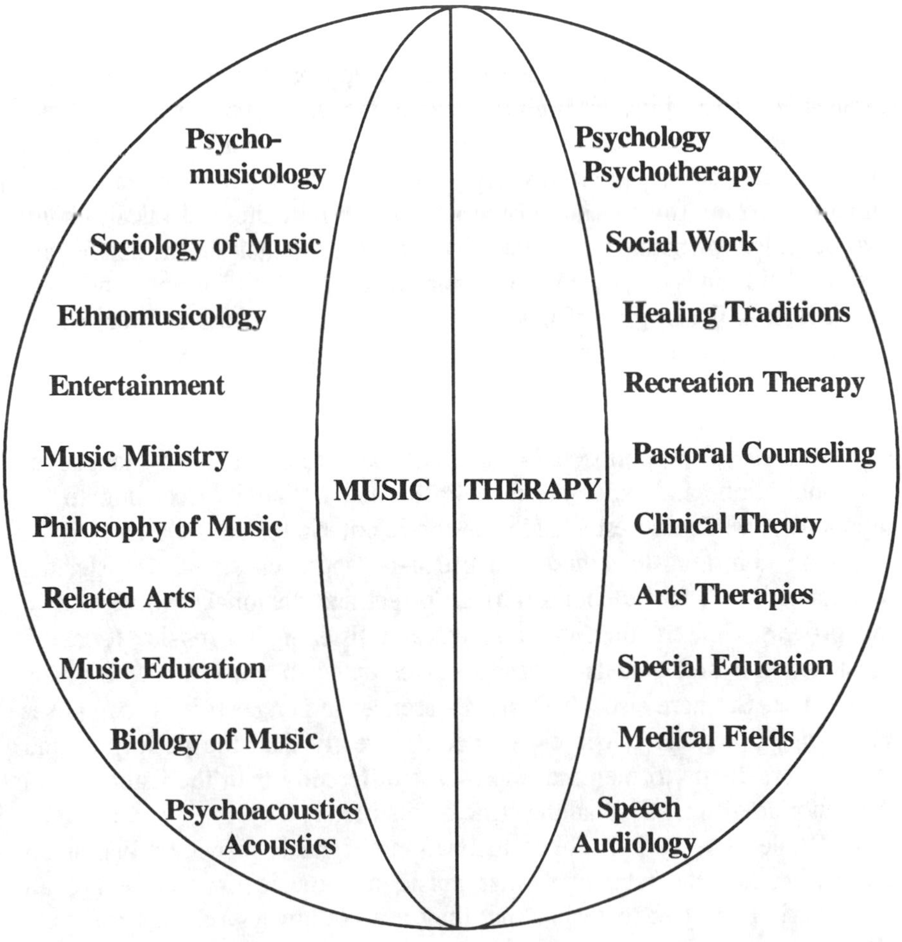

Psycho-
musicology

Sociology of Music

Ethnomusicology

Entertainment

Music Ministry

MUSIC **THERAPY**

Philosophy of Music

Related Arts

Music Education

Biology of Music

Psychoacoustics
Acoustics

Psychology
Psychotherapy

Social Work

Healing Traditions

Recreation Therapy

Pastoral Counseling

Clinical Theory

Arts Therapies

Special Education

Medical Fields

Speech
Audiology

And then there many other equally circuitous questions: Does music always involve sound? Does music include the organization of silence, noise, and vibrations? Is music strictly auditory? Does it always have to be experienced through the ear? Is it a musical experience to receive artistically organized sounds through the tactile senses?

Is music strictly human, that is, do all sounds in music have to be humanly made, or does music also include environmental or natural sources of sound? Are bird calls and whale songs music?

The answers to these questions can be approached from a variety of perspectives. The physicist might look at the objective attributes of the musical product itself, and as a result, define music according to structural or organizational relationships within and between sounds and other temporal events. The psychologist might look at how these physical, objective attributes of sound are experienced by the listener or musician, and therein define music according to experiential criteria. The anthropologist might look at the origins of music in each culture, and the commonalities in musical experiences across cultures, and define music according to its shared or universal properties. The sociologist might look at the roles and functions of music in society, and define it in terms of its collective significance. The philosopher might compare music to language, communication, and other art modalities, and define it according to its uniqueness, while also establishing aesthetic criteria for all the arts.

In contrast to these theoretical approaches, a musician's understanding of music comes through direct and personal involvement in the processes of creating, re-creating, and listening to music. It is the musician who understands what is most essential to music and the music experience. But here also, there are differences in perspective. A composer views music and the music experience differently than the performer and improviser, the performer and improviser differently than the listener, and the historian differently than the critic or instructor.

While these various conceptualizations of music provide a beginning foundation for understanding what music and music experience are all about, it is important to realize that they are not always relevant to actual clinical practice. There are many instances in the context of therapy when music has to be defined quite differently. Sometimes the music is less complete or less organized than what is required by conventional standards. Sometimes the process is not artistic or creative. Sometimes the experience is not auditory. Sometimes nonmusical elements and the other arts are added, so that the experience goes beyond what is conventionally defined as music. Sometimes, aesthetic standards are irrelevant or unimportant, and the music does not meet aesthetic criteria established in conventional definitions.

Thus, notwithstanding the insights of the physicist, psychologist, anthropologist, sociologist, philosopher, and musician, the most relevant question is how does a *music therapist* define music? What aspects of using it as a therapy can change one's fundamental notions regarding the nature of music and its boundaries? Exactly what is music within a clinical context?

Later in this book these questions will be addressed. For now, it is important to realize that when a music therapist defines music within a clinical context, several factors must be taken into account, including the boundaries of sound and varying levels of human organization and artistic merit.

PROBLEMS IN DEFINING THERAPY

Defining therapy is as difficult as defining music; in fact, the issues and problems are quite similar. The components of therapy, like the elements of music, are quite numerous and overlapping, and the experiences within therapy, like music experiences, are varied and multilayered. And similar to the difficulties in separating music from the arts, so is it difficult to distinguish therapy from education, development, growth, healing, and a host of other phenomena commonly referred to as "therapeutic." In short, setting criteria for what is therapy and what is not is as difficult as deciding what is music and what is not.

Therapy is traditionally defined in terms of its Greek root *therapeia* which means to attend, help, or treat. When taken together, these are certainly essential elements of therapy, however, a definition they do not make. To have an adequate definition of therapy, several issues have to be clarified. Does therapy involve any kind of attending, helping, or treating? Does anyone needing such support qualify for therapy? Does it matter who does the attending, helping, or treating, and does the person have to be specially trained? What is the process by which these supports are given, and changes take place as a result?

To be comprehensive, a definition of music therapy must therefore address several issues: 1) the health status or needs of the client that can be addressed in music therapy; 2) the respective roles and functions of the music and therapist; 3) the qualifications and responsibilities of the therapist; 4) the nature of the relationships that develop between client(s), music, and therapist; 5) the goals of therapy suitable for various philosophical orientations; and 6) a description of the therapeutic process that defines intervention and change without philosophical bias.

ART, SCIENCE, AND INTERPERSONAL PROCESS

As a fusion of music and therapy, music therapy is at once an art, a science, and an interpersonal process. As an art, it is concerned with subjectivity, individuality, creativity, and beauty. As a science, it is concerned with objectivity, universality, replicability, and truth. As an interpersonal process it is concerned with empathy, intimacy, communication, reciprocity, and role relationships.

Being both art and science practiced within an interpersonal context requires the integration of many seemingly contradictory elements. Music therapy can be both objective and subjective, individual and universal, creatively unique and replicable, intrapersonal and interpersonal, collective and transpersonal.

As an art, music therapy is organized by science and focused by the interpersonal process. As a science, it is enlivened by art and humanized by the therapist-client relationship. As an interpersonal process, it is motivated and fulfilled through art and guided by science. Of course, these paradoxes often blur the boundaries of music therapy and complicate its conception and definition. To define music therapy exclusively, as any one of these, is to ignore its very essence. Somehow music therapy has to be conceived in a way that embraces this multiplicity yet preserves its integrity. Similarly, music therapists have to be perceived in a way that acknowledges their unique abilities as artists, scientists, and therapists.

DIVERSITY IN CLINICAL PRACTICE

Music therapy is incredibly diverse. It is presently being used in schools, clinics, hospitals, residential centers, group homes, nursing homes, day-care centers, hospices, prisons, community centers, institutes, and private practices. Client populations include autistic and emotionally disturbed children, adults with psychiatric disorders, mentally retarded children and adults, individuals with visual, hearing, speech or motor impairments, learning disabled children, abused children, children with behavior disorders, prisoners, addicts, medical patients, senior citizens, terminally ill children and adults, and neurotic adults. Music therapy is also used to assist healthy individuals in stress reduction, childbirth, biofeedback techniques, pain management, self-actualization, and spiritual development.

Naturally, goals and methods vary from one setting to the next, from one client population to another, and from one music therapist to the next. Goals may be educational, recreational, rehabilitative, preventive, or psychotherapeutic, focusing on physical, emotional, intellectual, social, or spiritual needs of the client. Methods of treatment may emphasize listening, improvising, performing, composing, moving, or talking, and may include additional experiences in art, dance, drama, and poetry. Music therapists vary among themselves according to specialization areas and the various clinical orientations existing in that area. For example, music therapists who have a specialization in developmental disability may base their work on behavior theories, while others may use communication theory; some may work toward improving adaptive behavior, others may focus on academic learning, and still others may emphasize quality of life. Music therapists in a hospital or palliative-care setting may work within a biopsychosocial or transpersonal-healing orientation; some may focus on influencing the disease process and its effects, and some may address the wellness side. Music psychotherapists may operate within a variety of psychological theories, ranging from psychoanalytic to existential to cognitive to humanistic and transpersonal.

The implications of such diversity are enormous. How can such different clinical practices ever be contained within the same boundaries? Is there a common focus or basic idea that unifies the many goals, methods, and orientations? Is there any one thing that can be present and consistent in *every* definition of music therapy, regardless of population and setting?

DIFFERENCES IN PERSPECTIVE

So far we have only considered the problems of defining music therapy from a professional's point of view, that is, from the perspective of the therapist. But what meaning does a definition by professionals have for the clients they serve, even if it resolves the many theoretical issues raised here? How do clients define music therapy? Where do they place the boundaries of music and therapy? Do clients agree with how therapists define what they are both experiencing? Is a client's experience and understanding of music therapy the same as a therapist's? Is it possible to define music therapy collaboratively?

And taking this even further, differences in perspectives will also be found among professionals. A practitioner will define music therapy within a clinical context, which may be a different perspective from a researcher who defines it within a science context, which may be different from a theorist who defines it within a philosophical context.

Research would help a great deal in comparing and integrating these perspectives. Meanwhile, it should be kept in mind that most of this book deals with the perspective of a professional music therapist.

CULTURAL DIFFERENCES

Music therapy does not belong to any one culture, race, country, or ethnic tradition; it is global in its conception and manifestation. It is global not only because it exists as a profession in most industrialized nations around the world, but also, and more important, because the idea of using music as a healing art has existed for centuries, and in many different cultures. Moreno (1988) argues that music therapy, without being described as such, "is currently a flourishing practice in countless tribal and nontechnological societies in Asia, Africa, Australia, America, Oceania and Europe" (p. 271). He goes on to say that in most of these cultures, music and healing are practiced together within a shamanic tradition. A shaman is a priest or medicine man who uses rituals involving the arts to heal the sick.

So what bearing does all this have on defining music therapy? Everything! The way a culture defines and uses music determines whether it is considered relevant to medicine, healing and therapy; and similarly the way a culture views medicine, healing, and therapy determines how relevant music is considered to them. A good example is how Moreno (1988) describes the shaman. In most societies, he or she is multidisciplinary, that is, instead of being a specialist in only one art form, the shaman always integrates music, art, dance, and drama into a holistic approach to healing. The implications of this are that within a culture where music and the other arts are integrally related to one another, music therapy has to be defined very broadly; in contrast, in our own technological culture where music has clearly defined boundaries with the other arts and is often subdivided into subspecialties, music therapy has to be defined much more narrowly. Thus, we rarely expect a musician to be a painter, dancer, or actor, or a music therapist to also be an art, dance or drama therapist; and in fact, we are now moving toward even greater specialization within music therapy itself (e.g., improvisation, guided imagery, drumming, etc.).

Of course, cultural differences have many implications for defining music therapy other than how music and the other arts are related. Several important issues arise as the arts and arts therapies develop in different countries. Imagine how music therapy would be defined in cultures where music is regarded as purely recreational in nature. Would music therapy be accepted in countries that do not support music education in the schools? How would it be defined in countries where music is integrally linked to spiritual or devotional undertakings? When music is already related to divine healing, would there be a need for a profession of music therapy? Would the provision of music therapy services for money be regarded as a sacrilege, or at least a secularization of the sacred nature of music?

And last but not least, how would music therapy be defined in cultures that do not regard therapy as important or valuable, or where any form of psychological self-examination is taboo? We should not assume that the Western notions and attitudes about therapy are universal. Going to therapy is certainly not as popular or status-related in other cultures, and in fact, in some cultures the very idea of paying someone to help with one's personal problems is considered quite bizarre indeed.

DUAL IDENTITY

Music therapy has a dual identity. As a "discipline," it is an organized body of knowledge consisting of theory, practice, and research, all pertaining to the therapeutic uses of music. As a "profession," it is an organized group of people using the same body of knowledge in their vocations as clinicians, educators, administrators, supervisors, etc.

This dual identity poses several issues that affect how music therapy is defined.

> When conceptualized as a discipline, our identity is defined by the range of therapeutic applications music has, and our role boundaries are determined by the knowledge we have of them. When conceptualized as a profession, our identity is defined by our job titles and responsibilities, and our role boundaries are determined by the qualifications (and salaries) that others impose upon us (Bruscia, 1987b, p. 26).

Several questions arise. First, is one identity consistent with the other? Does the discipline have the same identity as the profession? Are theory, research, and clinical practice consistent with the public roles, titles, responsibilities, and standards that we adopt as a profession? Is the body of knowledge belonging to the discipline reflected in our professional employment as clinicians, educators, supervisors, and administrators?

Second, to what extent does one identity influence the other? Does the discipline define the profession, or is it vice versa? More specifically, do theory, research and practice determine professional roles, titles, responsibilities and standards, or does the professional image determine the boundaries of the discipline? This issue has been described in terms of "field-dependence" theory.

> When we define our identity in terms of the discipline, we are "field-independent"—we are who we are because of what *we* know about we do. When we define our identity in terms of the profession, we are "field-dependent"—we are what we do, and what we do is based on what *they* know. When we are field-independent, our major task is to educate ourselves; when we are

field-dependent our major task is to educate others. Herein lies the developmental struggle. Music therapy is struggling to exert its own identity at a stage of development when perceptions of others are still important. Hence, we are unable to be entirely field-independent or field-dependent. Our identity is being co-developed. The identity we give ourselves influences and is influenced by the identity given to us by others (Bruscia, 1987b, p. 26).

STILL DEVELOPING

Music therapy is still developing; it is still in the process of becoming. Though the idea of using music in therapy is thousands of years old, it was not until this century that a sufficient body of knowledge was gathered and documented to create a "discipline." Thus, as a formal discipline, it is still quite young. Theories are just beginning to take shape, and research needs are now becoming more clearly defined.

As a "profession," music therapy is only a few decades old. In the United States, the birth of the profession can be traced back to the founding of the National Association for Music Therapy in 1950—a mere fifty years ago. Because it is so young, its identity as a profession has not yet fully emerged within the education and health communities. The final job title and position description have not yet been written.

The implications for defining music therapy are manifold. Music therapy cannot be defined only in terms of its present status, but must remain open to its future possibilities, both as a discipline and a profession. "Music therapy is not only what it is today, it is also what it promises to be when fully developed" (Bruscia, 1987b, p. 26).

It should also be mentioned that music therapists have had to forge out their identity in a socioeconomic and political climate that is both demanding and changing. Music therapy has had to grow up in a "fast-lane" culture where health professionals are expected to produce results no less spectacular than space travel, and at a time when the values of intimacy and art are easily compromised by the prowess of science.

With these cultural challenges have come economic pressures. Governmental priorities for health care are constantly shifting, and funding streams appear and disappear in quickly changing landscapes. De-institutionalization and mainstreaming have been largely accomplished, but their effects are only now beginning to emerge. As a result, job markets have appeared and disappeared like mirages, and music therapists have had to stretch their professional identities to their limits in order to accommodate each wave of health reform. The goals and methods of music therapy have had to expand to meet the needs of new client populations and to accommodate the changing needs of more familiar populations. At the same time, music therapy is being revolutionized by current changes in the philosophy of science and the dramatic increase in holistic approaches to healing.

It is important to realize that environmental pressures are not unusual or necessarily detrimental to the process of identity formation. Without such pressures, music therapy might not have developed the incredible richness it has today; on the other hand, the price for such diversification may very well be a loss of boundaries and identity confusions. How far can music therapy stretch?

Music therapy is presently experiencing several identity problems (Bruscia, 1987b), and as a result, a number of educational questions have arisen. Should the undergraduate music therapy student be vocationally trained for the profession through very specialized studies in music and therapy, or should the student be educated broadly in the arts, sciences, and humanities? Should the music therapist be primarily a musician or a therapist? What kind of musician should a music therapist be? Is it better to be trained in classical or popular music? Is it better to be accomplished in one instrument or functional in several? Should the music therapist focus on being a performer or an improviser? What kind of therapist should a music therapist be, primary or adjunctive, specialist or generalist, teacher or therapist, activity therapist or psychotherapist? Is the music therapist primarily a clinician or researcher? Should a music therapist be self-defined or defined within the context of the job market?

Obviously, these questions are complex and difficult to answer, nevertheless, music therapy is at a stage of development when these identity problems must be examined. Perhaps the very fact that these questions have arisen at this time suggests that the profession is already grappling with them. It is hoped that by examining the identity issues involved in defining music therapy this book will contribute to the developmental task at hand.

IMPLICATIONS

Given all of the challenges inherent in defining music therapy cited above, it is very unlikely that a universally accepted or final definition will ever be formulated. Music therapy is too broad and complex to be defined or contained by a single culture, philosophy, treatment model, clinical setting, or individual definer. And this is precisely why there are so many different definitions of it, and why the definition offered in this book is called a "working one"! We are and we will always be in the process of defining for the answers to the diverse issues and questions raised here will always vary according to the definer and the context in which the defining takes place. The important point is that the purpose of creating a definition is not to determine once and for all what music therapy is; it is merely to establish a new perspective or approach to conceiving of it, another attempt to answer the basic core questions. Thus, every definition is important because, when we examine how the definer has answered all of these questions and challenges, we have an opportunity to broaden and deepen our understanding of music therapy. In the working definition that follows, all of the definitions in the Appendix have been brought into the discussion where relevant. This does not mean that the present definition agrees with or incorporates all of them—it does not!

Chapter Three

A WORKING DEFINITION

CAVEATS

Given all of the challenges inherent in defining music therapy cited in the previous chapter, it is very unlikely that a universally accepted or final definition will ever be formulated. Music therapy is too broad and complex to be defined or contained by a single culture, philosophy, treatment model, clinical setting, or individual definer. This is precisely why there are so many different definitions of it, and why the present chapter is entitled "Working Definition!" We are and we will always be in the process of defining, for the answers to the diverse issues and questions raised here will always vary according to the definer and the context in which the defining takes place. Furthermore, many of the issues reflect the paradoxes and vagaries which are indigenous to music therapy and which are impossible to resolve or clarify completely. The important point is that the purpose of creating a definition is not to determine once and for all what music therapy is, it is merely to establish a new perspective or approach to conceiving of it—another attempt to answer the basic core questions. Thus, every definition is important because, when we examine how the definer has answered all these questions and challenges, we have an opportunity to broaden and deepen our understanding of music therapy.

The purpose of this chapter is to offer a working definition of music therapy which attempts to address the many issues that have been raised so far, and which also synthesizes to the extent possible the various definitions found in the literature. Following this definition are brief explanations of each word or phrase. These explanations provide an overview for the in-depth discussions that follow in subsequent chapters.

The definition is a theoretical one. Its purpose is to enable professionals and students to examine conceptual issues involved in defining music therapy. It is not intended for lay audiences, and it may not be useful when describing music therapy to other professionals for the first time.

WORKING DEFINITION

Music therapy is a systematic process of intervention wherein the therapist helps the client to promote health, using music experiences and the relationships that develop through them as dynamic forces of change.

Systematic Process of Intervention

Music therapy is systematic in that it is goal-directed, organized, knowledge-based, and regulated; it is not merely a series of unplanned, random experiences that turn out to be helpful. Its three main procedural components are assessment, treatment, and evaluation.

Music therapy is a process that takes place over time. For the client, the time involves a process of change; for the therapist, it is a time-ordered sequence of interventions. For both client and therapist, this process over time can be described as developmental, educational, interpersonal, artistic, musical, creative, or scientific.

To be considered therapy, this process requires intervention by a therapist. An intervention is a purposeful attempt to mitigate an existing condition in order to affect some kind of change. In therapy, interventions must meet three criteria: the client must need outside help to accomplish a health objective; there must be purposeful intervention, regardless of outcome; and the intervention must be carried out by a therapist within the context of a therapist-client relationship.

What makes music therapy interventions unique is that they always involve both music and therapist acting as partners in the process. When music is used *as* therapy, music takes the primary role in the intervention, and the therapist is secondary; when music is used *in* therapy, the therapist takes the primary role, and music is secondary. When music is used by a client *without* a therapist, the process does not qualify as *therapy*; when a therapist helps the client *without* using music, it is not *music* therapy. Music therapy interventions are unique in that they focus on sound, beauty, and creativity.

Therapist Helps Client

A therapist is a person who offers his/her expertise and services to help the client with a health concern. By definition, a music therapist must have the necessary expertise to provide the service as well as recognition of such by an appropriate authority. The music therapist may serve as adjunctive or primary therapist, depending upon professional expertise and client need. The music therapist uses principles of personal and professional ethics to guide work with clients.

The music therapist is defined as the helper, and the client is defined as the person being helped. The client-therapist relationship is not reciprocal in this regard, though it is generally acknowledged that doing therapy affords many opportunities for therapists to meet their own needs at an unconscious level. Central to the client-therapist relationship is a contract for services that focuses on the client's health.

Music therapy provides very specific kinds of help to clients. Whether taking primary or secondary roles in the process, music and the therapist combine their resources to provide clients with opportunities for receiving empathy, understanding, validation, and redress; for verbal and nonverbal self-expression, interaction, and communication; for feedback on themselves and insights about their lives; for motivation and self-transformation; and for direct assistance and intervention.

A client is defined as a person who needs or seeks help from another person because of an actual, imagined, or potential threat to health, whether physical, emotional, mental, behavioral, social, or spiritual in nature.

To Promote Health

The goal of therapy is to promote health. Health encompasses and depends upon the individual and all of his/her parts (e.g., body, psyche, spirit), and the individual's relationship with the broader contexts of society, culture, and environment. There are two orientations to health: in the pathogenic orientation, health is an either-or condition, defined by the presence of illness; in the salutogenic, health is a continuum which includes all degrees of health. Going even further, the definition of health proposed here is the process of becoming one's fullest potential for individual and ecological wholeness.

Using Music Experiences

Music therapy is distinct from other modalities by its reliance on music experience as an agent of intervention. The way music therapists define "music experience" is based on the clinical contexts in which they work. Of particular importance is a nonjudgmental acceptance of whatever the client does musically, and clear priorities with regard to the purpose, value, and meaning of music within the therapy process.

Music is difficult to define for many reasons, and in therapy, the matter is further complicated by the notion that therapy depends upon not merely the music but the client's experience of it. Every music experience minimally involves a person, a specific musical process, a product of some kind, and a context or environment. Thus, the music used for therapy is not merely an object that operates on the client, rather it is a multifaceted experience involving the person, process, product, and context. For purposes of this book, music is defined as the human institution in which individuals create meaning and beauty through sound, using the arts of composition, improvisation, performance, and listening. Meaning and beauty are derived from the intrinsic relationships created between the sounds themselves and other forms of human experience, as well as the universe itself.

Four specific types of music experience serve as the primary methods of music therapy: improvising, re-creating, composing, and listening to music. These experiences can be presented with emphasis on various sensory modalities, with or without verbal discourse, and in various combinations with the other arts. Depending on how intrinsically musical the sounds and activities are, the experience may be described as premusical, musical, extramusical, paramusical, or nonmusical.

And the Relationships Formed Through Them

These varied kinds of music experience provide the client with opportunities to develop multifaceted relationships within and between the self and its various worlds. Accordingly, these relationships can be described as intrapersonal, intramusical, interpersonal, intermusical, and sociocultural. Of central significance to the therapeutic process is the client's relationships to the therapist and to the music.

As Dynamic Forces of Change

Music therapy can be likened to chemistry. Its main elements are the client(s), the music, and the therapist. These elements combine and interact in may ways, depending upon how the therapist conceives and designs the client's music experience. Thus, the key compound—determining how all the elements of the experience are related to one another—is the client-music interaction. Consequently, to analyze the dynamics of music therapy is to analyze the various ways in which the client experiences music. There are six dynamic models used, depending upon whether the music experience is objective, subjective, energentic, aesthetic, collective, or transpersonal.

The kinds of changes that can result from music therapy are myriad. Two important criteria are that they are health-related and that they actually result from the therapeutic process.

Chapter Four

SYSTEMATIC

Music therapy is a systematic process. It is not a series of random events or serendipitous experiences; it is not an unplanned or unmonitored process; and the outcomes are not merely happenstance. This seems to be an important point to make, considering the variety of adjectives that have been used in the literature to describe the process of music therapy. Some examples are: purposive, controlled, planned, prescribed, scientific, structured, integrated, and so forth.

While the word "systematic" seems to subsume most of these terms, it may imply more organization and control than desired or intended. It certainly does not convey the spontaneity and creativity that is nearly always present, even in the most planned and controlled music therapy situations. The path of any two people working together as client and therapist cannot always be completely charted out beforehand, and especially within a musical context. All kinds of things can and do happen when client and therapist interact through music; and many of them simply cannot be planned or predicted beforehand. Something unexpected, surprising, different, or novel is bound to happen when two people begin to experiment with and try new ways of being together or doing things differently—which of course is the very purpose of therapy.

The idea of using the word "creative" instead of "systematic" is a tempting one, but it may be unnecessary and somewhat misleading. Being systematic does not preclude being creative, and being creative always requires being systematic in some way. Furthermore, because the client and therapist are both engaging in music experiences, the process of music therapy can be presumed to be creative on some level. On the other hand, "creative" might give the wrong impression, as to some it would imply that music therapy is experimental or fanciful, and perhaps even unscientific. Using both terms seems futile also, because as will be seen in the next chapter, the process of music therapy has been described in many ways other than systematic and creative, and there is a limit to the number of adjectives that can be used.

The reason for finally selecting the word "systematic" was that it conveys many of the most important features of music therapy that are necessary to understand and to express to others outside the field. As will be explored now in detail, being systematic means that music therapy is purposeful, temporally organized, methodical, knowledge-based, and regulated.

PURPOSEFUL

Music therapy always has a purpose. The client comes to music therapy (or is referred) for a specific reason, and the therapist always works with the client with specific intentions or objectives in mind. Thus, music therapy is contractual; it always involves a shared commitment between client and therapist to achieve a purpose. Whenever possible, both the client and therapist are involved in determining what the goals of therapy are, and in some cases, they may even establish a written contract, stipulating goals and methods of treatment over a designated period of time, and the roles and responsibilities of each party.

As suggested earlier, being purposeful does not necessarily mean that all of the outcomes of music therapy can be predicted or specified beforehand. It often takes time and experience with one another until the client and therapist can formulate specific objectives for their work together, even though both parties are obviously committed to helping the client with a health need of some kind.

TEMPORALLY ORGANIZED

Music therapy is always organized in time. Notwithstanding those occasions when the process unfolds extemporaneously, there is always an effort to organize events and experiences into a meaningful, developmental sequence for the client. This is accomplished by having regularly scheduled appointments, by imposing time limits on sessions and the course of therapy, by organizing or managing each session so that the activities and experiences are timed appropriately, and by planning the overall process so that the client follows a developmentally meaningful sequence of learning, growth, or change.

METHODICAL

Music therapy always proceeds in a methodical fashion. Procedurally, it involves three basic steps or phases, which may be carried out separately or simultaneously. They are: assessment, treatment, and evaluation.

Assessment

Assessment is that part of the therapy process when the therapist engages and observes the client in various music experiences in order to better understand him/her as a person and to identify whatever problems, needs, concerns, and resources the client is bringing to therapy.

There are several approaches to assessment, depending on the therapist's objectives (see Bruscia, 1988b). When the assessment has "diagnostic" objectives, the therapist tries to determine whether the client has a particular clinical condition or problem, based upon whatever diagnostic criteria have been established within the health community, and then tries to explain and classify the client's condition according to its cause, symptoms, severity, etc. An example is when a music therapist tests the client's ability to imitate rhythm patterns in order to determine if there is any evidence of short-term memory or perceptual deficit.

When the objectives are "interpretive," the therapist tries to understand or explain the client's responses in terms of a particular theory, frame of reference, or body of knowledge. An example is when the therapist analyzes the client's song choices according to Freudian theory and proposes that he or she is expressing an unconscious need or wish for maternal love.

When the objectives are "descriptive," the therapist gathers as much information about the client as possible, and then tries to create a holistic picture of the client by synthesizing the information only in reference to that client, that is, without relating the information to other clients, diagnostic criteria, or theories. For example, the therapist may study all of the improvisations of a client, and summarize the findings by writing a portrait of the client which reflects his or her personal and musical characteristics. Or the therapist may even create an improvisation which incorporates and relates the most important musical characteristics of the client into a single piece.

When the objectives are "prescriptive," the therapist tries to determine what the client's specific treatment needs are, such as: whether music therapy is indicated or contraindicated; whether the client will be better served in individual or group sessions; whether therapy should involve active music-making or listening to music, along with the type of music making or listening that will be most suitable; whether the sessions should be scheduled once or twice per week; and so forth.

When the assessment has "evaluative" objectives, the therapist gathers baseline information so that the client's level of functioning at the beginning of therapy can be compared at various later stages, and ultimately at the end of treatment. An example is when the music therapist observes the frequency of acting-out behaviors in the first group activity, and then charts the frequency at various intervals thereafter.

Treatment

Treatment is that part of the therapy process when the therapist engages the client in various music experiences, employing specific methods and techniques in order to induce change in the client and his/her health. Most of the work in this phase involves planning and conducting the actual music therapy sessions themselves.

Much goes into planning music therapy. The therapist first establishes an overall direction for the work based on whatever needs, problems, and resources the client has revealed during the assessment. Goals may be broad or specific depending upon the client and the therapist's orientation. Whenever appropriate, the therapist will seek input from the client, the client's family, and other members of the treatment team in establishing the goals for music therapy.

Next, the therapist has to map out an overall treatment strategy. In music therapy, this usually involves selecting the types of music and music experiences that will be most relevant to the client and treatment plan.

Every music therapy session involves the client in a musical experience of some kind. There are four basic types:

- *Improvising*: having the client extemporaneously make up his/her own music while playing an instrument or singing;
- *Re-creating*: having the client sing a song or play a pre-composed instrumental piece of music, either by memory or using notation;
- *Composing*: helping the client to compose and notate a song, instrumental piece, or part thereof; and
- *Listening*: having the client listen and react to recorded or live music.

Much more will be said of these types of treatment later. For now, it is enough to realize that the basic tools of the music therapist are the various ways in which human beings engage in and relate to music.

Evaluation

Evaluation is that phase of the therapy process when the therapist determines whether the client and/or condition has in fact changed as a result of music therapy treatment. Two questions are inherent: Did music therapy work? And, did the client and/or condition improve? As with assessment, there are a variety of approaches and techniques, depending on the therapist's orientation and the characteristics of the client.

KNOWLEDGE-BASED

Music therapy is systematic for another important reason: it is based on a specific body of knowledge. This body of knowledge is comprised of many oral and written traditions in clinical practice, a variety of theories, and an ongoing stream of research. When these sources of knowledge in music therapy are integrated, clinical practice informs and is informed by theory and research; theory organizes and is organized by practice and research; and research enlightens and is enlightened by theory and practice.

One of the biggest challenges of any new discipline, and especially those which are hybrids of many different fields, is to define exactly what the knowledge base is. Here again, much depends upon how one defines and contextualizes music therapy. Consider for a moment how different the knowledge base would be if music therapy is defined as a branch of medicine, versus psychology, versus music. Much of the introspection and research on this topic has focused on identifying the specific competencies needed to practice music therapy. Since this is related to defining what a "therapist" is, it will be discussed in the next chapter.

REGULATED

Finally, music therapy can be considered systematic because the profession has established ethical and clinical standards which guide and regulate the conduct of its members when engaged in music therapy practice, theory, and research. These standards can be found in official codes of clinical practice and ethics published by the various associations throughout the world. These codes deal with several areas of common concern, including:

- *Competence.* Music therapists are expected to work within the boundaries of their qualifications, and make no claims beyond their abilities and levels of competence. At the same time, they are also expected to continually improve and expand their expertise through continuing education. The exact areas of competence that an individual must have to practice music therapy will be outlined later in the chapter dealing with the term "therapist."
- *Client Rights.* Music therapists are expected to respect all legal and personal rights of the client, including those related to safety, dignity, civil rights, treatment, self-determination, and confidentiality. To the extent possible, music therapists are expected to keep clients fully informed about their treatment, gain their consent, and invite their participation in decision-making.
- *Standards of Practice.* Music therapists are expected to strive towards providing the highest quality of service to their

clients, while also meeting all professional standards for referral, clinical assessment, program planning, treatment, evaluation, and termination of services.

- *Client Relationships*. Music therapists are expected to establish and maintain appropriate professional relationships with their clients. The client-therapist relationship should never involve sexual or inappropriate intimacy, exploitation, etc.
- *Other Relationships*. Music therapists are expected to respect the legal and personal rights of their colleagues and employers, while also observing all rules and regulations at their work site.
- *Research*. Music therapy researchers are expected to respect all legal and personal rights of individuals who serve as subjects or participants in their studies.
- *Fees*. Music therapists are expected to conduct their financial transactions with honesty, fairness, and integrity.

Chapter Five

PROCESS

THE TIME ELEMENT

Music therapy is a process that takes time: It is a sequence of experiences leading to a desired state, rather than a single event that has an effect. It is a series of interactions leading to a client-therapist relationship rather than a single interpersonal encounter; it is a layered progression of musical engagements rather than an isolated musical experience; it is a gradual process of change for the client, not merely a spontaneous or sudden cure; it is a sequence of interventions for the therapist, not merely a one-time maneuver or isolated therapeutic act. Thus, music therapy is evolutionary rather than momentary, sequential rather than singular, and gradual rather than sudden. It involves relationship rather than encounter, and engagement rather than manipulation.

By making these stipulations, two important criteria are being established for what qualifies as music therapy and what does not. First, music therapy is defined by the nature of the process, not merely the outcome. Every experience that turns out to be beneficial, health-enhancing, or even "therapeutic" does not qualify as "therapy." There are many events and experiences in life that lead to positive outcomes resembling the goals of therapy. Going to a movie, mountain climbing, white-water rafting, making love, singing a part in Handel's *Messiah,* attending a church service, talking to a friend, and eating chocolate chip cookies can all be regarded as therapeutic in some way; and under certain circumstances, they can even lead to significant changes in one's life—but none can be regarded as a "process" of therapy. There is a real difference between a single experience that has a therapeutic effect and the repeated engagements that typify the therapy process. Thus, having a powerful, transformative, or therapeutic music experience is not the same as entering into the process of music therapy, regardless of any similarities or differences in the depth, significance, or longevity of the outcomes.

Second, a distinction is being made between "process" and what might be called music therapy "services." The "process" of music therapy always involves *repeated* engagements in assessment, treatment, and evaluation. "Services" on the other hand, typically involve brief encounters that focus on a particular part or aspect of the entire therapy process. Examples of such services include diagnostic assessments, demonstration sessions, workshop experiences, consultations, etc. When engaged in the process of therapy, client and therapist commit themselves to a series of music experiences and to the development of a client-therapist relationship, both of which have the purpose of therapeutic change. These conditions can prevail even when the period of therapy is relatively brief (e.g., 3–6 sessions). In contrast, related services rarely require such commitments in time, engagements, or relationship.

Later we will see how these distinctions, and the clear-cut boundary being formed around therapy, will help us to further differentiate the various levels of music therapy practice.

TYPES OF PROCESS

Because music therapy is used in such a variety of clinical situations, the process has been described in many different ways, depending upon how it is applied, the type of client, the nature of the problem being addressed, and the therapist's theoretical orientation. This is quite evident when surveying the various definitions in the Appendix. Many adjectives have been used to describe the type of process involved in music therapy.

It is described as *developmental* when the sequence of changes or interventions parallels normal stages of growth, maturation, or development. For the client, this means that musical and nonmusical changes made during therapy are related to developmental age and corresponding levels of cognitive abilities, motor skills, motivation, emotional maturity, etc. For the therapist, this means that the goals of therapy are geared toward helping the client achieve appropriate developmental milestones, and that the treatment procedures are designed to parallel developmental tasks typical of the period.

The process of music therapy is *educational* when the sequence of changes or interventions is indigenous to the curricular subject matter or skill being learned, whether it be musical or nonmusical. For the client, this means learning things in steps according to levels of difficulty, starting from the simpler aspects of the material or task, and progressing to more complex ones. For the therapist, this means following the goals and learning activities of a curriculum or course of study.

The process is *interpersonal* when the sequence is based on stages in developing relationships with people. For the client and therapist, this means establishing rapport, making contact, exploring limits, gaining trust, defining roles, resolving conflicts, helping, separating, and so forth. All of these stages are accomplished through both musical and nonmusical interactions. These interpersonal processes have been described according to various treatment theories (e.g., psychoanalytic, humanistic, cognitive).

Because music therapy is a fusion of music and therapy, the process can also be described as artistic, creative, and scientific. As an *artistic* process, music therapy is concerned with the sequences involved in performing, composing, and improvising music. For the client, this may be stages in mastering an instrument, learning to sing or play, creating an improvisation, writing a composition, finding a way to express something through music, and so forth. For the therapist, it is the artistic process of bringing music to the client, of engaging the client in listening and music-making, and of musically interacting with the client. It is the art of hearing the client's music and understanding it in the context of his/her life. It is also the art of being a therapist and of making the therapeutic experience an aesthetic one.

As a *creative* process, music therapy is concerned with stages in identifying, exploring, testing, and selecting alternatives. For the client, this means solving problems and meeting one's own needs through new, creative ways. It is also the process of creating a new life, free from old conflicts and open to new challenges. For the therapist, this means finding creative ways of dealing with clients and their problems, seeing fresh alternatives for the client, searching for new methods of working, and evaluation, and being open to creative changes in oneself as a therapist.

As a *scientific* process, therapy involves the sequential steps of an experiment: defining and controlling variables, collecting data, analyzing the data to discover relationships among the variables, and interpreting the results. For the client, this means gaining more reliability in observing oneself and the world, and making more valid interpretations. It is the process of gaining more objectivity about one's own life and the forces that influence it. For the therapist, the scientific process involves ensuring that observations of the client are reliable and valid, and continuously evaluating the effects of therapy through objective means.

Of course, these different types of process often overlap in music therapy, and are therefore not mutually exclusive. A music therapist may conceive his/her work with the client as both developmental and scientific, or both artistic and interpersonal. At one point in therapy, the emphasis may be on artistic stages of growth; at another time, it may be educational. Even during the same session, one music therapy experience may be approached as a scientific process, and another may be approached as a creative or interpersonal one. Thus, much of the variety found in clinical practice can be understood in terms of how the process is conceived.

This leads to another important point. Because there are many different theories of development, education, creativity, and so forth, there are just as many ways to describe the process involved. For example, when a therapist takes a developmental approach, the process may be described according to the theories of Freud or Piaget, for example, and the focus may be sensorimotor, perceptual, emotional, cognitive, moral, social, or musical. Similarly, when an educational approach is taken, the process may be described in terms of behavioral theory or learning theory, and the focus may be on reading, writing, spelling, music-making, music listening, etc.

Finally, it should be said that everything that qualifies as a process does not qualify as therapy. Going through developmental milestones, following specific stages of learning, carrying out the sequential steps of science, and going through the various phases of artistic creation are not the same as engaging in the process of therapy. There are important differences in goals, experiences, and relationships, all of which will be discussed at various points throughout this book.

Chapter Six

INTERVENTION

CRITERIA

To intervene is to act upon someone or something in order to change the existing situation and thereby alter the course of events. It implies that a condition already exists, and that something is being done to abate or remedy it so that the anticipated outcomes are modified in some way. When understood in terms of its Latin roots, to intervene is to come between the various forces operating within a particular circumstance in order to affect them in some way. Thus, in terms of therapy, to intervene is to come between or mitigate those forces in the client's life which are affecting his/her health.

Including this word in the definition means that to be considered music therapy, the process must always involve an intervention of some kind by a therapist. Three very important points are being made here.

First, therapy implies that there is a need for outside intervention. The client *needs* help to mitigate those forces affecting his/her health. More will be said of this later, when the notion of "health" is discussed; for now, it is important to merely acknowledge that for whatever reason, therapy always implies that the client is unable to maintain, restore, or improve his/her health without some kind of outside help or added assistance.

Second, therapy is defined not merely by outcomes, that is, not merely by whether the client and his/her health has changed for the better. Therapy by definition requires an ongoing process of intervention. Thus changes that occur in the client or his/her condition which did not require any intervention (including those which are health-related), do not signify that therapy has taken place. Specifically, spontaneous cures and the unexplained disappearance of symptoms do not qualify as therapy unless they occur during or as the result of a process of intervention. Similarly, when clients undergo natural developmental change, maturational growth, or normal healing, the process cannot be considered therapy if intervention was not necessary.

On the other hand, therapy is also not defined in terms of whether the desired outcome or goal has been reached. If there has been a process of intervention and that process has not achieved the desired therapeutic results, or any identifiable change whatsoever, therapy has still taken place—it has just not been successful. Thus, what defines therapy is the *process* of intervention, not the *outcome*, whether it be positive or negative.

The third point is that by definition, therapy always involves a therapist. In order for *therapy* to take place, the process of intervention must be carried out by a person who, by qualification and intent, acts in the capacity of a "therapist;" it does not take place whenever helpful interventions are made by persons who are not therapists or who are not actual participants in the process. Of course, to say that therapy requires the efforts of a therapist does not mean that interventions from other sources do not take place during the process, and that they do not mitigate the therapeutic situation. Myriad forces prevail upon the client and his/her condition, both within and outside of the context of therapy, and many of them can affect the outcome in some way, either positively or negatively. When these forces operate outside of the context of therapy, or when they operate without the involvement of a therapist, the process of intervention cannot be considered therapy per se. Therapy is defined by the involvement of a therapist, not by the involvement of any other person or factor operating outside of the context of the therapy process.

AGENT OF INTERVENTIONS:
THERAPIST OR MUSIC?

When the above criteria are applied to music therapy, a core issue immediately arises. In music therapy, the therapist is not the only agent acting upon the client; in fact, sometimes, the therapist is not even the major source of intervention. Music plays an integral role in the therapy process, sometimes serving as a partner with the therapist, and sometimes facilitating or inducing change in the client with little or no help from the therapist. Zwerling (1984), noting the enormous power of the arts to be intrinsically healing in and of themselves, queried whether the role of an arts therapist should be to teach clients how to experience the arts and their healing properties, or to treat them through formal methods of therapeutic intervention employing the arts.

In terms of music therapy, should the therapist give the client access to the healing properties of music, or make intentional efforts to address the client's treatment needs through some combination of musical and personal interventions? In the former, it is the music that supplies the therapeutic remedy; in the latter, the therapist uses music as part of the remedy.

A useful distinction has been made between music *as* therapy and music *in* therapy (Bruscia, 1987a). In music *as* therapy, music serves as the primary medium and agent for therapeutic change, exerting a very direct influence on the client and his/her health. In this approach, the therapist's main goal is to help the client relate to or engage in the music, thus serving as a guide or facilitator who has the expertise needed to prescribe the appropriate music or music experience for the client.

In music *in* therapy, music is used not only for its own healing properties but also to enhance the effects of the therapist-client relationship or other treatment modalities (e.g., verbal discussion). Here music is not the only or primary agent of change, and its use depends upon the therapist. In this approach, the therapist's main goal is to address the needs of the client through whatever medium seems most relevant or suitable, whether it be music, the relationship, or other therapeutic modalities.

Perhaps the best way to understand the difference is to compare them in terms of what is the focus of therapy and what is the context which facilitates that focus. In music *as* therapy, *music* is the focus of therapy, thereby serving as the primary medium or agent for therapeutic intervention, interaction, and change; while the personal relationship between client and therapist and the use of other arts or therapeutic modalities provide a context which facilitates that focus. Conversely, in music *in* therapy, the focus is on either the personal relationship between the client and therapist, or an experience in a modality other than music, while music provides the context or background which facilitates that focus. Thus, when used *as* therapy, music is the foreground, and the relationship and other modalities are in the background; when used *in* therapy, music provides the background, while the relationship and other modalities serve as the foreground.

In terms of the present discussion, this distinction clarifies that while music can be naturally therapeutic or healing without the help of a therapist, music therapy requires the skilled application of music by a therapist. The therapist may choose to use music *as* therapy or music *in* therapy, however, in both instances the process involves intervention by a therapist.

In short, the present definition stipulates that for any process of intervention to be considered music therapy, it must involve *both* music and a therapist. Music therapy is not complete without either agent. Thus, any use of music for therapeutic benefit which does not involve a therapist is not considered music *therapy;* and any method of intervention which does not involve music in either assessment, treatment, or evaluation is not considered *music* therapy.

NATURE OF MUSIC INTERVENTIONS

The fact that music can serve as a partner to the therapist in the intervention process reveals much about the essential nature of music therapy. If the therapist can use music to accomplish therapeutic aims, either by itself or coupled with personal interventions, then there must be many similarities in the functions of the therapist and the music. That is, the processes of intervention used by the therapist must be very similar to processes found in music which act upon the client.

What then is the essential nature of intervention in music therapy? How do music and therapist act on the client in similar ways? Exactly what takes place in the therapeutic process, when the therapist and/or music intervene in the client's way of being? Exactly how do the therapist and music help the client?

In surveying the clinical literature, the author has identified many different kinds of interventions or ways that a music therapist typically helps clients. These interventions will be discussed in detail in the next chapter, entitled "Helps." The discussion belongs there because in actuality all interventions within a clinical setting are attempts of the therapist to help the client to achieve health.

What is important to address here is the unique nature of interventions in music therapy—where therapist and music work in tandem to help the client. In a sense, what we are really asking is what makes music therapy interventions different from those in any other form of therapy, or what interventions are truly indigenous and unique to *music* therapy. The answer to these questions lies in the combination of three elements that define and differentiate music therapy from all other modalities: sound, beauty, and creativity.

Sound-centered

Music therapy is sound-centered. It emphasizes the sensory modality of hearing—it is ear-oriented. Thus, in the truest forms of music therapy, most if not all of the interventions used center around the production or reception of sound, and particularly in the form of musical sounds. Ultimately, music therapy is a *sound* experience.

In *active* forms of therapy, when clients perform, improvise, or compose music, they express their problems through sound, they explore their resources through sound, they work through conflicts in sound, they develop relationships through sound, and they find resolution and fulfillment through sound. And all of this requires an ear orientation. How they sing and play is mediated by what they hear as they are doing it.

In *receptive* forms of therapy, when clients listen to music, they take in the sounds with their bodies, they apprehend sounds with their psyche, they hear themselves in sound, they hear the world of others in sound, they relive their experiences in sound, they remember in sound, they think in sound, and they approach the divine through sound.

This says much about what a music therapist's specialty is with regard to interventions. If clients need music therapy to sound off and to be heard, then a music therapist has to be a quintessential listener as well as an eloquent creator of sound. If sound is the primary medium of communication in music therapy, whether it be through vibrations, tones, sound forms, or music, then music therapists, by trade, have to be "sound" communicators.

Beauty-centered

Music therapy is beauty-centered. That is, the context for the sound experience in music therapy is always an aesthetic one—it is always motivated by the search for beauty, and the meaning that beauty brings to life through music. Thus, the very point of listening to or creating music as a therapeutic endeavor is to experience the beauty and meaning of life, and in the process, to learn how to work through the problems and challenges that are an integral part of the life experience. Just as music presents tension and conflict, and just as it moves toward change and resolution, so does the human being work to become whole and thereby live life more fully. And when this journey towards wholeness takes place within the exquisiteness of an art form, that is within an aesthetic context—the journey is made that much more poignant, potent, and memorable.

Clients come to therapy, no matter what their diagnoses, because they are having difficulties on this journey toward wholeness. At the most basic level, their problems have rendered them unable to find the beauty and meaning of their lives—they can no longer live their lives to the fullest.

What must never be forgotten then, is that regardless of its many applications and benefits, music therapy must always be an aesthetic endeavor. It is always and essentially concerned with beauty and meaning, and its primary mission by design is to help clients on their journey toward wholeness. Thus, whether music is being used to facilitate classroom learning, to teach adaptive behavior, to reduce physical pain, to stimulate reminiscence, or to build interpersonal skills—it is and must always be an aesthetic endeavor. Its greatest power lies in the beauty, meaning, and wholeness that it brings into the lives of clients; thus, without the aesthetic, music therapy ultimately loses not only its greatest potency but also its basic identity.

Creativity-centered

Music therapy is creativity-centered. The way sounds become beautiful and meaningful is through the creative process. When a client listens to or creates music, it involves being creative with sounds, exploring different ways the sounds can be arranged, perceived and interpreted. Thus we can say that the client's very participation in music therapy requires the creative process.

Therapists often draw parallels between the creative process and the therapeutic process. One reason is that both are believed to involve some kind of problem solving. Both therapy and the creative process involve: examining something in detail, identifying problems and challenges, exploring alternatives and options, playing with all the resources at hand, trying out what works best in solving the problem, selecting which options are more pleasing, and then organizing all the decisions into a product or outcome that is both beautiful and meaningful.

In music therapy, the process of solving "musical problems" is conceived as similar to the process of resolving "life problems," and the skills learned through finding musical resolutions are believed to generalize to life situations. For example, in improvisational music therapy, the client works on "discovering possibilities, inventing new options, choosing and testing alternatives, energizing, and projecting efforts through time" (Bruscia, 1987a, p. 364), and although these efforts take place within a musical framework, they can be seen as a metaphor for or even a direct manifestation of what the client needs to learn or accomplish in life.

Verbal psychotherapists have also cited the importance of creativity in the therapeutic process, even when treatment does not involve the manipulation of artistic media. Rollo May (1975) found direct links between the courage needed to be creative and the courage needed to live a healthy life. Zinker (1978) describes Gestalt therapy as treating a person like an art medium, and giving the person permission to be creative. The process involves "continuous invention of new models of seeing oneself" and "continuous behavioral testing of these innovative models in the safety of a creatively permissive environment" (p. 32).

Several definitions of music therapy stress the central role of creativity, some for the therapist and others for the client. The Association for Professional Music Therapists in Great Britain (1982) stipulates that the therapist uses music "creatively." The Canadian Association for Music Therapy (n.d.) states that "the nature of music therapy emphasizes a creative approach in work with handicapped individuals." The definition of music therapy published by the National Coalition of Arts Therapy Associations (1985) describes music therapy as the use of music as a creative and structured therapeutic tool. Finally, the Mid-Atlantic Music

Therapy Region (1988) of NAMT defines music therapy as the structured use of music as a creative process.

The issue of creativity also seems to be at the root of other distinctions in terminology. When grouping together art, music, dance, drama, and poetry therapies under a generic heading, terms such as "expressive therapy," "arts therapies," and "creative arts therapies" are commonly used. What is the difference? Is expressive therapy broader than the others because it includes media, materials, and processes that are not necessarily artistic or creative in nature? Does expressive therapy focus on the sensory modalities elaborated by the art form, rather than the art form itself? Are all of the arts creative? If not, why is the term "creative" included in some titles and excluded in others? Is creative arts therapies the most clearly delimited because it excludes anything that does not qualify as artistic and creative?

SUMMARY

An intervention is a purposeful attempt to mitigate an existing condition in order to affect some kind of change. In therapy, interventions are based on three criteria; 1) the client must need outside help to accomplish his/her health objective; 2) there must be purposeful intervention, regardless of the outcome; and 3) the intervention must be carried out by a therapist within the context of a therapist-client relationship.

What makes music therapy interventions unique is that they always involves both music and therapist acting as partners in the process. When music is used *as* therapy, music is the primary partner; when music is used *in* therapy, the therapist is the primary partner. When music is used as an intervention without a therapist, it is not music *therapy*; when a therapist does not use music in the intervention, it is not *music* therapy. Music therapy interventions are unique because they are sound-centered, beauty-centered and creativity-centered. Interventions in music therapy are carried out at two levels: using music experiences as the 'method' of therapeutic intervention, and establishing conditions which 'help' the client to enter into the therapeutic process.

Chapter Seven

THERAPIST

NEED FOR THERAPIST

In the last chapter, it was stated that therapy, by definition, requires intervention by a therapist. Now it is time to examine this conjecture in greater detail. Why is a therapist needed in order for therapy to take place? Can a person be a therapist to him or herself? Can one person assume the roles of both client and therapist? Does a client really need the help of a therapist?

These questions are particularly germane and perplexing for music therapy, where music is such an active agent in the therapeutic process, often supplanting the traditional functions of the therapist. Is a therapist really needed when music serves as the primary therapeutic agent, or can the client relate directly to the music without the aid of a therapist? Does music therapy refer only to those musical experiences which involve a therapist, or does it also include therapeutic experiences derived from the music alone?

It is interesting to find that in the literature, music therapy has often been defined simply as "the use of music," without any clear stipulation that a therapist is essential to the process. For example, see the definitions of Alley (1979), Alvin (1975), the Australian Music Therapy Association, Carter (1982), the National Coalition of Arts Therapy Associations (1985), Paul (1982), Schomer (1973, Sekeles (1985), and Steele (1977).

In contrast, there are several other definitions wherein the therapist is made a more essential ingredient. For example, the Association for Professional Music Therapists in Great Britain (1982) defines music therapy as a form of treatment whereby a mutual relationship is set up between patient and therapist. Bruscia (1986a) describes it as an interpersonal process involving therapist and client in certain role relationships and musical experiences. Codding (1982) cites both music and the therapist's skills as agents of change, and goes on to say that "the structure provided by the therapeutic environment, and the relationship between therapist and child, child and peers, facilitates the learning of necessary life skills" (p. 22). Boxill (1985) places the entire process of music therapy within the context of a client-therapist relationship, while the French Association for Music Therapy (1984) defines music therapy as "the use of sounds and music in a psychotherapeutic relation." And finally, in the present definition, the therapist helps the client through music experiences and the relationships formed through them.

These latter definitions imply that what makes the therapist an essential ingredient is the relationship that he or she develops with the client. Certainly this is true, but there are a number of fundamental questions still unanswered: What are the specific responsibilities of a therapist that define his/her role within that relationship? How does the client-therapist relationship differ from other kinds of relationships? What does a therapist do that other professionals, friends or relatives do not do or cannot do? What does a therapist bring to therapy that a client does not already have, or what does a therapist do that a client cannot do for him or herself?

DEFINITIONAL CRITERIA

According to Bloch (1982), "the person who makes himself available as a therapist is in effect a socially sanctioned healer who has been designated thus by virtue of his training and skills. The therapist is a professional who makes a commitment to help others in need of his expertise" (p. 4). When this definition of a therapist is considered in terms of the various roles and responsibilities ascribed to music therapists in the literature, one can identify several characteristics of a therapist which make him/her essential and unique to the process of therapy. A therapist is someone who: 1) helps the client, 2) on a contractual basis 3) with a health-related need, 4) within the context of a professional relationship, 5) which is based upon the therapist's expertise, 6) and governed by ethical rules of conduct. Let us now discuss each of these criteria separately.

Helper not Helped

A therapist is someone who makes a commitment to help another person, and to be available (as necessary and appropriate) whenever the person needs or seeks that help. Thus, a therapist is, by definition, the person who provides the help, and the client is the person who receives the help. While this seems blatantly obvious, there is something implied in this statement which needs to be said nevertheless. What makes the helping relationship in therapy a unique one, is that it is neither mutual nor reciprocal. That is, it is the therapist's responsibility to help the client—it is not the client's responsibility to help the therapist in return. The relationship of helper and helped in therapy is unidirectional and one-sided—it does not go both ways. It does not have the same give-and-take character of most personal relationships with family and friends. Notwithstanding financial remuneration for services, the therapist cannot expect the client to reciprocate *in kind* for whatever help s/he is offering as part of therapy. For example, if the client complains to the therapist about his/her problems or has a tantrum, the therapist does not have the right to do the same. Or if the client seeks support from a therapist during a life crisis, the therapist cannot expect the client to be there during his/her own crises.

When the roles in therapy are significantly reversed, that is, when the therapist needs or seeks help from the client, and/or when the client provides that help to the therapist, the therapist is no longer acting in the role of a therapist, and the client is no longer acting in the role of client—in short, therapy is no longer taking place.

Once it has been acknowledged that the client-therapist relationship is essentially one-sided with regard to help, it must also be recognized that the very act of doing therapy provides many opportunities for therapists to either meet their own needs, help themselves, or be helped by a client—either consciously or unconsciously, and either involving or not involving the client directly. The term commonly used for this phenomenon is *countertransference*. A discussion of countertransference is essential to understanding the nature of any helping relationship which is one-sided as with client and therapist—regardless of the therapist's philosophical orientation!

Although it was Sigmund Freud who first identified and named the phenomenon of countertransference, and although his initial definition of it was very limited in scope and applicable only to the psychoanalytic situation, it is now generally recognized as an essential concept of therapy, and a phenomenon which cannot be avoided in any client-therapist relationship, *regardless* of orientation (e.g., behavioral, developmental, psychodynamic, transpersonal), or goal of therapy (e.g., learning, behavior change, catharsis, insight, etc.). The reason is quite simple. If therapy involves or depends upon any kind of inter*personal* relationship between client and therapist, and if the therapist is a human being with the usual combination of body, psyche, and spirit, then there are bound to be personal feelings, attitudes, beliefs, biases, habits, or past experiences that a therapist has which influence who s/he is in that relationship and how s/he interacts with the client.

In its broadest conception, countertransference includes all conscious and unconscious predispositions and responses of a therapist to the client that have their origin in the therapist's personality and experience, both past and present. It can have both positive and negative effects. Countertransference has a positive effect when the therapist can use personal similarities with the client to gain greater insight and rapport. It has a negative influence when the unconscious needs of the therapist interfere with effective intervention. The result is that the therapist meets his or her own needs instead of, or at the expense of, meeting the client's needs, and is unaware of doing so. The most common examples are: when the therapist projects his/her own needs onto the client and then treats the client for those needs rather than the client's real needs; when the therapist distorts or misinterprets information about the client to match his/her own beliefs; when the therapist gets overly involved in the client's problems and loses his/her personal boundaries; or when the therapist mistreats or neglects a client because of unconscious feelings of anger or revenge at significant people in his/her own life. Keep in mind that these are only a few of the possibilities.

Unfortunately, because this term was originally coined by Freud and then further developed conceptually by psychoanalytic therapists, many therapists with different orientations assume that countertransference is not relevant to their work. This is a very dangerous assumption indeed. Every therapist, regardless of philosophical orientation or area of practice, has an ongoing responsibility to take the precautions necessary to avoid negative countertransference. Indeed, this is one of the most important ethical responsibilities every therapist has.

A detailed discussion of countertransference in music therapy (and its partner, transference) can be found in Bruscia (1998).

Contractual Relationship

If the therapist is defined as the helper and the client is defined as the person seeking help, and if this arrangement is not based on mutuality or reciprocity in kind, what is the nature of their relationship? What is the essential agreement between the two parties which makes it possible for them to work together? Why is the therapist agreeing to be the helper in such a situation? Does the client agree to do anything in return, and if so what?

The main point being made above about the lack of reciprocity is that in a therapist-client relationship, the therapist is expected to provide a certain kind of help that the client is not expected to return *in kind*. Clients do not give therapy to the therapist in return for the therapist's services. This does not mean that there is not a contractual agreement.

The therapist agrees to help the client with a particular health objective by providing a particular kind of service, and the client (or the agency or institution acting on behalf of the client) agrees to accept that service and to remunerate the therapist in some way for them. By definition then, therapists provide their services within a contractual agreement with clients or their guardians, and this agreement is based on remuneration (which can be of various kinds), but not reciprocity in kind.

A therapist is a professional, which means that, s/he earns money and makes a living by providing services to clients. Thus, the very basis for therapy is an agreement between the therapist and client (or guardian) that the therapist will be remunerated for the help that s/he provides to the client. Therapy is not something that is given away, and a therapist is not a volunteer who donates his/her services. Of course, this does not mean that therapists do not sometimes volunteer their services or give free sessions to clients or trade their services with other therapists. All of these are clearly exceptions to the rule, sometimes warranted and sometimes not, sometimes ethical and sometimes not. Judgment is always needed. But for theoretical purposes, a therapist is not defined as someone who offers his/her services without remuneration. The exceptions to this do not define the rule. Therapists provide therapy as a profession, and therefore expect to be remunerated for their services to clients.

Given the altruism and caring that is often necessary for therapy to be effective, it might seem rather crass to emphasize the financial aspects of their relationship. But this crass fact is a rather important one in defining the role boundaries of a therapist. A therapist does not provide help to clients whenever clients express a desire or need for their services, or whenever a therapist might want to help a client. Therapy always proceeds on the understanding that a therapist does not provide therapy unless such help is requested, as evidenced by an agreement by the client or guardian to pay for the therapist's services. When something is given freely, without payment, there is always a doubt as to whether the client wants what the therapist is providing, or whether the therapist is helping the client for personal rather than professional reasons.

Health Focus

Therapy is not defined as just any kind of help, and a therapist is not just any kind of helper. Therapy, by definition, is an effort to promote health; and a therapist, by profession, is a person who helps others to do so. Thus, the specific kind of help that a therapist gives to a client is first and foremost health related. That is, when a therapist acts in the capacity of therapist, it always involves helping the client to address specific health concerns. As will be discussed later, health is defined very broadly, to include the physical, mental, emotional, social, and spiritual well-being of the client, as well as the myriad factors which bear upon such well-being; nevertheless, it is important to realize that the therapist's role responsibilities have boundaries, and that these boundaries are essential for therapy to take place.

Two questions are important to ask in maintaining these boundaries. First, is the therapist helping the client with regard to his/her health; and second, is the therapist providing services of a professional nature? Other kinds of help that a therapist might provide to a client—that is, any kind of help that does not seek to restore, maintain or improve the client's health—are not considered therapy. It should also be noted that the kind of help provided by the therapist is professional rather than personal in nature. That is, the therapist helps a client through specific types of professional services as defined by the therapist's discipline or area of expertise. Notwithstanding the myriad needs of a client that may arise during the course of treatment, and the emphasis currently given to interdisciplinary programming, a therapist does not provide help of a personal nature or help which goes beyond his/her professional boundaries.

To be more specific, the professional services of a music therapist are defined and delimited by those health concerns of the client that can be addressed through music. Although this may seem obvious and redundant to say, the primary job of a music therapist is to provide clients with music experiences aimed at promoting health. Any job which relates to health but not music, or music but not health are outside the boundaries of professional music therapy. The implications are that, notwithstanding the personal needs of a client or the job demands of the agency taking responsibility for a client, the services of a music therapist do not include running errands or doing personal favors for clients; they do not include seeing the client socially or participating in private family events; they do not include doing what other professionals are qualified and supposed to do, such as being a lifeguard at the pool, or coaching the basketball team, or cooking meals for the clients, or teaching clients in another field.

When music therapists give clients services which are beyond the limits of their field, it is important for them to realize that what they are doing is not music therapy. Music therapy cannot be defined to include all the services that every music therapist might choose to give their clients or agencies. Music therapy has its own specific and clearly defined boundaries which are indigenous to its mission. Moreover, music therapists should always be vigilant that what they offer to client is always within the boundaries of a professional relationship, as well as their expertise. This leads us to the next parts of this discussion.

Expertise

One of the most important characteristics of a therapist is expertise. Clients usually seek help from a therapist because the therapist has the knowledge or skill that the client needs to deal with a health concern. That is, a therapist is usually an expert with regard to a particular health problem or method of treatment.

A therapist, by definition, has specific knowledge and skills, and offers his/her expertise to help the client. To function as a therapist, one has to have the expertise needed to assume the role responsibilities required by the particular form of therapy being provided and the client population being served. In music therapy, the expertise needed at the entry level—that is, to begin practicing as a beginner—falls into three main areas: musical foundations, clinical foundations, and music therapy. See Table 1 for a shortened version of "Essential Competencies for the Practice of Music Therapy" (Bruscia, Hesser, Boxill, 1981). Originally developed in 1974, this inventory of entry-level competencies was officially adopted by the American Association for Music Therapy and used as evaluative criteria for endorsing undergraduate degree programs and for certifying individuals entering the field. Advanced competencies have also been formulated for learning in-depth models of clinical practice, theory, research, supervision, teaching, and administration (Bruscia, 1986b).

Credentials

Not only must a therapist have the necessary knowledge and skill, s/he must also be designated as such by an appropriate authority. That is, a music therapist has to be recognized as a "trained professional" through some official mechanism or authority (e.g., certification or registration by a professional association or state licensing board). This serves to ensure prospective clients that the therapist is qualified to practice music therapy.

In the United States, there has been three such credentialing associations: the National Association for Music Therapy (NAMT) who granted the title "Registered Music Therapist" or "RMT" to qualified individuals; the American Association for Music Therapy (AAMT) who granted the title "Certified Music Therapist" or "CMT" to qualified individuals; and the Certification Board for Music Therapists (CBMT) who grants the title "Music Therapist-Board Certified" or "MT-BC" to qualified individuals who pass its national examination. As of January 1, 1998, the NAMT and AAMT unified to become the American Music Therapy Association (AMTA), yielding all responsibility for credentialing of individuals to the CBMT, while still retaining its role in the accreditation of undergraduate and graduate degree programs which prepare the individuals.

Similar associations exist in many other countries throughout the world, all concerned with the development of standards and requirements for training music therapists and granting them credentials. For a comprehensive account of these associations, see Maranto (1993).

Defining the specific competencies of a music therapist has been an important development in a field which is by its very nature so interdisciplinary. There are many musicians who do similar kinds of work in clinical settings but are not qualified fully as music therapists; similarly there are many therapists in other clinical fields who use music in their practice, but are not qualified fully as music therapists.

This situation has raised a very interesting dilemma in defining music therapy. Is music therapy defined by the type of training the therapist has, or by the type of service the therapist provides? If a psychotherapist uses methods of music therapy, should the service be called psychotherapy or music therapy? Or conversely, if a music therapist uses methods of psychotherapy, is the service classified as psychotherapy or music therapy? These questions are made even more difficult when musicians who are not trained in therapy and therapists who are not musicians do intense training in one particular area or method of music therapy and become quite competent to practice it.

They may be doing music therapy, and quite competently, but should they be defined as music therapists?

Several definitions of music therapy have tried to grapple with these issues, either by stipulating the need for training, or by specifying the nature of the services provided. A few definers call for a professional music therapist who is specially trained. Bright (1981) says that music therapy is "carried out by a trained music therapist working in the context of a clinical team" (p. 1). Rudenberg (1982) and Peters (1987) stipulate that music therapy is provided under the direction or supervision of specially trained professionals.

Some definitions go even further and spell out specific role responsibilities of the music therapist. The Canadian Association for Music Therapy (n.d.) states that the "professional music therapist participates in the assessment of client needs, the formulation of an approach and programme for the individual client, and then carries out specific musical activities to reach the goals." The National Association for Music Therapy (1980) cites the same responsibilities. Kenny (1982) says that the music therapist "serves as a resource person and guide, providing musical experiences which direct clients towards health and well-being" (p. 7). The Uruguayan Association (UAMT, 1984) describes the music therapist's role as using music to stimulate the client to make the changes necessary for better integration with the environment. Finally, in her discussion of the role of the music therapist, Peters (1987) says: "The music therapist carefully selects the music or music activity to be used with a particular client, based on the therapist's knowledge of the effects of music on human behavior and the particular client's strengths, weaknesses, and therapeutic goals. The music therapist also often plays a very active role in helping the client derive a therapeutic experience from involvement with music and music activities. By creating a success-oriented, non-threatening atmosphere, establishing a growth-promoting relationship with the client, and structuring the environment to help the client achieve certain therapeutic goals, the music therapist transforms mere music activity into music therapy" (p.7).

Related to this issue is the capacity of a music therapist to serve as a primary therapist. When serving in an ancillary capacity, the music therapist stays within the boundaries of music, and works with team consultation or supervision by a primary therapist. When serving as the primary therapist, the music therapist may address goals from other disciplines within the limits of his/her expertise, and with the appropriate consultations. Obviously then, educational background, training, and competence are important determinants of the role boundaries of a music therapist.

If the therapist has to be a professional with expertise in the designated area, then obviously s/he does not go beyond his/her area of expertise in helping the client. A music therapist is not, for example, a speech therapist or psychotherapist–unless specifically trained and officially designated as such. Thus, a music therapist does not use assessment, treatment, or evaluation procedures from other disciplines without the necessary training or expertise, and does not offer clients any kind or level of health-related service that goes beyond his/her specific area of expertise.

All of these conditions point to the most important issue in defining a therapist—professional ethics. A therapist is, by definition, an expert who uses principles of personal and professional ethics to guide his/her work with clients. In music therapy, these principles are concerned with matters such as competence, professional conduct, client rights, and research.

Table 1.

ESSENTIAL COMPETENCIES
FOR THE PRACTICE OF MUSIC THERAPY
AT THE ENTRY LEVEL

Musical Foundations

- *Music Theory and Music History:* ability to analyze elements, structure and style of music aurally and visually; understanding of characteristics of music from various periods, styles and cultures; ability to recognize standard works from classical and popular literatures; ability to solfege, and take aural dictation.
- *Composition and Arrangemen:* ability to compose and arrange simple songs and nonsymphonic instrumental pieces.
- *Performance:* ability to sing or play a major instrument with considerable proficiency and interpretive understanding.
- *Keyboard:* ability to play intermediate pieces, sight-read simple pieces, and play and sing basic repertoire of traditional folk and popular songs; ability to play basic chord progressions in all keys, to harmonize melodies and transpose at sight and by ear.
- *Guitar:* ability to strum and pick basic chords and accompany self while singing a basic repertoire of traditional folk, and popular songs; ability to harmonize melodies and transpose at sight and by ear.
- *Voice:* ability to sing in tune with pleasing quality and by memory a basic repertoire of traditional folk and popular songs; understanding of basic vocal techniques.
- *Nonsymphonic Instruments:*ability to play autoharp and wide variety of melodic and percussive nonsymphonic instruments.
- *Improvisation:* ability to extemporaneously invent and develop musical ideas on major instrument, voice, keyboard or guitar, and nonsymphonic instruments, in solo and ensemble settings.

- *Conducting:* ability to conduct small vocal and nonsymphonic instrumental ensembles.
- *Movement:* ability to express self through movement and dance, and to move expressively to music.

Clinical Foundations

- *Exceptionality:* understanding of various exceptionalities, their causes, symptoms, personal implications; understanding of normal development and psychopathology.
- *Dynamics of Therapy:* understanding of dynamics and processes of client-therapist relationship, individual and group treatment process, and various models of psychotherapy.
- *Therapeutic Relationship:* Understanding of client's perspective; recognition of own impact on client; ability to establish therapeutic relationships and use self effectively in individual and group therapy.

Music Therapy

- *Foundations and Principles:* understanding of the nature of music and rationale for its use in therapy; understanding of musical characteristics of various client populations; understanding of purpose of music therapy with different populations; understanding of basic principles in music therapy assessment, treatment and evaluation; knowledge of history of profession.
- *Client Assessment:* ability to identify assessment needs, and implement effective methods of client assessment through music; ability to evaluate and apply assessment findings.
- *Treatment Planning:* ability to identify treatment needs, formulate appropriate goals and objectives, develop effective treatment strategies for individual and group music therapy.
- *Treatment Implementation:* ability to create conducive environment, develop appropriate musical materials, lead various kinds of musical experiences, spontaneously engage client in music, organize sessions, and identify significant events.

- *Therapy Evaluation:* ability to recognize and record significant changes, set realistic time frames for evaluation, design effective methods of determining client progress, and utilize evaluation findings.
- *Therapy Closure:* ability to determine appropriate time for terminating therapy; ability to provide client with closure.
- *Communication about Therapy:* ability to communicate with client, significant others, and treatment team about therapy, through both oral and written means.
- *Interdisciplinary Collaboration:* understanding of the role of other disciplines in relation to music therapy; ability to relate client's programs to those of other disciplines, and to collaborate with team members.
- *Supervision and Administration:* ability to participate beneficially in supervision; ability to administer clinical music therapy programs in various settings.
- *Ethics:* ability to interpret and apply ethical standards of practice.

Chapter Eight

HELPS

Help is such a common word that it may seem unnecessary to question what it means. But when placed so prominently within the definition of a health profession it becomes a key word to define. If the main purpose of music therapy is to help the client, it seems essential to know precisely what the nature of that help is. And in the real world, there is a fundamental question that must be answered for every client that enters the music therapy room and for every referral made by another health professional: Exactly what can a music therapist do to help this client that cannot be done by another kind of health professional? Of course, the most obvious answer is to engage the client in therapeutic music experiences. But exactly how does engagement in music help the client in a therapeutic way?

Earlier it was explained that music is used in two basic ways: as therapy and in therapy, that is, with the music taking the primary role of helper and the therapist being secondary, and with the therapist taking the primary role of helper and the music being secondary. Thus, it is not entirely accurate to say that it is just the music that makes music therapy unique—it is the combination of the music and therapist in the role of the helper that differentiates it from other disciplines.

The implications of this for understanding how music therapy helps the client are myriad. Simply stated, depending on client need and circumstances, the therapist can help in certain ways and the music can help in others; sometimes they can help in the same ways, and sometimes they cannot; sometimes only the therapist can provide the specific kind of help needed by the client, and sometimes only the music can provide it; and sometimes both therapist and music have to be combined to provide the help needed.

With this in mind, let us examine clinical practice to discover exactly how music therapists use music and their personal selves to help clients.

What follows is a brief description of the kinds of help that the author identified in the first edition of this book as types of interventions. While these ways of helping can be implemented musically, verbally, or nonverbally, emphasis will be given here to the musical implementation, as this is most germane and indigenous to music therapy.

EMPATHY

Empathy is the capacity to identify with or understand what another person is experiencing. This may include going through similar body experiences, feeling the same emotions, taking the same perspective on something, thinking the same thoughts, doing the same thing together, and so forth. Empathy is accomplished through the process of identification, when one person identifies with the other and then imagines what that person must be experiencing. Or as commonly expressed, it is when we "walk in someone else's shoes."

Music is a medium par excellence for empathy. In fact, in many ways, it is unmatched by any other medium. When we sing the same song together, we live in the same melody, we share the same tonal center, we articulate the same lyrics, we move ahead according to the same rhythm—moment by moment, sound by sound, through an ongoing awareness of the other, and through continuing efforts to stay together and thereby become one within the experience. Meanwhile, we are also receiving the same feedback as we listen to ourselves: we hear the same sounds and words as we sing them, and feel the same ebb and flow as we shape each phrase. When the song is sad, we share that sadness, we live through it together; and when the song is joyful, we celebrate together, we share the same occasion to rejoice. Our actions are synchronized in time, our bodies resonate to the same vibrations, our attention is riveted on the same focus, our emotions are reflected in one another as well as in the music we are making, our thoughts are one.

What makes music particularly conducive to empathy is that it not only unites the musicians in the same sensorimotor activity, it also holds the musicians and listeners together in the same auditory space and time, while taking them through the same realms of human experience in a very intimate way. Music holds us in its presence because when sound enters the environment, it infuses it completely and cannot be ignored or blocked out as easily as other kinds of stimuli.

Empathic techniques can be found in both active and receptive forms of music therapy. For example, in active music therapy (when the client is engaged in music-making), the therapist can use techniques such as: imitating (e.g., echoing a rhythm or melody after being presented by the client); synchronizing (e.g., playing the same melody or rhythm at the same time); reflecting (e.g., musically depicting the client's moods, attitudes, feelings); and incorporating (e.g., using one of the client's musical motifs as part of the music) (Bruscia, 1987a).

In receptive music therapy (when the client listens to music), the therapist demonstrates empathy by selecting the music according to the "iso-principle" (i.e., by matching the music to what the client is experiencing, either physically, emotionally, or mentally). For example, the therapist may select music that "entrains" the client (e.g., matches autonomic responses such as the heart beat), music that "resonates" with the client (e.g., vibrates at the same frequency), music that "reflects" the client's feelings, moods, or attitudes, or music that "expresses" what the client is expressing at a conscious or unconscious level.

Empathy is essential in the therapist-client relationship; in fact, it is the basis for all the interventions that a therapist uses to help the client. Through empathy, the therapist establishes rapport with the client, builds understanding of the client's resources and needs, secures the client's trust, and prepares the client for all the other kinds of help the therapist will be offering.

Aside from the direct benefits of receiving empathy from the therapist, the client also gains a model for empathy. By experiencing and observing the therapist's empathy, the client can be motivated to empathize with others, and in the process develop the sensitivity and skills needed.

OPPORTUNITIES FOR SELF-EXPRESSION

Clients often come to therapy because they need to express what they are experiencing inside, and because music provides myriad opportunities for helping them to do so. Music therapists engage clients in a wide variety of activities and experiences aimed at helping them to externalize, enact, release, ventilate, represent, project, or document their inner experiences. The media may be musical, verbal or nonverbal; however, of all these, it is musical self-expression which distinguishes music therapy from other modalities. Only in music therapy does a client have an opportunity to express him/herself through singing, playing instruments, and through the creative acts of improvising and composing. Music is the art of expressing oneself in sound; through it, we turn inner body sensations, movements, feelings, and ideas into external sound forms that can be heard.

Making and creating music provides opportunities for self-expression at many levels. At the most primitive level, it enables us to sound our bodies—to vibrate and resonate its various parts so that they can be heard. When we sing or play instruments, we release our inner energy into the outer world, we sound our bodies, we give form to our impulses, we voice unspoken or unspeakable ideas, and we pour our emotions into descriptive sound forms.

When we listen to music we express ourselves vicariously, through the composer and performers of the piece. Vicarious self-expression is very important when we have difficult feelings to express, feelings that we are unable to shape into a suitable form, as well as feelings that we reject or do not want to own as ours. When we hear the composer and performers expressing their feelings, we can either identify with them and experience the release as ours as well as theirs, or we can be a part of their release but not identify the feelings as our own.

Musical self-expression often leads quite naturally to other forms of expression, depending on the client's abilities and proclivities. Clients who are verbal frequently want to talk about what they expressed in their music, or what they heard being expressed in the music of others; clients who are more nonverbal sometimes want to move or draw to music which they have found to be self-expressive. More will be said about this shifting of modality in the next section.

Before leaving this discussion, it should be said that musical self-expression is not merely about externalization and release of feelings, it also requires a host of sensorimotor, perceptual, and cognitive skills. Music therapists therefore often use singing, playing instruments, and listening as enjoyable and rewarding ways to acquire and improve skills in self-expression.

INTERACTION

Self-expression is different from interaction and communication. When one expresses oneself, it does not have to be directed towards someone or something outside; it can involve merely the release of what is inside, without any concern for whether the expression is understood by the outside world, and without any concern that it will offend or harm anyone or anything. Self-expression, as used here, is essentially a private matter. In contrast, interaction is concerned with engaging the outside world in a give-and-take of mutual influence; it is a process of acting upon and being acted upon by others in a reciprocal way.

Music therapy by its very nature, regardless of goal or orientation, involves interaction, either between the client and therapist or between different clients. The reason is that creating and listening to music is a very natural and easy way of relating to others. When we sing or play an instrument with someone, we have to take specific parts in order for the music to make sense. If one person is the soloist and another the accompanist, each person has a specific role in relation to the other: the soloist leads and the accompanist follows. On the other hand, if the music is a round or canon, every person takes exactly the same role, but each one sings or plays it at a different time. Music is full of these kinds of role relationships; in fact, we can say that every composition or improvisation is like a diagram which specifies each person's part and the relationships between each part and the whole.

An important component in carrying out these role relationships is listening to one another. It is not enough to play out one's role without regard for what others are doing. Each musician has to listen to the other(s), and adjust one's own singing or playing to stay together in tempo, pitch, dynamics, and so forth.

For all these reasons, music provides infinite models for interaction, and music therapy provides an opportunity to experiment with each of them. Certainly, other forms of therapy have the very same aims, however, here again, the unique advantage of music therapy is the use of sound and music as the primary modality or context for interacting and relating with others.

COMMUNICATION

While interaction involves taking roles in relation to others and then engaging them in mutually reciprocal ways, communication goes one step further. It involves exchanging ideas and feelings with others. One person has an idea and conveys it to another person, who then responds by conveying his/her idea, and so forth. As such, communication is interaction with a particular purpose: to encode and decode and thereby exchange messages or information with others.

In music therapy, the mode of communication may be musical, verbal, or nonverbal/nonmusical, with special emphasis given to musical modes. The reason is that there is a core belief that musical communication is different from verbal communication in both content and process, that is, not only in what can be communicated with any reliability, but also in the way it is communicated. What we are able to communicate in music, we are not always able to communicate in words, and vice versa: and the ways in which we are able to communicate musically we are not always able to use verbally, and vice versa. Essentially this means that musical communication stands on its own without parallel or overlap, and as such cannot be replaced or superseded by any other modality of interaction and communication.

But this is only half of the picture. Just as often, musical communication overlaps with verbal and other nonverbal modes of communication, and can serve as a bridge between them. Music is not only nonverbal sound, it can also include words, movements, and visual images. Thus, music does not only communicate something that is uniquely musical, it can also enhance and enlarge verbal and other nonverbal forms of communication. Think of how many ways music leads into or incorporates other modalities of communication. We can set words, movements, or visual images to music, we can talk about music and our experiences with it, we can move to music, and we can draw to music.

Having the flexibility to move from verbal to musical to other nonverbal channels of communication is a hallmark of music therapy. "Music can provide a nonverbal means of self-expression and communication, or it can serve as a bridge connecting nonverbal and verbal channels of communication. When used nonverbally, [music] can replace the need for words, and thereby provide a safe and acceptable way of expressing conflicts and feelings that are difficult to express otherwise. When both nonverbal and verbal channels are employed, the [music] serves to intensify, elaborate, or stimulate verbal communication, while the verbal communication serves to define, consolidate, and clarify the [musical experience]" (Bruscia, 1987a, p. 561).

FEEDBACK

Musical self-expression enables us to externalize what is internal, to bring what is inside outside. This externalization is significant in that it helps us to make what is latent manifest, to bring what is unconscious into consciousness, and ultimately to turn our inner images into outer realities. In the process, we are afforded significant opportunities to reflect upon ourselves—to hear how our inner urgings and difficulties sound, to hear who we are. In other words, making music always involves a feedback loop: we put sounds out there, and then we hear them; we sound ourselves and then we hear ourselves sounding. This kind of feedback is essential to therapy, as it is the basis upon which the client can recognize the need for change, and then identify the specific kinds of changes needed.

In addition to receiving feedback from one's own expressions, clients in music therapy also get feedback from their musical interactions with the therapist. In fact, one of the main reasons why client and therapist make music together is to enable the client not only to hear him/herself, but also to hear how others in the external world perceive and react to what s/he is expressing. The therapist can do this by musically mirroring what the client is doing musically, or by reacting and responding to it.

Feedback is essential to therapy for two reasons. First, it provides the client with insight. Hearing oneself through one's own ears and through the therapist's ears helps the client to recognize the need for change, and then identify the specific kinds of changes that need to be made. Second, feedback is a way of testing and dealing with reality. Once externalized, the client's self has to negotiate with the demands of the world. This process of give-and-take is exquisitely carried out through musical interactions.

EXPLORATION

Health has often been described as wholeness—that way of being when the parts work together toward becoming increasingly more complete as a human being. Thus when the parts are not working, either alone or together, there is a threat to health; our potential for wholeness has been reduced. When considered in this light, every health threat can be defined as a loss of potential—a reduction in the alternatives needed to become a fully functioning human being. And following from this, every form of therapy can be defined as an attempt to restore the alternatives and potentials that a client has lost. The ongoing job of a therapist then is to help clients explore the alternatives and potentials they need.

Exploring the client's alternatives and potentials is indigenous to the creative process of making and listening to music. When clients make music, they take on a particular musical challenge or problem (e.g., performing the score, improvising around a particular rhythm or melody, writing a song) and then begin to explore what musical options are available given the inherent limits placed on the task. Then they have to evaluate the options, make decisions, and work them out. Making music is always about trying out different things, deciding what is best, and then working it all out, eventually using whatever resources are found to be relevant and available. And similarly, listening to music always involves deciding what to listen to, how to listen, what the music means, and so forth. Music listening is the process of exploring a piece of music and one's own imagination at the same time.

Creative exploration is also a way of working with the feedback that a client gets from his/her own music-making. As explained above, hearing one's own sounds, and hearing how others respond to them help to illuminate the kinds of changes the client needs to make; but before such changes can be made, the client has to explore the various options, and to rehearse the change itself. It is the exploratory, creative nature of music that enables such experimentation.

MAKING CONNECTIONS

An important characteristic of wholeness, both in health and in music, is harmony. Harmony is when everything fits and works together as parts of a whole, which are parts of another whole, and so forth. For this reason, a common goal in music therapy, whether the orientation be educational, medical, or psychotherapeutic, is to help the client make connections of all kinds, to put the parts back together into a harmonious whole. The connections that need to be made may be between various parts of the self (e.g., body, mind, spirit), between various parts of the body (e.g., hands and eyes or ears), between various parts of the psyche (e.g., conscious and unconscious; thoughts, feelings, images, memories, attitudes, beliefs), or between self and nonself (e.g., other people, objects, the universe, etc.).

Music is useful in making such connections because it involves and requires every kind! When we sing or play an instrument, we are called upon to connect our ears with our minds, our eyes with our hands, our thoughts with our feelings, unconscious fantasies with our conscious intentions, our beliefs with our actions, our inner worlds with the outer world, and ourselves to others. And similarly, when we listen to music, we feel the vibrations in different parts of the body, we hear how ideas and feelings fit together, we experience the past with the present, we hear how the world is connected. Music is a model of human harmony—it provides the necessary maps and routes to connect the various parts of our existence and experience.

Of course, the connections that are inherent in music can also be enhanced or facilitated through verbal and nonverbal means. Music therapists often engage clients in discussions that identify connections that need to be made or explored in music, or they may ask clients to discuss connections that have already been experienced within the music. Music therapists may also use other modalities such as moving and drawing to make connections before or after the music experience.

REDRESS

Clients often come to therapy because they have suffered a loss, injury, or deprivation of some kind, and as a consequence have basic human needs which have not been met in the past or are not being met in the present. These needs may be physical, emotional, mental, social, or spiritual in nature. For example, clients who grew up in a deprived environment may need the therapist to provide sensory stimulation and affectionate touch; clients who have not had adequate parenting may need for the therapist to temporarily serve as a surrogate mother or father; clients who were never allowed to play as a child may need the therapist to give them permission and encouragement to be playful; clients who have not been given boundaries or limits may need for the therapist to provide the necessary structure and containment. The possibilities are endless.

Redress is any form of intervention wherein the therapist tries to help the client by meeting his/her unmet needs, as appropriate to the therapist-client relationship. This might include providing the client with whatever has been deprived of him or her in the past, making restitution for something or someone the client has lost, or finding ways to compensate the client for an injury, illness, or trauma.

While this kind of help is given in many forms of therapy, music therapy provides the additional possibility for the client to receive redress from the music as well as the therapist. Often, it is within the music experience that the client has his/her needs met, as in the above examples, for sensorimotor stimulation, playful experiences, affectionate contact with others, structure and containment, or encouragement and hope. "Musical redress" may be provided to the client through active involvement in music-making or through more receptive listening experiences. A particularly caring form of musical redress is when the therapist makes a gift of music to the client, either through actually singing or playing for the client, or by giving the client a piece of music, recording, instrument, etc.

INFLUENCE

Clients always come to therapy because they need help in making the changes necessary to achieve health. Depending on the nature of these changes, it is sometimes appropriate for the therapist to provide this help by exerting direct influence over the client, as opposed to providing the conditions necessary for the client to change him/herself. This may be done by specifying to the client what change is needed, guiding the client to identify the change, or actually acting upon the client in a way to induce the change.

In music therapy, such influence can be exerted by the therapist as a person (either verbally or nonverbally) or by the music. For example, if the client needs to stop a particular behavior, the therapist may personally intervene by physically preventing the client from doing it or by verbally directing the client to stop; or alternatively, the therapist may engage the client in a music experience that precludes the possibility of the client behaving in that way, or detracts from the client's motivation to continue. Or in a completely different setting, a client may need to learn specific skills and the therapist may either teach them to the client verbally or through the music. And in yet another setting, the client may need to calm down, both physically and emotionally, and the therapist may try to help the client through verbal discussion, or by doing a music relaxation exercise. In all of these examples, the therapist tries to help by acting directly upon the client to induce the desired change.

MOTIVATION

The irony of therapy is that clients may come to it without the necessary motivation to invest in the therapeutic process or make the desired changes. In fact, lack of motivation can often be the main reason why a client needs therapy.

In music therapy, clients are motivated by the sheer joy of making and listening to music. Music is such a pleasurable and rewarding activity, that it motivates both therapist and client to reach beyond their limits, to explore new horizons, to find new resources, to take new risks, and to try out new ways of being in the world. And beyond that, the transcendent beauty of music leads us into those wonderful peak experiences that reaffirm the beauty of life.

VALIDATION

Clients often come to therapy because they have lost sight of their value as human beings and as individuals, or because they have always lacked a sense of self-worth. In fact, health problems themselves can wear a person down, and call into question whether one has the resources to conquer them. And of course, therapy itself is also hard work; it challenges who we are and what we can do. It is not easy to change ourselves, our environment, or our lives. In the process of trying, clients often become weary and need support, praise, acceptance and encouragement. Such forms of validation are sometimes the most valuable kind of help that a therapist can offer to clients.

In music therapy, validation may come from the therapist on a personal level, or it may come from the music. When a client makes music, and when that music brings attention and praise, the experience is very self-validating; the success of making music builds self-confidence and self-esteem. When clients listen to music, a different kind of validation is provided. Sometimes the way the client feels is validated by what the music is expressing, almost as if the music is saying, "Yes, this is the way it feels." Sometimes the music is validating because it offers emotional support and reassurance. It creates and sustains a holding environment for us to feel safe. Ultimately, whether the therapist or music provides validation, it is one of the most treasured kinds of help a client can receive.

POSTSCRIPT

Before leaving this chapter, it is important to point out that in the present definition, the phrase "helps a client" is followed by the phrase "to promote health." What this implies is that the therapist can only help. The therapist cannot make the necessary changes for the client, nor can the therapist force the client to make the necessary changes, no matter how much influence and motivation are applied. Thus, all the kinds of help described above essentially give clients the conditions they need to change themselves and their health. Certainly a therapist can help the client to be healthy, and may even induce the healing process, but ultimately, it is the client who has to take the necessary steps to achieve and maintain health.

Bateson (1980) captures the limits and needs for a therapist by taking an old adage one step further: "You can take a horse to the water, but cannot make him drink. The drinking is his business. But even if your horse is thirsty, he cannot drink unless you take him. The taking is your business" (p. 80).

Chapter Nine

CLIENT

Now that the terms "therapist" and "help" have been defined, further clarification is needed on what a "client" is. Who goes to a therapist for help? What role conditions are necessary for someone to be a "client?" What characterizes the person on the receiving end of therapy?

In the minds of most lay people, the need for therapy often implies that a person has a sickness of some kind, and needs help in dealing with it. For various reasons, having certain kinds of illnesses or problems, or needing certain kinds of help from others often carries a stigma in our society. This is particularly true when the problem is mental or emotional in nature, or when the illness is contagious or related to a taboo.

Health professionals have tried to circumvent such stigma by creating new terms for individuals who need therapy. Hence, in current jargon, therapy recipients may be called "clients" instead of "patients," or "residents" instead of "clients," or "consumers" instead of "residents," or "person with a disability or challenge" instead of "disabled person."

Often, the terminology reflects the setting in which therapy is provided and the philosophical orientation of treatment. For example, "patients" are found in hospitals where the orientation is medical, "clients" are found in individual therapy situations where the orientation is nonmedical and egalitarian, "students" are found in special schools where the orientation is educational, and "residents" are found in group homes or nursing facilities where treatment is milieu-oriented.

Notwithstanding the well-meaning motives for using such jargon, the basic questions remain. Are recipients of therapy by definition sick? Can someone who is healthy still be a client? What conditions qualify a person for the kind of help a music therapist gives?

In surveying definitions of music therapy, it is interesting to discover how these questions are addressed. Most say that the recipients of music therapy are adults and children who have one or more type of disorder, handicap, need, or problem. The problems most often cited are physical, emotional, psychological, intellectual, behavioral, motor, and social in nature, which certainly covers a broad spectrum of populations and pathologies. Besides adults and children, the recipients of therapy are also called clients, patients, pupils, human beings, and human organisms.

Although not specifically mentioned in many definitions, it is important to remember that therapy is also provided to groups of people, including couples, families, and peer groups. There is also a growing trend to provide therapy to entire communities. A good example is the work of Stige (1993) who prepared a group of clients to take part in a community music group, and then worked with the community group to make them more open to the individuals with disabilities. Going even further, Kenny (1982) believes that in addition to individuals and groups, "society" is also a beneficiary of therapy. Following in the same line, Boxill (1988) has formed an organization to advance peace in the world through music therapy.

This expansion in the definition of clientele for therapy is consistent with a growing realization in medicine, psychology, and many other health professions of the importance of the entire ecology system. Every form of therapy is inextricably linked to ecology. We cannot understand or help human beings achieve health without also examining and treating the various contexts or environments in which they live. Thus, the clients of therapy will increasingly be not only the individual with a health concern, but all those ecological units impinging upon him or her, and all those groups, communities, and systems that are in turn affected by one individual with a health problem in their midst.

In sharp contrast to naming the recipients of therapy, it is very interesting to find that in some definitions, the recipients of therapy are not mentioned at all, and that in others "human behaviors" (Hadsell, 1974; Codding, 1982) and "learning" (Steele, 1977) are cited as targets of therapy.

Since there are so many different conceptions of who should receive therapy, it is important that any definition of music therapy include criteria for participation. More specifically, the health status or needs of music therapy candidates must be clearly delineated, along with the needs addressed by the therapeutic process.

In the present definition, a client is 1) any individual, group, community, or environment that needs or seeks help from a therapist 2) because of an actual, imagined, or potential threat to health, whether physical, emotional, mental, behavioral, social, or spiritual in nature. A "threat" to health may be mild, moderate or severe, or it may be manifested as a health "need," "concern," or "objective." The person may even be essentially well, but still need help in preventing health problems from taking place. As Bloch (1982) says, "Sometimes the need is far from clear and may amount only to a general sense of dissatisfaction. But no matter how covert the problems, the essential point is that an individual designates himself [or a group designates itself] as in need of help and chooses someone who has been socially sanctioned as able to provide that help" (pp. 4 5).

Of course, not all clients actively seek out help, despite their obvious needs. Individuals who do not have the mental or physical capacity to recognize their own health problems or to seek help from a therapist also qualify as clients. In these cases, parents, legal guardians, or clinical agencies may act on behalf of the clients in contracting the necessary therapeutic services.

Chapter Ten

TO PROMOTE HEALTH

IS HEALTH THE PRIMARY AIM?

The present definition states that the primary aim of music therapy is to help clients promote health. While this might seem like a safe generalization to make, a review of definitions in the Appendix raises many questions. Many say simply that music therapy is the use of music for "therapeutic aims," without specifying the outcomes, and surprisingly, only a few definitions even mention health. The most well-known one is: "Music therapy is the use of music in accomplishment of therapeutic aims: the restoration, maintenance and improvement of mental and physical health" (NAMT, 1980). It is also interesting to find that many definitions state the desired outcome in other terms, such as well-being, wellness, full functioning, integration, maximum potential, and self-actualization; and an even greater number describe the outcome in terms of pathology rather than health. These definitions describe music therapy as the treatment or rehabilitation of illness, disease, disorder, disability, problems, and needs.

One explanation for these differences is that music therapy is used with so many different client populations that it is impossible to cite the same aims across various clinical settings. Thus, music therapists working in a school setting have different therapeutic aims than those who work in a hospital, rehabilitation center, or nursing home. As a result, they not only define music therapy differently, they also have completely different notions about what constitutes health for their particular clientele. Thus, as populations and settings vary, so do therapeutic aims and philosophies, and as these vary, so do definitions of music therapy and conceptions of health.

Obviously, a comprehensive definition of music therapy has to take these differences in clinical perspectives into account, and an attempt must be made to recognize and understand the philosophies of health underlying them.

A central task for music therapy then is to define health in a way that illuminates and embraces the myriad variations in clinical perspectives. To do this, four fundamental questions have to be addressed.

- What does health encompass and include?
- Is health an either-or condition or a continuum?
- What conditions characterize health?
- How are these conditions created?

WHAT DOES HEALTH ENCOMPASS?

Webster's dictionary (1974) defines health as a "condition of being sound in body, mind, and spirit." This statement is quite a significant one in that it implies that health is a holistic condition. It is not defined or determined by the state of the body alone, but is the overall soundness of all parts of us. Thus, health is being sound of body *and* being sound of mind *and* being sound of spirit.

Of course, one might very well ask whether health includes anything else. What else has to be sound? What other entities might be an integral part of one's health? Ruud (1998) points out that health is a phenomenon that extends beyond the individual to encompass society and culture. An individual cannot be sound of body, mind, and spirit in a society and culture that is not healthy; and conversely, a society and culture cannot be healthy if individuals within them are not sound in body, mind, and spirit. Moreover, an individual needs the support of society and culture to be healthy, and every individual's health has an impact on society and culture. And going even further, it can also be argued that the health of any individual, society, and culture is integrally linked to the environment. Thus, health encompasses and depends upon the entire ecological system, from body, mind, and spirit, and their interactions within the individual, to the broader contexts of the individual's relationships with society, culture, and environment.

IS HEALTH A
DICHOTOMY OR CONTINUUM?

The next important question is whether health is an either-or, dichotomous condition (either well or ill, healthy or sick) or a graduated continuum ranging from unhealth to health, with no definitive boundaries between the two polarities. This question certainly has implications for how one defines "client."

Antonovsky (1987), a medical sociologist and leader in health studies, outlines two orientations that can be taken in answering this question, pathogenic and salutogenic.

Pathogenic Orientation

In the pathogenic orientation, health is a state of well-being or homeostasis that we continually try to maintain, but that continually gets disrupted by illness, injury, disease, and so forth. In this orientation, health is a dichotomous, either-or phenomenon: we are either healthy and successfully maintaining a state of homeostasis; or we are unhealthy because that state has been disrupted or lost by the intrusion of a pathology. Thus, health is regarded as the usual or normal state of being (even though somewhat ideal and elusive), characterized by the absence of pathology, while unhealth is an abnormal, unusual, and undesirable state, characterized by the presence of pathology.

There are many different types of pathology that can disrupt health, and when they are defined and compared, we can learn much about what constitutes health. The following list includes some of the most commonly used terms in the pathogenic orientation.

- *Trauma:* any injury or harm brought about an environmental event or condition (e.g., being injured during birth, getting hurt in an accident, being victimized or abused, witnessing a very painful event, being involved in a disaster or war).
- *Deficit:* the lack of something necessary or essential to structural completeness or functional adequacy (e.g., the absence or loss of a limb or other part of the body).

- *Disease:* the loss of health due to the collapse, disruption, malfunctioning, or deterioration of organic structures or processes; any illness, sickness, or malady (e.g., cancer, Alzheimer's disease, Multiple Sclerosis, etc.).
- *Syndrome:* any health problem defined by a particular group of symptoms and/or etiologies (e.g., Cerebral Palsy, Schizophrenia). Syndromes usually define a particular client population.
- *Disorder or impairment:* any loss, disruption, or disturbance in normal human functioning (e.g., aphasia, paralysis, blindness, allergies, immune disorders, sleep disorders). Sometimes the term disorder is used interchangeably with syndrome (as in the *Diagnostic and Statistic Manual*), but for the sake of clarity, syndrome is defined here as a group of disorders. Thus, all clients within a particular population have the same syndrome, but each client may have different disorders related to the syndrome.
- *Abnormality:* any structural or functional irregularity, or any deviation from normal expectations or prescriptions (e.g., microcephaly, sociopathy).
- *Disability:* any loss of capacity to perform specific acts resulting from any of the above. As such, a disability is an outcome or result of the other health threats. This term is often used interchangeably with impairment and handicap.
- *Handicap:* any restriction in the full performance or experience of an activity; any limitation in the potential to perform a task to its fullest. This includes common activities such as driving a car, participating in sports, living independently, etc.
- *Exceptionality:* a broad term for any exception to the rule, norm, or standard, including any extremes (e.g., exceptionally high or low IQ, special talents, being extremely small or large in physical size, etc.).
- *Problem in Living:* any difficulty in everyday life that stems from any of the above (e.g., problems with job, relationships, finances, etc.).

Obviously, there are many overlaps and boundaries between these terms; however, within the pathogenic orientation, making such distinctions can be very helpful in ferreting out the various layers of a client's health problem or pathological condition. For example, cerebral palsy is a "syndrome" of motor "disorders" (e.g., spasticity, ataxia, etc.), which are the result of a "trauma" to the brain at birth. The disorders result in various kinds of "disabilities" (e.g., speech, walking), and "handicaps" (inability to drive a car), which in turn cause many "problems in living" (e.g., isolation, depression). Taking another example shows that every clinical condition has a completely different configuration. Depression resulting from a "trauma" is a "problem in living;" depression resulting from an imbalance in brain chemistry is a "disorder." The inability to speak is a "disability" in cerebral palsy because it is the result of the motor "disorders," but in other conditions, speech problems are "disorders or impairments."

While those who subscribe to the pathogenic orientation are quite concerned with diagnosis and classification of the client's pathology, they also can take two distinct positions: one that focuses on health and one that focuses on disease. Antonovsky (1987) explains: "Those who adopt the former position [i.e., a health emphasis] would allocate attention and resources to keeping people healthy, preventing them from becoming sick. Those who take the latter stance [i.e., a disease emphasis] focus on treating those who are sick, seeking to prevent death and chronicity and to restore health if possible" (p. 3). This distinction is important because it points out that interest in prevention and health maintenance can still stem from a pathogenic rather than salutogenic orientation.

Salutogenic Orientation

In the salutogenic orientation, a person's health can be described along a continuum, depending upon how well the person is resisting, combating, or coping with the continual health threats described above, or what Antonovsky calls life stressors of all kinds, ranging from the microbiological to the societal-cultural. In this orientation, health is a state of heterostasis rather than homeostasis, that is, health exists in the presence of (and in spite of) ongoing health threats or life stressors. Thus, health is not a normal homeostatic state that we have to continually maintain by staying free from disease, rather it is an ongoing process of building "generalized resistance resources" to the normal threats to health. In the salutogenic orientation, disease is not an abnormal occurrence, and very far from an unusual one; moreover, life's stressors are not necessarily the cause of disease, but in fact, may be the very source of health. The reason is that life stressors enable us to build the resistances we need to move from the dis-ease end of the continuum to the health/ease end. Antonovsky is unequivocal in stating the two fundamental assumptions of the salutogenic orientation: The first is that "heterostasis, disorder, and pressure toward increasing entropy" is "the prototypical characteristic of the living organism" (p. 2); the second is that "disease, however defined, is very far from an unusual occurrence" (p. 2).

It is important to point out that, notwithstanding the names given to these two orientations, the main difference is *not* that the pathogenic focuses exclusively on unhealth and the salutogenic focuses exclusively on health. This is not the case. Rather there are two important other distinctions. First, in the pathogenic, health is considered usual, and unhealth is considered "unusual;" in the salutogenic, health and unhealth are both considered usual. Second, in the pathogenic, health is an either-or state, while in the salutogenic health is an ongoing process of managing unhealth.

HEALTH AS A WAY OF BEING

Antonovsky's notion about health as process helps us to realize that health is more than something that we either have or do not have, depending upon the presence or absence of disease; it is what we do with whatever we have and do not have. But even this notion has to go one step further. What we "do" with respect to our health is part of who we are as individuals. Thus, health is a way of being, rather than merely a state of having or a process of doing. Interestingly, Webster's definition suggests the same idea; it describes health as a condition of *being* sound rather than a *soundness* of mind, body, and spirit. This implies that health is more than an attribute that a particular structure of the individual either has or does not have, it is an active process that the individual undertakes through these structures, and even more, it is the individual's way of being with those structures, in whatever state they happen to be at the time. Thus, health is not something to have, it is something we do, and even further, it is who we are; and the same can be said of unhealth.

Conceiving health as a way of being has two significant implications. First, health and unhealth are not defined for us according to objective determinations of whether we have a disease, rather we define where we are along the continuum of health/unhealth as it constantly emerges. Health is a choice we actively make, not a condition that happens to us. Second, as a choice, health depends upon how we experience wherever we are along the continuum. It is more than an attribute belonging to us as objects, it is how we subjectively experience ourselves as persons. It does not reside in our structures, nor is it merely reflected in our actions. Health is more than an objective condition: it is intrinsically subjective, and it depends largely upon how we define and experience ourselves and our world. In short, health is who we are as we experience ourselves, and as we shape those experiences. It is as Ruud (1998) puts it, our whole "quality of life" or what might be more accurately called our whole *quality of living*.

Aldridge (1996) has already put forth many of these ideas in reference to music therapy, and goes even further to describe health as a personal identity that we create through the lifestyle that we choose. He says

> In modern times, health is no longer a state of not being sick. Individuals are choosing to become healthy and, in some cases, declare themselves as pursuing the activity of being well. This change, from attributing the status of "being sick" to engaging in the activity of "being well," is a reflection of a modern trend whereby individuals are taking definition of themselves into their own hands rather than relying upon an identity being imposed by another . . . While personal active involvement has always been present in health care maintenance and prevention . . . a new development appears to be that "being healthy," being a "creative" person, being a "musical" person, and being a "spiritual" person are significant factors in the composition of an individual's "lifestyle." Rather than strategies of personal health management in response to sickness, we see an assemblage of

activities like dietary practices, exercise practices, aesthetic practices, psychological practices, spiritual practices designed to promote health and prevent sickness. These activities are incorporated under the rubric of "lifestyle" . . . (p. 20).

HEALTH DEFINED

So far we have reached three fundamental conclusions about health. The first is that it is holistic, going beyond the body to include mind and spirit, and going beyond the individual to include one's society, culture, and environment. The second is that health exists along a multidimensional continuum of constant change, ranging from unhealth to health; it is not an ideal, dichotomous state of homeostasis that differentiates wellness from illness. We are not in or out of health, we are related to both health and unhealth on many different levels and in many different ways. The third is that health is not something we have, it is an active process and our very way of being in that process.

With these conclusions stated, we can now move to an even broader, far-reaching definition—one which is brief but requires considerable elaboration of each of its components.

Health is the process of becoming one's fullest potential for individual and ecological wholeness.

Process of Becoming

Health is developmental and evolutionary; it is a process of moving beyond the present way of being into increasingly richer and fuller ways. It is not a state of being in the past or present, it is an active and intentional emerging into the future—a continually striving to become who we can be.

Wilber (1995) has described this process of becoming in terms of four basic operations:

- *Preservation.* The individual has to maintain and protect from harm all those aspects of self that define his or her identity, and thereby provides the foundation for further growth. This includes taking responsibility as an individual to act on one's own behalf to achieve individual wholeness, independent of environmental factors, and in the process, utilizing and assimilating external resources to the extent necessary for survival and self-preservation.

- *Adaptation.* An individual is always part of a larger wholeness, and therefore is continually called upon to adapt and accommodate to the various environments and contexts of his or her existence. This includes communing with other wholes, and trying to adapt one's wholeness to fit into them as a part.
- *Transcendence.* The individual continually creates a new self, going beyond the past and present, to become a more expansive and different person. This is the process of creative growth. Change is indemic to health.
- *Dissolution.* The process of growth is always kept in check and stimulated by forces of destruction and decay. Just as wholes are built up, they can break down and dissolve; and in fact, the destruction of parts provides an impetus to the building of new wholes. Thus, development and evolution can move forward or backward, through growth and decay, through birth of the new and through death of the old.

These forces work in continual tension, through opposite pulls that the individual must seek to balance. In preservation, the pull is toward self and away from nonself; in adaptation, the pull is toward nonself and away from self; in transcendence, the pull is towards creating new selves; in dissolution the pull is toward letting go of previous selves.

Fullest Potential

A potential is any alternative or possibility that exists which is desirable or preferred with respect to development and evolution. It is the next rung on any of the many ladders of growth—for body, mind, spirit, individual, society, culture, or environment (or for whatever entities we define as components of our health universe).

Human beings have three layers of potential: universal, collective, and individual. The universal layer is the potential that humans have as a species; it is largely unknown, yet often used to set limits or norms for what is possible with regard to health. Undoubtedly, the possibilities of health for the species is greater than what we have envisioned so far.

The collective layer is the potential formed when individuals gather into groups of various sizes, from family to nation. This layer of potential is constantly being explored but remains largely unknown. The possibilities of health at this layer are nearly limitless, as they depend upon the combined potentials of each individual belonging to the group.

The individual layer is the unique potential that each person has based on circumstance, the various contexts in which the person lives, and developmental status. No two individuals have the same alternatives or possibilities for health; consequently, at this layer, health must be conceived as relative rather than universal, individual rather than collective, and idiographic rather than nomothetic. Thus, individual health is not defined by whether a person has more or less potentials when compared to another person or to expected norms of a group or species. Rather, health is the extent to which each individual reaches his or her own unique potentials at whatever developmental stage the individual is. This means that a person with cancer may be healthier than a person without cancer, and a person with schizophrenia may be healthier than a person experiencing a spiritual crisis. What defines health, then, is not the severity of the challenge (if that could ever be determined), but rather the way a person uses his or her developmental potentials at the time in meeting the challenge.

Individual and Ecological Wholeness

Wholeness (or holism) is an ideal of completeness that can never be attained, but nevertheless, is always present. It is the eternal quest of finiteness for infinity. As such, wholeness is the fundamental thrust for all developmental and evolutionary growth. Every part or entity contributes to a whole, which becomes part of a larger whole, which becomes part of larger and larger wholes, ad infinitum. Wilber (1995) calls these layers or components of reality "holons" and describes their constellations as "holarchies."

All evolutionary and developmental patterns proceed by holarchization, by a process of increasing orders of wholeness and inclusion, which is a type of ranking by holistic capacity . . . the higher or deeper dimension provides a principle, or a "glue" or a pattern, that unites and links otherwise separate and conflicting and isolated parts into a coherent unity, a space in which separate parts can recognize a common wholeness and thus escape the fate of being merely a part, merely a fragment (Wilber, 1996, pp. 29–30).

Wholeness can be viewed as individual and ecological. Individual wholeness is comprised of all the various part/wholes (or holons) that make up the person, in whatever ways they are defined and differentiated. For example, Webster's dictionary cites the main parts of the person as mind, body, and spirit, whereas Wilber (1996) divides the person into object (exterior holons), and subject (interior holons), both of which include Spirit. Similarly, ecological wholeness is usually conceived as consisting of society, culture, and environment, whereas Wilber (1996) divides the ecosystem into the collective exterior (the objective biosocial sphere) and the collective interior (the subjective sociocultural sphere).

Threats to Health

Based on the above definition, the following are ways in which health may be compromised:

- The absence, loss, or destruction of any part of the individual or ecology that dismantles wholeness or obstructs development.
- Failure to integrate any part of the individual or ecology into a meaningful whole (e.g., fragmentation, splitting off, or dissociation of part from whole).
- Any imbalance in the four basic operations involved in the process of becoming, for example: more preservation than adaptation (and vice versa), more transcendence than dissolution (and vice versa).

- Any reduction or denial of one's own potentials.
- Any stagnation in the past or present (e.g., any developmental fixation or delay) or any form of resistance towards developmental or evolutionary growth.

Individual Differences

Earlier it was emphasized that no two individuals have the same alternatives or possibilities for health, and that what defines health is not the severity of the health threat, but the extent to which the individual can use his or her full potentials in dealing with it. We know, of course, that people vary considerably in this capacity: some individuals seem able to deal with any health threat that besets them, regardless of severity, while others seem unable to deal with even minor threats.

Antonovsky (1987) proposed that to understand this difference we have to look not at what factors led to or caused the health threat, but what the individual did to resist or overcome the threat, and thereby move once again toward the health end of the continuum. His initial term for this was the person's "generalized resistance resources," which he defined as any aspect of the person's life that helped to fight off various health threats. To study this further, he interviewed survivors of the Holocaust to see if he could identify any differences between those survivors who were in relatively good emotional and physical health in spite of their horrendous experiences and advancing age, and those who were not. What he found was a difference in dispositional orientation. Specifically, those who were in good health had what he called a better "Sense of Coherence" than those who were in poor health. Antonovsky defined this Sense of Coherence as "a global orientation that expresses the extent to which one has a pervasive, enduring though dynamic, feeling of confidence that 1) the stimuli deriving from one's internal and external environments in the course of living are structured, predictable and explicable; 2) the resources are available to one to meet the demands posed by these stimuli; and 3) these demands are challenges, worthy of investment and engagement" (1987, p. 19). Antonovsky named these three elements comprehensibility, manageability, and meaningfulness respectively, and described their relationships as follows:

The motivational component of meaningfulness seems most crucial. Without it, being high on comprehensibility or manageability is likely to be temporary. For the committed and caring person, the way is open to gaining understanding and resources. Comprehensibility seems next in importance, for high manageability is contingent on understanding. This does not mean that if resources are at one's disposal, meaningfulness will be lessened and coping efforts weakened. Successful coping then depends on the SOC [Sense of Coherence] as a whole (p. 22).

Antonovsky also points out that these three components are manifested in behaviors, attitudes, ideas, feelings, spiritual beliefs—or the person's entire way of being which in turn are rooted in the sociocultural and biosocial environments in which the person lives.

Chapter Eleven

USING MUSIC

The phrase "using music experiences" is a short one, but loaded with issues and implications. The first challenge is to formulate a definition of music which is consistent with the basic premises and practices within music therapy; the second is to define and differentiate the myriad levels and types of music experiences used for therapeutic purposes.

The present chapter focuses on defining music. We will begin by surveying how music therapists conceptualize music, as indicated in their definitions of music therapy. We will then identify those factors operating within a clinical context that shape these conceptions. At the end, a definition of music will be offered for consideration within the context of music therapy.

Why is it important for music therapists to deal with such matters? Because how we define music has a profound impact on how we conceptualize music therapy. If what gives music therapy its uniqueness is its reliance on music, then we need to have a very clear understanding of what music is and what it is not. Otherwise, we will be unable to define what music therapy is and what it is not. And without clear boundaries for music therapy, we will be unable to specify what music therapists do that other therapists do not do, and what competencies they have that other therapists do not have!

HOW MUSIC THERAPISTS
CONCEPTUALIZE MUSIC

It is obvious, both from definitions of music therapy and from clinical practices described in the literature, that music therapists use a broad spectrum of music experiences in working with clients, and in so doing, conceive the boundaries of music very expansively. While many definitions leave the matter open to interpretation by citing "music" as the primary agent of therapy, other definitions use more detailed phrases, such as "musical activities" (Carter, 1982; Rudenberg, 1982; Bang, 1986), "musical experiences" (Bruscia, 1986a), "structured music learning and participation exercises" (Steele, 1977), "the elements of music and their influences" (Munro & Mount, 1978), "the unique properties and potentials of music" (Hadsell, 1974), and "the healing aspects of music" (Kenny, 1982). Gertrude Orff (1974) describes music therapy as the use of "musical materials" such as "phonetic-rhythmic speech, speech, free and metric rhythm, movement, melos in speech and singing, [and] the handling of instruments" (p. 9).

Several music therapists have pointed out that music therapy also relies upon interpersonal components, such as "the therapist" (Bonny, 1986; Priestley, 1975, 1994), "the therapist's skills" (Codding, 1982), and "the various relationships formed through the music" (Bruscia, 1987a). Alvin (1978) concluded that music therapy involves the exhaustive use of everything contained in music, including vibrations, resonances, and all manifestations of responses to both music and the therapist.

In surveying clinical practice, one finds that some music therapists go beyond the traditional confines of music as an art form, and employ sounds, vibrations, and energy forms as part of the therapeutic process. For example, Benenzon (1981) defines music therapy as the clinical use of the "sound-man complex" whether the sound is musical or not. Sommer (1961) suggested the use of sound effects as a form of "music therapy without music" for psychiatric patients. Many therapists use sound effects as stimuli for projective personality tests (Benenzon, 1981; Bruscia & Maranto, 1985).

In Brazil, the music used in therapy includes any "rhythmic sonorous expression" (Barcellos, 1982). Colon (Bruscia, 1985) builds therapy around "the sonorous musical complex world every human being has internally" (p. 15).

In Norway, a new avenue being explored is vibroacoustic therapy or the "music bath," which involves the direct application of musical vibrations to the client's body (Skille, 1983). A similar approach is being used in the United States with the Somatron, a specially designed chair in which the client listens to music and receives its vibrations (Somasonics).

In China, music therapy involves: 1) listening to music (simple music therapy), 2) listening to music while receiving an electrical current transformed from the musical signal (music electrotherapy), and 3) listening to music while receiving an electrical music current and acupuncture (music electroacupuncture) (Hongshi, 1988).

"Toning" is the use of vocal sounds to restore vibratory patterns of the body within a perfect electro-magnetic field, thereby enabling the body and all of its parts to function in harmony (Keyes, 1973).

Halpern (1978) composes music that "as an energy, can work on the energy body of an individual and speak in the vibrational language, the mother tongue, to the various organs and systems, to help bring that body into physical alignment and attunement with its own perfect pattern of perfection" (p. 24).

One might question whether sounds and vibrations are "music" in the truest sense, and whether the application of these elements of music can be considered part of "music" therapy. Eagle (1978) argues that music is the organization of sounds and silences in time, and that like everything else, sounds are made up of vibrations. He believes that the study of vibrations and even unorganized sound will reveal much about the nature of music and its influences on human and infrahuman behavior.

So what can be concluded from all these diverse conceptualizations of music within clinical practice? Simply that, if the myriad therapeutic potentials of music are to be exploited to the fullest, we must go beyond the traditional definitions and boundaries of music established within other fields. This leads to the next major issue: What factors in clinical context are most important to consider when conceptualizing music?

FACTORS IN DEFINING MUSIC
WITHIN A CLINICAL CONTEXT

Philosophers, physicists, psychologists and musicians have struggled for centuries with the elusiveness of music to definition, each taking a very different perspective on what it is. The challenge for music therapists is that these perspectives are not always relevant or expansive enough for the world of clinical practice. There are many factors operating within a therapeutic context that influence how we define and delimit music. The most important ones are:

- The client's musical preferences, abilities, and achievements are always accepted nonjudgmentally; as a result, aesthetic and artistic standards in music therapy are broader and more inclusive than those in other music professions.
- The client is the main priority of therapy, not the music.
- Music therapy operates on the assumption that music experience is meaningful to clients, and that clients can use music to make meaningful changes in their lives.
- In music therapy, music is more than the pieces or sounds themselves; every music experience involves a person, a specific musical process, and a musical product of some kind.
- The multisensory aspects of music are fundamental to its therapeutic application, but stretch the boundaries of music experience.
- Similarly, the overlaps and relationships between music and the other arts are often exploited for therapeutic purposes, and this also calls for more inclusionary boundaries for the music experience.

Nonjudgmental Perspective

Notwithstanding the wide array of music experiences used, candidates for music therapy are not limited to those clients who have extensive musical backgrounds, and participation in music therapy does not require clients to have special musical abilities or skills. In fact, clients are mostly untrained in music, and sometimes they have problems that can interfere with their ability to make or experience music fully.

Because of this, their musical efforts do not always compare favorably with those of trained musicians. Sometimes clients are unable to play or sing with technical proficiency; sometimes their music lacks rhythmic or tonal control; sometimes they do not always sing or play the right notes; sometimes clients engage in an exploratory, playful process rather than an artistic, creative process, and sometimes the results are sounds rather than music. In many cases, clients lack the necessary training and skills to make their music sound the way they would like, or the way trained musicians would like it to sound.

Aside from the skill issues, clients also come to therapy with their own musical preferences and tastes and are not always interested in listening to or making music that the therapist has selected for its therapeutic benefits or aesthetic qualities. There are also times when clients are not emotionally ready to experience music to the fullest, as this would bring them too close to their problems. Sometimes, even the best music presents a world of experience that a client cannot handle—physically, emotionally, or mentally.

For all these reasons, the client's musical abilities and preferences must always be accepted nonjudgmentally. While striving to help each client to achieve his/her musical potentials, music therapists strive to accept the client's musical efforts at whatever level they are offered, whether consisting of sound forms or music and regardless of their artistic or aesthetic merits, recognizing that as therapeutic progress is made, the client's music will become more fully developed. Essentially this means that, in a therapeutic situation, the client's needs, the client-therapist relationships, and the goals of therapy take precedence over externally imposed aesthetic or artistic standards. Moreover, in a clinical context, music must be selected or created first for its clinical relevance, usefulness, and appeal for the client, and then according to more traditional artistic values.

This is not to say that the quality of the music experienced in therapy is unimportant; it is of utmost concern, even when priority is given to therapeutic concerns. When therapy involves listening to music, it is essential to consider whether the music has the aesthetic qualities needed to motivate the client to engage in the therapeutic process, as well as whether it has the physical and psychological qualities needed to induce positive changes. Because every piece of music presents and engages a person in a world of physical, emotional, mental, and spiritual experiences, there must be considerable attention to the kinds of worlds that a therapist wants to present to a client!

When therapy involves the client in making music, it is often in the quality and beauty of the music that the client's therapeutic growth can be heard. Imagine for a moment how a group of hyperactive, impulsive children would sound if they were performing in a bell choir. When they are acting out, the music will sound disjunct and unharmonious; whereas when they control their impulses, pay attention, and cooperate with one another, the music will have flow and stability. Every note will be heard in its place; every note will have value in relation to one another. Their music will have all the desired positive qualities. Similarly, anyone who has ever witnessed the musical triumphs of a client who has had to overcome multiple disabilities to play a single melody line can hardly claim that the resulting music is not beautiful. The beauty of music lies beyond its surfaces and structures, it also emanates from the soul, and when a client is able to find the soul in music, or make it sing, the music is beautiful—regardless of whether the beat is steady and the notes are in perfect rhythm. As we will discuss below, music is more than a product; thus the quality of music resides in much more than that.

The main point of all this is that the music therapist has to accommodate and accept the client's musical efforts, works, and tastes without judgment, for it is in this basic respect, this unconditional positive regard, that rapport can be established and a therapeutic relationship can be built. At the same time, during the course of therapy, the therapist will continually be working to further develop the client's musical potentials, recognizing that it is in this process of musical expansion that therapy takes place. With every therapeutic step the client takes, the client's music will move closer to the client's full musical potential. It is important to realize that nonjudgmental acceptance does not mean that the client does not have greater, as yet unmet, musical potentials, and that these potentials should not be further developed in therapy. Unconditional positive regard means that the therapist accepts the client wherever s/he is, while also helping the client to move forward in meeting his/her full musical and therapeutic potentials.

Priorities of Therapy

In music therapy, the main priority is to address the client's needs and problems through music; it is not to produce an enduring work of art that will have significance and relevance outside of the therapy context, nor is it to promote or perpetuate music as an art form for its own sake. This does *not* mean that when client and therapist make or listen to music they do not care about its beauty; nor does it mean that they are not interested in making music for its own sake; nor does it mean that the music created or heard in therapy characteristically has no aesthetic value! Often the music for therapy is of exceptional artistic quality and aesthetic merit, not only when judged according to conventional standards of professional musicians and critics, but also based on the broader criteria of artistry embraced in music therapy. Anyone who has heard the exquisite musicianship of Paul Nordoff can hardly claim that music therapists are not concerned with the quality of music! His improvisations stand on their own as works of art, and his clinical successes were the first to demonstrate a basic principle in music therapy: the better the music, the better the client will respond, and the more clinically effective music therapy will be. Similarly, anyone who has examined the music programs developed by Helen Bonny (1978) for use in Guided Imagery and Music (GIM) will realize how important the quality of music is in therapy, and not only the compositions, but the performances as well.

But aside from the extent to which music therapists themselves meet and adhere to conventional standards of aesthetic values, Aigen (1995a) argues that broader criteria have to be embraced in music therapy. Using the theory of John Dewey, he proposes that "music as a fine art" and "music as a therapeutic art" are not really any different because "the aesthetic qualities of music [are] connected to the basic processes of life and nature" (p. 238). He goes on to say that what brings people to therapy is the inability to experience the various parts of themselves and their lives as "components of a larger whole, the sense of which adds meaning and purpose in life," and that it is "the aesthetic properties of music— incorporating the inherent dynamisms of melodic, harmonic and rhythmic structures—[that] have the ability to frame raw experience into a whole experience" (pp. 240–241). A key factor in this wholing experience is the tension indigenous to life that is also integral to music and therapy, along with the various processes by which this tension is accumulated, sustained, resolved, and released.

Later it will also be argued that music goes beyond intrinsic structures within the work itself, to include the process, person, and context. Meanwhile, let us examine the issue of meaning in music.

The Meaning of Music in a Therapeutic Context

While scholars all agree that music has meaning, there are different theories on what gives music its meaning, and what kinds of meaning are possible to derive from it. These theories raise important questions for music therapy because as a discipline we assume that clients can find music meaningful in some way and that this meaningfulness is essential to the process and effectiveness of therapy. Another reason is that on a daily basis, we witness and help our clients work though myriad disabilities and problems in order to find or give meaning to their music experiences. Thus, music therapy brings a perspective on meaning-making in music not found in any other discipline—the perspective of how meaning is created under circumstances which are not always ideal, circumstances when the musicians or the listeners are struggling with physical, emotional, mental, social, or spiritual problems.

There are three main theories on meaning in music which are important to consider as music therapists: absolute formalism, referentialism, and absolute expressionism. For an in-depth discussion of these theories, see Meyer (1958) and Reimer (1970). According to Reimer, the absolute formalists believe that

> the "meaning" of an art work is like no other meaning in all the experience of man. Aesthetic events, such as sounds in music, mean only themselves; the meaning is sui generis completely and essentially different from anything in the world which is non-musical . . . The experience of art, for the Formalist, is primarily an intellectual one; it is the recognition and appreciation of form for its own sake. This recognition and appreciation, while intellectual in character, is called by Formalists "an emotion"— usually, the "aesthetic emotion." But this so-called "emotion" is a unique one—it has no counterpart in other emotional experiences (pp. 20–21).

Thus, all meanings found in music are indigenous to music and music alone, and as such are entirely independent and different from meanings found in the other arts or the world outside of art.

This position is largely untenable in music therapy for two reasons. First, it denies the importance of any relationship that may exist between music and the universe, the human condition, or individual ideas and feelings. This eliminates the very possibility that music can be meaningful or beautiful within a therapeutic context. Or put differently, for the absolute formalist, when music is used in therapy, it cannot be considered an art, for it is not deriving its meaning strictly from an intellectual appreciation of its formal beauty. Second, the absolute formalists are essentially elitists. They believe that most people are unable to achieve a truly aesthetic experience of music unless they have the necessary musical training and talent, and thus, for the masses, music serves primarily as a means of entertainment (Reimer, 1970). This certainly rules out the possibility that music could be aesthetically meaningful to individuals who are struggling to overcome disabilities and health problems! (It bears mentioning here that music therapy is very likely to be rejected or denigrated as a profession by musicians, conservatories and university music programs that hold this position).

In contrast to the absolute formalists, the referentialists believe that the core meanings of music and music experience are found outside of the work itself—in nonartistic or extramusical phenomena, events, ideas, feelings, etc., communicated through the music. For them, music embodies meaning by representing, symbolizing, expressing, or referring to the (nonmusical) world of human experience. Compositions, improvisations, and performances provide listeners with messages about life, the universe, human experience, and the individual musicians involved in creating them; and the process of composing, improvising, performing, and listening provide us with opportunities to live and work through various aspects of the human condition. For this reason, there is a direct and close relationship between music and musician. Unlike the absolute formalists, the referentialists believe that music is a reflection of the musicians involved in creating it, and every music listening experience is a reflection of the listener.

The referentialist position is very consistent with the basic premises of music therapy, and especially those schools that emphasize the use of music in therapy. The referential music therapist believes that music is a universal language that individuals can use to express the human condition as well as their own unique ideas, feelings, and identities. They also believe that the value of music is that it extends beyond itself as well as the entire realm of art and aesthetics. For them, music experience leads into and facilitates nonmusical experience of all kinds. Reimer (1970) explains that for referentialists,

> the values of art and being involved with art are nonartistic values. Art works serve many purposes, all of them extraaesthetic. If one can share these values one becomes a better citizen, a better worker, a better human being, to the extent that art influences one in non-artistic ways and these influences are assumed to be beneficial (p. 20).

The third position, held by the absolute expressionists, is an integration of absolute formalism and referentialism. Reimer (1970) summarizes their views as follows

> the aesthetic components in a work of art are similar in quality to the quality inherent in all human experience. When one shares the qualities contained in an art work's aesthetic content, one is also sharing in the qualities of which all human experience is made. The relation between the qualities of the art work and the qualities of human experience is felt by the perceiver of the work as "significance." To the degree that an art work contains aesthetic qualities which are convincing, vital, keen, and to the degree that these qualities can be experienced by the perceiver, the significance of the experience—the relation of the aesthetic qualities to the qualities of life—will be convincing, vital, keen. The residue of sharing the significant aesthetic qualities of the art work is a deeper sense of the nature of human life (pp. 24–25).

This position is also consistent with the basic premises of music therapy, and in particular those schools of practice which emphasize the use of music as therapy. Reimer (1970) provides another eloquent summary of the absolute expressionist which is relevant to the idea of using music as therapy. He says:

> the experience of art is related to the experience of life at the deepest levels of life's significance. One can share the insights of art not by going outside of art to non-artistic references, but by going deeper into the aesthetic qualities the art work contains. It is in the aesthetic content of the art work that insights can be found, and the deeper the experience of the aesthetic qualities the deeper can be the sense of significance gained. If the experience of art is to be significant for life, the experience of art must be aesthetic experience (p. 25).

Music as Person, Process, Product, and Context

Every music experience minimally involves a person, a specific musical process (i.e., composing, improvising, performing, or listening), a musical product (i.e., a composition, improvisation, performance, or perception), and a context (e.g., the physical, emotional, interpersonal environment). In music therapy, these components are integrally related if not inseparable; in fact, the very point of music therapy is finding the relationships between them. When a client takes the role of improviser, and engages in the process of extemporaneously creating an improvisation, the music therapist will always seek ways to relate the client to the client's process, and the resulting product to both the client, the specific process used by the client, and the context in which the process and product exist. And the same holds true for when the client takes the role of performer, composer, or listener.

While the relationship between person, process, and product in music might seem obvious, it is not universally accepted, and in music therapy, it raises a number of fundamental questions with regard to aesthetics: Exactly where does the music reside—in the person, the process, or the product—and how does this determine the boundaries of music experience? On which of these should aesthetic or artistic standards be applied? Does the meaning and beauty of the music reside in the person of the client, the process that the client undergoes to participate in the music, or the actual musical product that results?

In the author's opinion, there is only one way to answer these questions from a music therapy perspective: The boundaries of music includes the person, the process, the product, and the environment (e.g., nature, the universe); music resides in all of these components at the same time, and inseparably; the meaning and beauty of music can always be found in one of these components, if not another; aesthetic standards for one of these components cannot be universally or objectively applied to the others.

Thus, within a clinical context, the meaning and beauty of the client's musical efforts are always to be found either within the client, the process, the product, or the context. When the client has difficult feelings inside, the musical product may reflect these difficulties; but the beauty will lie in the process that the client underwent to express these feelings. When the client has to overcome disabilities to engage in the process, the musical product becomes beautiful, not because the music is perfect but because the client's victory is beautiful.

A maxim of all therapies is to seek the best in every client. Thus, in music therapy, the therapist must always search for the meaning and beauty of whatever the client brings forth within the music experience. We always assume that meaning and beauty are present; and within this perspective, aesthetic and artistic standards are very different in focus and criteria.

The converse of seeking the very best in every client is avoiding judgment. This too affects how the music therapist views the music experiences of clients.

Multisensory Applications

Music engages all of the senses. Though we typically think of music as an "auditory" art form, it also provides visual, tactile and kinesthetic stimulation, and it affords us opportunities to respond through these sensory channels. When we go to a concert, we can respond to the sounds of the music, the sight of the musicians playing, and the vibrations of the instruments or voices. As listeners, we can hear, see, and feel the music. When we play an instrument, we feel the shape and texture of the instrument, we receive kinesthetic feedback from our motor movements, we look at the musical score and other players, we hear the music we are making, and we feel the sound vibrations being produced. Thus, as a "stimulus," music can provide multisensory *input,* and as a "response," music can provide multisensory channels for *output.*

The multisensory aspects of music make it ideal for therapeutic use, especially if one considers how many disabilities and handicaps involve specific sensory or motor impairments. Music therapists, then, are continuously concerned with which sensory modality needs to have greater input or output, and how music can provide the stimulation or response medium to accomplish this. Often, music activities or experiences are needed to stimulate and exercise all the senses; however, with certain clients, the auditory aspects of music might be emphasized, and with others, the visual, tactile, or kinesthetic channels might be emphasized.

As the therapist manipulates the music activity to focus on different sensory channels, the basic nature of music and the music experience can change considerably. When visual or tactile rhythms are used to stimulate motor-impaired clients, does their experience qualify as musical? When hearing-impaired clients hear only certain sound frequency bands of a recorded composition, is their experience truly a musical one? When clients respond to music through visual images or body movements, are their responses musical, or do they go beyond its borders?

Obviously then, the multisensory applications of music have important implications for defining it in a therapy setting. When used clinically, music may be less or more than sound stimulation and auditory experience.

Related Arts Modalities

Based on the above discussion, music can be heard, seen, and felt; it can be transmitted through sounds, visual forms, and sensations, and it can be verbal and nonverbal. This wide range of input and output modalities leads to a final issue in defining music. Where are its outer boundaries? How does it relate and overlap with other kinds of experiences?

The problem here is that music is not always just music. It is often intermingled with other art forms. Songs combine music and poetry. Operas integrate music, drama, dance, and the visual arts. Symphonies can be based on stories or artworks. Singers mime and act while they sing. Conductors use gestures and movements to shape and direct the music. Listeners can move, dance, mime, dramatize, tell stories, paint, draw, or sculpt as a means of reacting to music. Or, one can create music as a means of depicting dance, drama, stories, poetry, mime, painting, etc.

Many of these "interrelated" art forms and experiences are used in music therapy. The most common examples are song-writing, musical story-telling, musical dramas, movement to music, musical rituals, and drawing to music, to name a few.

The use of these activities poses many questions regarding the boundaries of music therapy. Is song-writing within the realm of music therapy, poetry therapy, or both? Is musical story-telling an activity for bibliotherapy, drama therapy, or music therapy? Is moving or dancing to music within the realm of movement/dance therapy or music therapy? Is painting to music an activity for art therapy or music therapy?

PRESENT DEFINITION OF MUSIC

Given the many factors that shape how a music therapist conceives of music, it is important to offer a definition that is consistent with clinical practice and its basic philosophical premises. Toward this end, the following definition is offered:

Music is the human institution in which individuals create meaning and beauty through sound, using the arts of composition, improvisation, performance and listening. Meaning and beauty are derived from the intrinsic relationships created between the sounds themselves and from the extrinsic relationships created between the sounds and other forms of human experience. As such, meaning and beauty can be found in the music itself (i.e., the object or product), in the act of creating or experiencing the music (i.e., the process), in the musician (i.e., the person), and in the universe.

Let us now further elaborate on each part of the definition.

- Music is essentially a human undertaking, regardless of whether it is inspired by the Creator, or whether it originates from nature.
- Music is an institution. Like the other arts, music is an organized and enduring pattern of human interaction centered

around a set of values that are shared by a community and reciprocally related to that community with specific functions, aims, customs, traditions, and rules. When defined as an institution, music is species-specific and therefore universal; however, the criteria by which it is defined as an art form are culture-specific.

- Individuals create music. Thus, its meaning and beauty are always original and unique to each individual, and always invented anew.
- The art of music is both active and receptive in nature, with composition, improvisation, performance, and listening each having equally significant roles. Thus, the meaning and beauty of music reside both in the real world of sound as actually created by the composers, improvisers, or performers, and in the imaginal world of the listeners.
- Music conveys meaning and beauty both in reference to itself and in reference to the world beyond it. Its significance is both referential and nonreferential.
- Music is product and process, material and experience, real and imaginal, personal and transpersonal. Its meaning and beauty can be found in any of these aspects, and cannot be limited to any one of them.

Chapter Twelve

LEVELS OF MUSIC EXPERIENCES

WHY MUSIC EXPERIENCE
RATHER THAN MUSIC

One of the distinctive features of the present definition is that it stipulates that music therapy is not merely the use of music, rather it is the use of music *experiences*. The implications of adding "experience" to "music" are subtle but important nevertheless. What it implies is that the agent of therapy is seen as not just the music (i.e., an object which is external to the client); rather it is the client's experience of the music (i.e., the interaction between person, process, product, and context). Thus, the task of the music therapist is more than prescribing and administering the most appropriate music; it also involves shaping the client's experience of that music.

Another implication is that music therapy becomes an "experiential" form of therapy, that is, one which relies upon experience as both the agent and outcome of therapy. The main idea underlying experiential therapies is that the client accesses, works through, and resolves the various therapeutic issues directly through the medium (e.g., music, art, dance). For example, when the goal of music therapy is educational in nature, the client is engaged in music experiences that present the learning challenge and then provide options for its achievement. That is, the client experiences "what" is to be learned through the music, while also experiencing the learning process itself, again within the music. When the goal is psychotherapeutic, the client is engaged in music experiences that evoke the feelings and interpersonal dynamics that are problematic, while also experiencing their resolution or transformation through the music. Thus, what makes music therapy unique is not merely its reliance upon the music, but its reliance upon music experience as the primary aim, process and outcome of therapy.

A third implication is that the experience may include more than the music. As will be discussed later, the client's experience may be premusical, musical, extramusical, or even nonmusical, depending upon the extent to which music is involved. Any one of these experiences may be therapeutic. Thus, to say that music therapy involves only the use of music, rather than all of the other possible components of the music experience, is to largely deny the richness of music experience and its myriad potentials for therapy.

A fourth implication is that methodology in music therapy is based on what the client experiences, rather than by what the therapist does to shape that experience. For example, if a therapist is improvising and the client is only listening, the method is "receptive" rather than "improvisational." To be considered improvisational, the client must be improvising, regardless of what the therapist is doing at the time, whether it be improvising, listening, or performing. In short, it is the client's experience that is at the center of therapy, not the therapist's actions, and because of this, all methodological decisions are based on what the client needs to experience through music.

This brings us to an even more fundamental premise: music therapy itself is defined and delimited by the extent to which the client's experience involves music, not according to whether the therapist is actively engaged in making the music, nor whether the therapist has the musical competencies needed to do so! When a client listens to pre-recorded music, and the therapist merely selects the music and shapes the client's listening experience, it is still music therapy; and this holds true regardless of whether the therapist created the music, or whether the therapist is a trained musician or music therapist. Similarly, when a client makes music alone, and the therapist simply listens, it is still music therapy, regardless of the therapist's involvement and training. Music therapy occurs when the client experiences music therapeutically within a client-therapist relationship; it is not dependent on what the therapist knows or does.

Now that the significance of the entire phrase "music experiences" has been explained, it is time to examine the various types of experiences characteristically used in music therapy.

LEVELS OF MUSIC EXPERIENCE

Because music therapists frequently bend and shape the above four types of music experience to include all elements that have therapeutic potential, and because these experiences may additionally involve verbal discussion and other arts modalities, a constant and disturbing question has always been: When does the client's experience go beyond the limits of music and music therapy? To be sure, some experiences that music therapists give clients are more intrinsically "musical" than others. But exactly how "musical" does a client's experience have to be in order to be considered within the boundaries of music therapy, especially when we adopt the definition of music offered previously?

Perhaps the most efficient way to answer this question is to first identify those criteria that determine whether an experience is intrinsically musical. In surveying the various experiences used in music therapy, the following criteria seem to be most relevant: 1) whether the input or output is human or nonhuman, random or orderly, and controlled intentionally or unintentionally; 2) whether the input or output is auditory, vibrational, or visual; 3) whether the input or output are organized according to sound parameters or other parameters (e.g., motor patterns, speech patterns); 4) whether the sounds make meaningful forms; 5) whether any aspect of the experience is aesthetic in nature.

Based on these criteria, five levels of music experience can be discerned in clinical music therapy: premusical, musical, extramusical, paramusical, and nonmusical. Before defining these, we must first acknowledge that music therapy involves the client in both active and receptive music experiences, and that because of this, the intrinsic musicality of any experience may vary according to the nature of the musical input as well as the client's output. Thus, criteria for both types of experiences are needed. What follows is a description of each level of music experience, differentiated according to whether the client is engaged in a receptive or active experience.

Premusical

Premusical inputs are those that are insufficiently developed, organized, or complete to be considered intrinsically musical, or which function as communicative signals rather than purposeful musical expressions. Examples include: random vibrations, vibrational forms, musical vibrations, musical electric signals, motor rhythms, visual rhythms, environmental or natural sounds, animal sounds, unorganized body or instrumental sounds, random vocalizations, music or speech babble, and prosody.

Premusical outputs are those reactions to music that have insufficient awareness or intentionality to qualify as musical. Examples include autonomic and reflexive responses to music, changes in level of consciousness or arousal due to music, and sensorimotor schemes triggered by music.

Musical

Musical inputs are sounds that are sufficiently controlled or organized that they create relationships that are intrinsically meaningful. Although the sounds may represent, depict, or refer to something beyond themselves, their primary meaning or significance lies in the musical relationships that exist between the simultaneous and successive sounds themselves. These intrinsic relationships are evident when the materials are organized according to the basic musical elements (e.g., pulse, rhythm, scale, tonality, melody, harmony, texture, timbre, dynamics), and when the materials create musical forms (e.g., motifs, phrases, improvisations, compositions, performances).

Musical outputs are intentional efforts to listen to or make music. Listening is a musical experience when efforts are made to apprehend and experience the relationships and meanings intrinsic in the music. This usually entails a variety of covert processes, such as attending, perceiving, discriminating, analyzing, remembering, evaluating, interpreting, feeling, preferring, and so forth.

Creating sounds is considered a musical experience when efforts are made to control, manipulate, and organize them so that there are meaningful relationships among and between them. Typically, this involves activities such as improvising, performing music, composing, and the various covert activities involved therein.

Extramusical

Extramusical inputs are essentially nonmusical aspects of music or music experience which stem from, affect, or derive their meaning from the music (e.g., lyrics, programs, stories, or dramas depicted in the music). Such elements may be meaningful in and by themselves, or they may be dependent upon the music for their meaning. The music, on the other hand, is independent of such extramusical elements for its essential meaning, yet is enhanced and made more significant because of them. That is, the sounds themselves are no less meaningful or related from a musical standpoint, yet these essential musical meanings and relationships are somehow illuminated or enhanced by their extramusical denotations.

Because of this dual layer of meanings, the listener may put the music in the foreground of the experience and derive meaning primarily from it, with the extramusical element serving as a background, or do the reverse, that is, focus on the extramusical element for meaning with music in the background.

Extramusical outputs are essentially reactions or behaviors to music which do not involve making music, but derive their meaning from the music being experienced. Examples include responding to music by moving, miming, dramatizing, drawing, painting, sculpting, imaging, fantasizing, talking, writing, etc. Here again the person may put music in the foreground and shape the accompanying behavior accordingly, or do the reverse, focus on the extramusical behavior and put music in the background of the experience.

Paramusical

Paramusical inputs are those aspects of the music environment that impinge upon the individual while listening to or making music, but are not intrinsically related to the music, and do not depend upon the music for their meaning. Usually these forms of input occur independently of the music yet coincide with it, or they are stimulated by the music in some tangential way. Paramusical inputs serve as a foreground for the client's experience with music in the background, and therefore may include all nonmusical inputs that occur in conjunction with musical inputs. Examples of paramusical inputs include: 1) people, objects, furniture, lights, and props in the music environment; and 2) dance, drama, artworks, poetry etc., created independently of music, but still in the music environment.

Paramusical outputs are behaviors or reactions that occur within the context of musical activity but are nonmusical in their intent or content. Such responses may emerge or stem from the music, music environment, or experience thereof, yet they are not intrinsically related to or controlled by the music, and they are not dependent upon it for their meaning. Examples include daydreaming, being distracted, talking or engaging in another art activity with music in the background, etc.

Nonmusical

Nonmusical inputs are those aspects of the music therapy environment that impinge upon the client but that do not arise from, affect, or derive meaning from any of the previous kinds of stimuli or responses.

Nonmusical outputs are those behaviors or reactions that have no musical intent or significance, and which do not stem from, affect, or derive meaning from any type of musical activity.

CAVEATS

Music therapy sessions contain myriad inputs and outputs at various levels of intrinsic musicality. Sometimes the input is premusical and the output is musical; sometimes the reverse is true. Each session varies from moment to moment, and each client operates on a different level of musicality. Sometimes it is difficult to determine what the client is experiencing at all, let alone categorize the experience according to the above levels. It is important to realize that music is a pervasive human experience which does not always fit so easily into the confines of such categories, and furthermore, that its use in therapy is enhanced by taking *full* advantage of its breadth. On the other hand, there is an advantage to recognizing that some experiences are more or less intrinsically musical than others. These distinctions can guide the therapist in shaping the client's experiences, and also serve as a reminder that, although music therapy involves all levels of music experience, the closer the client's experience is to the purely musical level, the more certain we can be that it is truly *music* therapy.

Chapter Thirteen

TYPES OF MUSIC EXPERIENCES:
THE FOUR MAIN METHODS
OF MUSIC THERAPY

In the last chapter, music therapy was described as an experiential form of therapy because it focuses on and utilizes the client's music experience as its primary methodology. Essentially this means that, in music therapy, the client undergoes the processes of assessment, treatment and evaluation by engaging in various types of music experiences.

In music, there are four distinct types of experience. They are: improvising, re-creating (or performing), composing and listening. Each of these types of music experience has its own unique characteristics, and each is defined by its own specific process of engagement. Each type involves a different set of sensorimotor behaviors, each requires different kinds of perceptual and cognitive skills, each evokes different kinds of emotions, and each engages a different interpersonal process. Because of this, each type also has its own therapeutic potentials and applications. Thus for example, listening to music has certain therapeutic potentials and applications, which are different from those of improvising; and similarly, improvising music has different potentials and applications from performing a composed work.

To understand how music therapy works, then, requires an understanding of each type of music experience. The purpose of this chapter is to identify and define the various ways that improvising, re-creating, composing, and listening experiences are shaped by music therapists to meet client needs.

Before we proceed, we have to clarify some terms related to methodology that are often confused. In the literature, one often finds that the terms method, approach, model, procedure and technique are used interchangeably, as if they all mean the same thing. This has led to considerable confusion and arguments over who has originated what method, and which technique belongs to whom. While there is no obvious or singularly correct way to define each of these terms, they do need to be differentiated. And so, the selection of terms and definitions proposed here may be somewhat arbitrary; what is more important is that they have been differentiated and clarified. To understand the differences, we will use improvisation as an example throughout the discussion.

A *method* is here defined as a particular type of music experience used for assessment, treatment, and/or evaluation. Since there are four main types of music experiences (improvising, re-creating, composing, and listening), these are considered the four main methods of music therapy; and since there are many different ways of designing these four experiences, each of the methods have many *variations*. Thus, the various ways of engaging the client in extemporaneous music-making fall under the category of "improvisational" methods; the various ways of engaging the client in reproducing music fall under the category of "re-creative" methods; the various ways of engaging the client in composing are called "compositional" methods; and the various ways of engaging the client in listening experiences are called "receptive" methods.

In order to engage the client in these music experiences, the therapist uses various procedures. A *procedure* is an organized sequence of operations and interactions that a therapist uses in taking the client through an entire music experience. As such, procedures are the basic building blocks of a music therapy session; they are the various things that a therapist does to organize and implement the method. For example, if the method is improvisation, and the variation is "instrumental group," the therapist may use the following procedural steps in carrying out the session: 1) clients select instruments; 2) group experiments with instruments freely; 3) therapist presents a structure or play rule for the improvisation; 4) group improvises according to the play rule; 5) group discusses the improvisation; and 6) the same steps are repeated until the end of the session.

Within each of these procedural steps, the therapist may use a variety of techniques. A *technique* is a single operation or interaction that a therapist uses to elicit an immediate reaction from the client or to shape the ongoing, immediate experience of the client. Thus, a technique is a smaller, single operation within a procedure, while a procedure can be viewed as a series of techniques. In our improvisation example, the therapist may use a variety of musical techniques when the group is improvising together, such as "grounding," "pacing," "incorporating," and so forth (Bruscia, 1987). Similarly, when the group discusses the improvisation, the therapist may use a variety of verbal techniques such as "probing," and "reflecting."

When a therapist begins to develop a systematic approach employing one or more of the four main methods in a particular way, following specific procedural sequences, and relying upon certain techniques, a model is being developed. A *model* is a comprehensive approach to assessment, treatment, and evaluation which includes theoretical principles, clinical indications and contraindications, goals, methodological guidelines and specifications, and the characteristic use of certain procedural sequences and techniques. Examples of improvisationl models of music therapy are: "Creative Music Therapy," the model developed by Nordoff and Robbins (1977) or "Analytical Music Therapy," the model developed by Mary Priestley (1994). Notice that a model is much more comprehensive than a method; in fact, a model is the specification of how a method can be used, usually with certain client populations. Also notice that there are only four main methods of music therapy, and that these methods vary endlessly with regard to procedures and techniques, depending upon the model. Also, a method carries no particular theoretical orientation, whereas a model always implies one. A therapist can use improvisation within many different theoretical orientations, but as soon as improvisation is implemented in a particular way, according to any kind of principle, a theoretical orientation is implied.

To summarize: a method is a particular type of music experience that the client engages in for therapeutic purposes; a variation is the particular way in which that music experience is designed; a procedure is everything that the therapist has to do to engage the client in that experience; a technique is one step within any procedure that a therapist uses to shape the client's immediate experience; and a model is a systematic and unique approach to method, procedure and technique based on certain principles.

With this in mind, we can now examine the four main methods of music therapy in greater detail. What follows is a brief outline of each method, including: definitions, uses, variations, and the clinical goals that are most relevant to it, given its intrinsic nature.

IMPROVISATORY EXPERIENCES

Definition and Uses

In improvisation experiences, the client makes up music while playing or singing, extemporaneously creating a melody, rhythm, song or instrumental piece. The client may improvise alone, in a duet, or in a group which includes the therapist, other clients, and sometimes family members. The client may use any musical medium within his/her capabilities (e.g., voice, body sounds, percussion, stringed or wind instruments, keyboard, and so forth). The therapist helps the client by providing the necessary instructions and demonstrations, offering a musical idea or structure upon which to base the improvisation, play or sing an accompaniment that stimulates or guides the client's improvising, or presents a nonmusical idea (e.g., image, title, story) for the client to portray through the improvisation.

The clinical goals of improvisation experiences may include:

- Establish a nonverbal channel of communication, and a bridge to verbal communication
- Provide a fulfilling means of self-expression and identity formation
- Explore various aspects of self in relation to others
- Develop the capacity for interpersonal intimacy
- Develop group skills
- Develop creativity, expressive freedom, spontaneity, and playfulness with various degrees of structure
- Stimulate and develop the senses
- Develop perceptual and cognitive skills

Many different client populations manifest therapeutic needs in these areas: from obsessive-compulsive children to adults with borderline or narcissistic personality disorders; from autistic nonverbal children to aggressive adolescents; from impulsive, acting out children to inhibited depressed adults; and from developmentally delayed or physically disabled children to children free of handicap.

Variations

Instrumental Nonreferential: The client extemporizes on a musical instrument without reference to anything other than the sounds or music. In other words, the client improvises music for its own sake, without trying to make it represent or describe anything nonmusical. Three subtypes are: solo, duet and group, each of which poses different kinds of musical challenges.

Instrumental Referential: The client extemporizes on a musical instrument to portray in sound something nonmusical (e.g., a feeling, idea, title, image, person, event, experience, etc.). Subtypes include solo, duet, and group, each which has implications for how the nonreferential idea is perceived and musically projected.

Song Improvisation: The client extemporizes lyrics, melody, and/or accompaniment to a song. Subtypes are solo, duet and group song improvisations. Given the prominence of melody in song, and the close relationship between melody and lyrics, the addition of other improvisers can significantly complicate the process.

Vocal Nonreferential Improvisation: The client extemporizes a vocal piece without words or images. Subtypes are solo, duet and group.

Body Improvisations: The client improvises by making various kinds of percussive body sounds (clapping, snapping, patschen). Subtypes include solo, duet and group.

Mixed Media Improvisations: The client improvises using voice, body sounds, instruments, and/or any combination of sound sources. Subtypes include solo, duet and group.

Conducted Improvisations: The client creates an improvisation by giving directive cues to one or more improvisers.

RE-CREATIVE EXPERIENCES

Definition and Uses

In re-creative experiences, the client learns or performs precomposed vocal or instrumental music or reproduces any kind of musical form presented as a model. Also included are structured music activities and games in which the client performs roles or behaviors that have been specifically defined. The term re-creative is used here rather than performing because the latter often implies singing or playing a piece before an audience. Re-creative is a broader term which includes rendering, reproducing, realizing, or interpreting any part or all of an existing musical model, whether done with or without an audience.

Clinical goals may be to:

- Develop sensorimotor skills
- Foster adaptive, time-ordered behavior
- Improve attention and reality orientation
- Develop memory skills
- Promote identification and empathy with others
- Develop skills in interpreting and communicating ideas and feelings
- Learn specific role behaviors in various interpersonal situations
- Improve interactional and group skills

Primary candidates for re-creative experiences are those clients who need structure to develop specific skills and role behaviors. They are also indicated for clients who need to understand and adapt to the ideas and feelings of others while still retaining their own identity, as well as clients who need to work with others toward common goals.

Variations

Instrumental Re-creation: The client may be involved in any of the following kinds of experiences: sounding an instrument in a prescribed way, sight-playing some kind of notation, performing precomposed instrumental pieces, rehearsing in an instrumental ensemble, taking private lessons, performing imitative tasks on an instrument, or playing an instrumental part with a recording. The essence of all these tasks is the reproduction of structured or precomposed musical materials using a musical instrument.

Vocal Re-creation: The client may be involved in any of the following: vocalizing in a prescribed way, sight-singing, singing songs, chanting, choral-speaking, rehearsing choral groups, taking voice lessons, vocally imitating or learning melodies, or lip-synching recorded songs. The essence of all these tasks is the vocal reproduction of structured musical materials or precomposed songs.

Musical Productions: The client is involved in the planning and performance of a talent show, musical play or drama, recital, or other kind of musical production involving an audience. The essence of these tasks is performing for an audience, and all the preparations involved.

Musical Games and Activities: The client participates in musical games (e.g., name that tune, musical charades, musical chairs, etc.) or participating in any activity that is structured by music.

Conducting: The client directs the live performance of music by providing gestural cues to the players as dictated by a score or other notational plan.

COMPOSITION EXPERIENCES

Definition and Uses

In composition experiences, the therapist helps the client to write songs, lyrics or instrumental pieces, or to create any kind of musical product such as music videos or audiotapes. Usually the therapist takes responsibility for the more technical aspects of the process, and gauges the client's participation to his/her musical capabilities. For example, the client may generate the melody on a simple bar instrument, while the therapist provides the harmonic accompaniment; or the client may produce the lyrics while the therapist composes the melody and harmony to go with them.

The main clinical goals are to:

- Develop organizational and planning abilities
- Develop skills in creative problem solving
- Promote self-responsibility

- Develop the ability to document and communicate inner experiences
- Promote the exploration of therapeutic themes through lyrics
- Develop the ability to integrate and synthesize parts into wholes

Variations

Song Parodies: The client changes words, phrases, or the entire lyrics of an existing song, while maintaining the melody and standard accompaniment.

Song-Writing: The client composes an original song or any part thereof (e.g., lyrics, melody, accompaniment) with varying levels of technical assistance from the therapist. The process includes some form of notation or recording of the final product.

Instrumental Composition: The client composes an original instrumental piece or any part thereof (e.g., melody, rhythm, accompaniment) with varying levels of technical assistance from the therapist. The process includes some form of notation or recording of the final product.

Notational Activities: The client creates a notational system and then composes a piece using it, or the client notates a piece that has already been composed.

Music Collages: The client selects and sequences sounds, songs, music, and fragments thereof in order to produce a recording which explores autobiographical or therapeutic issues.

RECEPTIVE EXPERIENCES

Definition and Uses

In receptive experiences, the client listens to music and responds to the experience silently, verbally, or in another modality. The music used may be live or recorded improvisations, performances, or compositions by the client or therapist, or commercial recordings of music literature in various styles (e.g., classical, rock, jazz, country, spiritual, new age). The listening experience may be focused on physical, emotional, intellectual, aesthetic, or spiritual aspects of the music, and the client's responses are designed according to the therapeutic purpose of the experience.

The main clinical goals are to:

- Promote receptivity
- Evoke specific body responses
- Stimulate or relax the person
- Develop auditory/motor skills
- Evoke affective states and experiences
- Explore ideas and thoughts of others
- Facilitate memory, reminiscence, and regression
- Evoke imagery and fantasies
- Connect the listener to a community or sociocultural group
- Stimulate peak and spiritual experiences

Candidates for listening experiences are those clients who have the attentional abilities and receptivity needed to take in the music, and who will benefit therapeutically from responding to the music in a particular way (e.g., analytically, projectively, physically, emotionally, spiritually).

Variations

Somatic Listening: The use of vibrations, sounds, and music in various elemental and combined forms to directly influence the client's body and its relationship to other facets of the client. Subtypes include:

- *Entrainment:* The use of vibrations, sounds, and music in various elemental and combined forms to establish synchronicity in autonomic or voluntary body responses: between client and music, within parts of the client's body, and between the client and another person. The stimuli used may be recorded, or created by therapist and/or client, instrumentally or vocally.

- *Resonance (Toning):* The use of vibrations, sounds, and music in various elemental and combined forms to vibrate parts of the client's body at various frequencies or frequency patterns, and to establish sympathetic vibrations between the stimulus and the client. The stimuli used may be recorded, or created by therapist and/or client, instrumentally or vocally.
- *Vibroacoustic Music:* The administration of vibrational frequencies to the client's body while listening to music; or the application of the vibrational patterns of music directly to the client's body (e.g., musical acupuncture).
- *Music Biofeedback:* The use of music to provide moment by moment auditory feedback on autonomic body functions (e.g., blood pressure, heart rate, hormone levels, gland secretion, etc.). The purpose is to facilitate the client's use of biofeedback technology and to thereby provide greater awareness and control over the body. Music may also be used to facilitate the relaxation process in biofeedback.

Music Anesthesia: The use of music listening: to enhance the effects of anesthetic or analgesic drugs, to induce insensibility to pain without anesthesia, to reduce or control pain, and to reduce anxiety associated with pain.

Music Relaxation: The use of music listening: to reduce stress and tension, to reduce or countercondition anxiety, to induce body relaxation, or to facilitate entry into altered states of consciousness.

Meditative Listening: The use of music to assist in meditation or in the contemplation of a particular idea. The music may be recorded or created live by client and/or therapist, and used in the background or foreground of the experience.

Subliminal Listening: The use of sounds or music to mask the delivery of subliminal verbal messages or suggestions to the unconscious mind.

Stimulative Listening: The use of music listening: to stimulate the senses, to bring alertness, to establish reality orientation or contact with the environment, to increase energy level, to elicit sensorimotor activity, to increase sensory perceptions, or to elevate mood.

Eurhythmic Listening: The use of music to rhythmically organize and monitor the client's motor behaviors, including speech, breathing, fine and gross movement sequences, body exercises, and formalized dance steps. Note that in this method, the client's motor behaviors are much more prescribed and structured than in projective movement to music. The method is also different from action listening in that the rhythm of the music is used to organize the motor behavior rather than to cue or direct which motor behavior is to be performed.

Perceptual Listening: The use of music-listening exercises to improve skills in auditory attention, perception, discrimination, and conservation, and the relationship between auditory and other sensory modalities.

Action Listening: The use of song lyrics or musical cues to elicit specific behavioral responses (e.g., motor movements, daily living activities, verbal responses).

Contingent Listening: The use of music listening as contingent reinforcement for behavior change.

Mediational Listening: The use of music as a mediational strategy in learning and recalling information. Music is paired to various types of information or to a particular experience in order to make it more concrete, memorable and retrievable.

Music Appreciation Activities: The therapist presents music-listening experiences that will help the client to understand and appreciate the structure, style, historical significance, and aesthetic value of the music.

Song (Music) Reminiscence: The use of music listening to evoke memories of past events and experiences in the client's life. The music may be vocal or instrumental, recorded or performed live, and selected by either client or therapist according to its association or temporal relationship to the time period in the past of interest. After listening (or performing the music), the client and therapist reminisce about the client's past.

Song (Music) Regression: The therapist selects music that will enable the client to re-experience the past, not as a reminiscence of it in the present, but as a reliving of the past in the past. Often, the client listens to the music in a relaxed, quiet state.

Induced Song (Music) Recall: When induced *consciously,* the therapist asks the client what song (or music) comes to mind in reference to a particular topic, issue, or event in the ongoing therapeutic process; when induced *unconsciously,* a song (or piece of music) unexpectedly and spontaneously comes into the therapist's or client's awareness in response to a particular topic, issue, or event (Diaz de Chumaceiro, 1998a, 1998b).

Song (Music) Communication: The therapist asks the client to select or bring in a recorded song (or other piece of music) which expresses or discloses something about the client that is of relevance to therapy; or, the therapist selects a recording that communicates something of relevance to the client. Then both parties listen to the recording and explore what the music communicates about the client, the client's life, or therapeutic issues.

Song (Lyric) Discussion: The therapist brings in a song that serves as a springboard for discussion of issues that are therapeutically relevant to the client. After listening to the song, the client is asked to analyze the meaning of the lyrics, and to examine (in dialogue with the therapist or other clients), the relevance of the lyrics to the client or the client's life.

Projective Listening: The therapist presents sounds and/or music and asks the client to identify, describe, interpret, and/or free associate to them through either verbal or nonverbal means. Specific projective listening techniques include:

- *Projective Sound Identification:* The client listens to ambiguous sounds and identifies what they are.
- *Free Association:* The client listens to sounds or music and speaks or writes whatever comes to mind, paying no attention to their cohesion or meaning.
- *Projective Storytelling:* The client listens to sounds and/or music and makes up a story accordingly, either orally or in writing.
- *Music Dramatization:* The client acts out what s/he hears in the music.
- *Song Choices:* The client selects and listens to favorite or preferred songs, or song with which s/he has a strong identification or connection. (See Song Communications and Induced Song Recall.)
- *Projective Movement to Music:* The client listens to music and extemporizes expressive movements accordingly.
- *Projective Drawing to Music:* The client draws while listening to music.

Imaginal Listening: The use of music listening to evoke and support imaginal processes or inner experiences, while in a nonordinary state of consciousness. Specific types include:

- *Directed Music Imaging:* The client images what the therapist presents while listening to music, usually in an altered state of consciousness. The image may be selected by therapist or client, and may be mental or physical in nature. The image may be specific, personalized, or general, and the therapist's guiding may be spaced at various intervals.
- *Unguided Music Imaging:* The client images freely while listening to music while in an altered state of consciousness without direction or dialogue with the therapist. With or without the focus, music is usually short.
- *Guided Music Imaging:* The client freely images to music while in an altered state of consciousness and dialoguing with the therapist.
- *Guided Interactive Music Imaging:* The client co-creates images to music with other clients under the guidance of the therapist.

Self-Listening: The client listens to a recording of his/her own improvisation, performance, or composition, to reflect upon oneself and the experience.

Chapter Fourteen

RELATIONSHIPS

In music therapy, the therapist uses both music experiences and the relationships that develop through them as therapeutic agents. This part of the definition suggests that, in addition to its direct therapeutic effects, music also helps the client to develop various kinds of relationships, and further, that these relationships have their own therapeutic effects. Thus, both music and relationships are integral and interdependent parts of the intervention process.

The relationships that emerge within music therapy are multifaceted. They can be between elements within a person, between people, between a person and an object, or between objects. Each of these can be manifested and experienced physically, musically, mentally, behaviorally, socially, or spiritually. Thus, for example, relationships might be explored between two opposing feelings a client has, between different parts of the client's body, or between the client's music and his/her feelings about a significant other. Or, relationships in therapy might be examined between the client's feelings and therapist's feelings, between the client's music and the therapist's music, or between the client's thoughts and the feelings of another client.

The following are convenient ways of categorizing these myriad relationships. Although described only in terms of the client, these relationships also exist for the therapist as well.

- *Intrapersonal* relationships are those found within the person between any parts of the self, such as between: the client's body and the client's emotions; the client's visual response and the client's auditory response; the client's thoughts and the client's feelings; the client's behavior and the client's music; the client's personality and the client's music, and so forth.
- *Intramusical* relationships are those that exist within a person's music, such as between: the client's rhythm and the client's

melody; the client's melody and the client's accompaniment; the client's timbre and the client's volume.

- *Interpersonal* relationships are those that exist between one person and another, or among persons in a family or therapy group. These relationships are not within the musical realm. Examples are between: one client's behavior and another client's feelings; the client's behavior and the therapist's behavior; one client's tone of voice and another client's verbal response; the client's body language and the therapist's body language.
- *Intermusical* relationships are those found between one person's music and the music of one or more other persons, such as between: one client's rhythm and another client's rhythm; one client's rhythm and the group beat; the client's timbre and the therapist's timbre; the client's melody and the therapist's harmony.
- *Sociocultural* relationships are those between the individual and any community to which the individual belongs (e.g., work groups, social organizations, religion, ethnic or racial groups, society, culture). This includes both personal and musical realms, such as between: the client's music and the music of his heritage; the client's thoughts and the client's religion.
- *Environmental* relationships are those found between the individual and the various physical environments in which the individual lives.

These relationships can serve several important functions in therapy. If health is enhanced by harmony and balance, then therapy is the process by which harmonious and balanced relationships are explored and developed within the client's world. Thus, the relationships that are formed through music experience can help to give the client an awareness of which of the above relationships are harmonious and balanced and which are not, while also providing the motivation and support needed to do something about them. Thus, relationships can be the target of change or the condition necessary for change.

Of all the relationships that can develop in music therapy, two are of greatest methodological significance: how the client relates to music (his/her own as well as the therapist's), and how the client relates to the therapist (both personally and musically). It is from these relationships that the others are accessed, explored and developed.

Both relationships can be characterized as either: 1) a "transference" relationship (when the client relates to the music or therapist as a person from the past [usually parents]); or 2) as an "authentic" relationship (when the client relates to the music or therapist as they are and for what they offer in the present). Though these types of relationships seem most relevant to psychotherapeutic approaches, they have wide implications for other orientations as well. The reason is that in every application of music therapy, the music and the therapist are helping the client in some way, and a helping relationship of this kind seems to elicit these kinds of parental or interpersonal issues, regardless of whether the goal of therapy is physical, emotional, mental, or spiritual health.

The relative emphasis given to the client-therapist and client-music relationship depends greatly upon whether music is used *as* therapy or *in* therapy, and upon the theoretical orientation of the therapist. When music is used *as* therapy, the client-music relationship serves as the primary vehicle or agent for therapeutic change, and the client-therapist relationship is facilitative and supportive to that end. Here the therapist's main role is musical in nature, and his/her identity is more "musician as therapist." In this case, the client-therapist relationship can be characterized as essentially music or activity based.

When music is used *in* therapy, the reverse is true. The client-therapist relationship serves as the primary context for change and the client-music relationship facilitates that end. Here the therapist's main role is interactional in nature and often verbal, and his/her identity is more "therapist as musician." In this case, the client-therapist relationship can be characterized as more interpersonal than musical.

Chapter Fifteen

DYNAMIC FORCES

Although the term "dynamic" is usually associated with psychoanalytic theory, every form of music therapy regardless of its orientation can be described in terms of "dynamic" elements and forces. The reason is that music therapy always involves the client in some kind of encounter or interaction. For therapy to take place, someone or something must act in some way on the client to effect an outcome, while the client is continually acting and reacting. There is always a reciprocal exchange of action and reaction: the therapist may act upon the client, the music may act upon the client, the client may act upon him or herself, or the music may be the medium for therapist and client to act upon one another, and so forth. These interactions or encounters comprise what is commonly called the "dynamics" of therapy.

The dynamics of therapy can be likened to chemistry. Just as chemical elements can be combined to form compounds, and then further combined to produce various reactions and changes, so can the various elements of the therapeutic situation. In music therapy, the basic elements that are used in various combinations include: the client, the therapist, the music (in all of its various manifestations), and in some cases, other clients. Also included may be significant people in the client's life, and other art forms and artifacts.

While these elements can combine and interact in many different ways, the key element is music. In terms of our analogy to chemistry, music is the most important ingredient; it determines how all the other elements and compounds combine, interact, and affect one another. And even more specifically, it is how the *client's music experience* has been designed that determines what reactions and relationships are possible between the other elements and compounds. *Thus, the client-music interaction lies at the very core of music therapy, shaping the dynamics of all other relationships.*

This has very significant ramifications. It implies that to analyze the dynamics of music therapy is to analyze the various ways in which the client experiences music! This makes perfect sense, because the whole premise of music therapy, as a unique treatment modality, is that music experiences are used in some systematic and purposeful way to meet specific therapeutic needs of the client.

Upon analyzing clinical practices in music therapy, the author has identified six basic models for designing the client's music experience, with each model casting the client, therapist, and music into a particular dynamic configuration, and each model specifying their roles and functions in relation to one another, as well as their desired interactive effects. What defines each model is the particular aspect or property of music that is emphasized within the client's experience (regardless of whether the experience involves improvising, composing, re-creating or listening). Specifically, the six dynamic models are differentiated according to whether the client's experience focuses on the 1) objective, 2) universal, 3) subjective, 4) collective, 5) aesthetic, or 6) transpersonal properties of music. Each of these will be discussed in detail, however, before proceeding an overview may be helpful.

Figure 2 shows the six models in relation to one another. Models one through four have been diagramed based on Wilber's theory of evolution (1996), which differentiates exterior and interior realms (the right and left halves of the circle) of individual and collective development (the upper and lower halves respectively). As shown:

- When the client's experience is focused on the *objective* properties of music (i.e., stimulus, organismic, or response variables), the model is concerned with the *exterior individual* realm. The exterior individual realm includes all those aspects of a person that can be observed and measured, such as body structure and activity, behavior, and so forth.
- When the client's experience is focused on the *subjective* properties of music (i.e., as a process or representation referring to self/other), the model is concerned with the *interior individual* realm. The interior individual realm includes all those aspects of a person that are concerned with value and meaning.

Figure 2.

THE SIX DYNAMIC MODELS
OF
MUSIC THERAPY

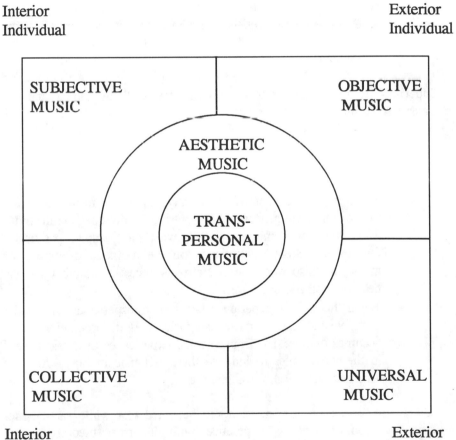

Interior
Individual

Exterior
Individual

SUBJECTIVE
MUSIC

OBJECTIVE
MUSIC

AESTHETIC
MUSIC

TRANS-
PERSONAL
MUSIC

COLLECTIVE
MUSIC

UNIVERSAL
MUSIC

Interior
Collective

Exterior
Collective

- When the client's experience is focused on the *universal* properties of music (i.e., the natural, organic patterns inherent in sound and music), the model is concerned with the *exterior collective* realm. The exterior collective realm deals with all aspects of the "objective" physical world that are shared by communities of individuals.
- When the client's experience is focused on the *sociocultural* properties of music (i.e., as ritual, identity, or archetype of a community), the model is concerned with the *interior collective* realm. The interior collective realm deals with all aspects of the "subjective" world that are shared by communities of individuals.

Superimposed over these four models are the aesthetic model and the transpersonal model.

- When the client's experience is focused on the *aesthetic* properties of music (i.e., as an art object or artistic process), the model is concerned with the appreciation of beauty and meaning either in the music itself, or in any realm of life to which the music refers (e.g., exterior, interior, individual, collective). Thus, this model emerges not only when the therapist specifically focuses the client's experience on the aesthetic properties of music, but also when the music experiences in the other models become aesthetic in nature.
- When the client's experience becomes transpersonal, the model goes beyond any of these categories and differentiations, and becomes unitive. The transpersonal experiences of music appear in the very center to indicate that, in music therapy, they are accessed through the aesthetic realm.

Before any further discussion, it should be noted that while each model defines an entire school of practice with its own theoretical and methodological perspective, the models are not mutually exclusive. A therapist can move from one to another with the same client depending upon the situation, and as this occurs the therapeutic process gains breadth and depth, thereby leading to more pervasive changes in the client. This in turn moves the therapeutic effort from adjunctive to more primary levels of intervention.

MUSIC AS OBJECTIVE EXPERIENCE

Music consists of organized sounds and vibrations; it is energy and matter heard in motion. It therefore has specific physical and acoustical properties that can be used for therapeutic purposes. When the therapist uses these properties of music to directly influence the client's body or behavior in some observable way, or when the therapist uses nonmusical stimuli to induce specific musical responses from the client, the dynamic can be described as the use of music as an objective experience. The experience is objective because the variables of primary interest (on both the stimulus and response sides of the equation) can be operationally defined, observed, and measured.

In this dynamic model, qualities of the therapist, client, and music are objectified, that is, operationally defined in terms of measurable stimulus, organismic or response variables, and then utilized to produce the desired effects on one another. Thus, the therapist, client, and music are seen as separate entities that are related to one another in various stimulus-response and cause-effect relationships. Two different configurations are most commonly used: music as stimulus and music as response.

Music as Stimulus Condition

In this configuration of the objective model, specific properties of the music are used as stimulus, mediator, or reinforcer to induce observable, nonmusical responses in the client. The musical stimulus is designed to evoke an immediate nonmusical reaction which either is therapeutic in itself or is prerequisite to therapeutic change. In this dynamic, the therapist and music are both located on the causal side of the exchange, as separate or combined stimulus objects that have been designed to effect change, while the client is located on the effect side as a separate object that has been targeted for change.

Typical examples of this dynamic include: the use of music listening to effect physiological changes, the contingent use of music to influence nonmusical behavior, and the use of music as mediator in nonmusical learning. Here the effectiveness of therapy depends upon the extent to which the stimulus conditions can induce the desired response, and then be either faded away or generalized.

Music as Response Modality

In this configuration of the objective model, the therapist uses either nonmusical or musical stimuli, usually in the form of an activity, to elicit specific musical responses from the client deemed to be therapeutic (e.g., imitation of a rhythm, pitch-matching). Notice that the target response is musical, and that it is operationally defined as the therapeutic objective. Thus, for example, correct imitation of all aspects of rhythm patterns of varying lengths is used as an operational definition of short-term memory, and the patterns themselves can be operationally defined to reflect different types of mnemonic strategies. Here the effectiveness of therapy depends upon whether the activity used as a stimulus can elicit the desired musical response, and the extent to which the musical response can generalize to nonmusical areas of functioning.

Therapist's Role

In the objective model, the therapist needs considerable knowledge of the research literature. Of particular relevance is an understanding of how stimulus, organismic, and response variables are related. More specifically, the therapist has to know how the various stimulus properties of music can be therapeutically applied with different therapeutic problems and client groups, as well as how various musical responses within a particular client group are indicative of therapeutic change in nonmusical areas of functioning.

Within the session, the therapist has these main responsibilities: taking all relevant organismic variables into account, to pinpoint and operationally define the desired therapeutic response (whether musical or nonmusical), to utilize the appropriate stimuli to produce that response, to establish the kind of interpersonal and physical environment that is conducive to therapy, to observe and whenever possible measure the client's responses, and to determine in an objective way client progress and the effectiveness of various therapeutic procedures.

Given the nature of these responsibilities and the expertise needed to carry them out, the therapist typically takes a more directive role in conducting the session, while also being sensitive to the needs and wishes of the client. The therapist is ideally warm and supportive toward the client, while also maintaining objectivity and the appropriate professional distance. Essentially, the therapist is a sensitively empirical clinician, who utilizes scientific research on the therapeutic potentials of music as the basis for assessment, treatment, and evaluation.

MUSIC AS UNIVERSAL ENERGY FORM

In the objective model, music is conceived as a human creation; an object made by people with specific properties that can be used for therapeutic purposes. In the present model, music is still part of the object world, but is conceived as something more than a human creation; rather it is a condition of the universe itself. Here music is a living energy form that precedes and presupposes the earthly musical creations of individual human beings. With this in mind, Kenny (1988) asked:

> Could we image that music is at the root of our existence; that music is the formative element, not an epiphenomenon; that music is not something we create, but something we notice and record? Could we imagine that the "creator" of the sound merely listens to a larger pulse of natural life and informs us about these rhythms, patterns, textures, and tones, providing a blueprint, a landscape of the greater pattern of life? (p. 52).

Three basic notions underlie the use of music as a universal energy form. The first is that the universe itself, like music, is patterned vibration, George Leonard (1978) explains:

> At the root of all power and motion, at the burning center of existence itself, there is music and rhythm, the play of patterned frequencies against the matrix of time . . . we now know that

every particle in the physical universe takes its characteristics from the pitch and pattern overtones of its particular frequencies, its singing. And the same thing is true of all radiation, all forces great and small, all information (pp.2–3).

Inherent in this notion is that all matter is energy and all energy is matter; or as Eagle (1991) says in his discussion of the quantum theory of physics, "all being can be described equally as particle and wave at the same time"

The second basic notion is that all parts of the universe are integrally related, and that every macrosm contains and is contained in a microcosm. Bohm (1980) calls this concept "holonomy" and asserts that: "In the 'quantum' context, the order in every immediately perceptible aspect of the world is to be regarded as coming out of a more comprehensive implicate order, in which all aspects ultimately merge" (p. 156).

Putting all this together, Eagle and Marsh (1988) explain how the universe, the person and music are all interrelated:

The laws of the universe "out there"— in the environment outside of the human body—are equally applicable to the function of the universe "in here"—inside the body. "Out there" and "in here" are both composed of vibrations and vibro-magnetic fields, the analytical and perceptual interpretative parts of which are frequencies/pitches, intensities/loudnesses, wave forms/tone qualities (timbres), durations/times, and locations/localizations. Of such stuff is the body made and music composed (p. 23).

The third notion is that, because music is a manifestation of the order, balance, and harmony inherent in the universe, it has the potential for restoring such qualities to any part of the universe that becomes disordered, unbalanced, or unharmonious through disease or illness. Thus, music and its basic structural components (sound, vibrations) are inherently healing to all living things.

These basic notions, taken together, have spawned two basic approaches within the universal model, one which we will call "elemental" and the other which we will call "musical."

Elemental Approach

In the elemental approach, sounds and vibrations are used for healing purposes in isolation, that is, without music or outside of a music experience. Thus, healing takes place within the client's experience of the structural components of music rather than real music per se. As such, the client experiences parts of the music which in no way resemble the whole. These practices are best described as "sound healing" or "vibrational healing," both of which are defined in a later chapter. What is important to point out here is that both practices are not concerned with music experience per se, and therefore do not belong within the boundaries of music therapy or music healing.

Musical Approach

In the musical approach, therapy or healing takes place within the client's experience of *music* and all of its components, including sound and vibration as well as melody, rhythm, and harmony. The premise here is that all the elements and relationships found in music created by human beings are a replica of organic elements and relationships found in nature. Thus, a created piece of music is an explication of the implicate order of the universe (see Eagle 1991), and every experience of music is a re-creation of the universal life experience. The practices in this approach are best described as "music healing" and "music therapy in healing," both of which are defined in a later chapter.

Therapist's Role

The therapist's role in this model is similar to that when music is used as a therapeutic stimulus and response. In fact, both music and therapist are used in similar ways. Music is the primary agent of change, operating directly on the individual within a cause-effect paradigm, while the therapist is a scientific healer, who uses theory and research as the basis of practice. In this model, however, the therapist needs special expertise in physics and metaphysics, and an acute understanding of how energy forms within the universe relate to and affect energy forms within the species under conditions of health and disease. (See Summer [1996] for a comprehensive discussion of the knowledge base needed in this model, and the many fallacies that have crept into that knowledge base).

The client-therapist relationship is ideally warm and supportive, but is of relatively less dynamic significance than music because it is not the chief determinant of therapeutic change. The client is essentially "healed" by the music of the universe, with the therapist in a secondary role. The dynamic is sometimes considered "self-healing," because the client responds naturally to natural forces within the universe, but it can be argued that this is still an intervention from an outside force, and thus would be more accurately called "sound-, vibrational- or music-healing."

MUSIC AS SUBJECTIVE EXPERIENCE

Making and listening to music are always uniquely personal experiences; no two persons sing or play a piece in the same way, no two persons improvise or compose in the same way, and no two persons hear a piece of music in the same way. Thus, the way a person makes or listens to music is a direct manifestation of that person's unique identity as a human being, reflecting not only who the person is but also how he or she deals with various situations as exemplified in the music. Similarly, when two or more persons make or listen to music together, their shared music experience is equally unique to themselves; no other two persons will interact, communicate, and relate to one another in the same way.

Because of this, therapists can use music to help clients experience and explore various aspects of themselves and how they relate to the world. To use music in this way, the therapist designs the music experience according to whatever the client needs to explore and experience, or what might be more accurately called, the therapeutic issue. For example, a therapist may ask a client to improvise alone in order to explore how the client organizes and relates various aspects of the self, or how the client makes decisions when alone; in contrast, the therapist may improvise with the client to explore how independent or flexible the client is making decisions when others are involved.

Two basic approaches may be taken in configuring the dynamics of music within a subjective experience, one focusing on the process of making or listening to music, which we will call "music-as-process," and the other focusing on musical products (i.e., the recorded or scored improvisation, composition, or performance resulting from the musical process), which we will call "music-as-representation."

Music-as-Process

When music is used as process, the ongoing, moment-to-moment experience of creating, re-creating or listening to music provides the client with opportunities to discover, experience, and transform various aspects of the self, others, and/or the self-other relationship. Music-as-process can also be used to explore events, objects, images, symbols, inner experiences, or any aspects of the client's world. In this model, it is the process of making or listening to music that is itself the process of therapeutic change. In comparison to the previous models, this use of music is not predetermined according to stimulus-response bonds and specific therapeutic outcomes, rather it is exploratory, extemporaneous, and open to whatever emerges. The process is also not necessarily aesthetically driven, as the main purpose is to use music as a very personal expression or reflection of each individual involved.

The primary focus for the client in music-as-process may be anywhere along the continuum of self to other, depending on how the process is designed. Thus, music may reflect the self-process or the self-other process.

- *Music-as-Self-Process:* On one end of the self-other continuum, the process may be designed so that the client makes or listens to music alone, that is, with the therapist (or other clients) present but not participating directly in the experience, with the primary focus being the intrapersonal self. Here the primary goal is to provide the client with opportunities: to discover and experience various aspects of the self (past and present); to examine and work through feelings, thoughts, images, etc.; to identify and explore alternate ways of being; and to work out and make the necessary changes. Of course, even when the primary focus is on the self, others are implicated, as are external events and objects. The mere presence of others as listeners and the unfolding of the musical process in the external world provides a broad context for the client's exploration, including both the world of others, as well as the world of objects. In addition, the intrapersonal self already includes and implicates others and objects, either because the experience itself focuses on the self in relation to them, or because the self always contains internal representations of them (viz., introjects). Nevertheless, the dynamic is still music as "self-process" because the client is accessing, expressing, working through, and reintegrating all aspects of the music without the help or influence of anyone else.

- *Music-as-Self/Other-Process:* On the opposite end of the continuum, the client makes or listens to music with others actively participating in the process, with the main focus being on who the other persons are in relation to the self. Here too objects and events may be implicated. In the middle of the continuum, the client may make or listen to music alone or with others, with the main focus on either the interpersonal self, or the self in relation to others. Both of these variations can be called music-as-self/other-process, because the unfolding of the music is the unfolding of the self-other relationship, with possibilities for focusing on self, other, or both sides of the relationship. In the process, the client gains opportunities to discover existing patterns, to explore alternative ways of relating, and to make the necessary changes.

When music is used in either way, the therapist provides what is sometimes called a "transitional [musical] space," a term originating from Winnicott's theory (1953) of object relations, and later applied to the various creative arts therapies. The concept of "music as process" goes beyond the concept of transitional musical space in several ways, and though there is no room to discuss these in detail, it is important to at least cite what they are. The following are areas of "music-as-process" not traditionally included in discussions of transitional musical space: solo music-making by the client, that is, without active participation by the therapist; expression of all aspects of the self instead of mere psychological projection of only unwanted parts; and receptive as well as active forms of musical endeavor.

Music-as-Representation

Whenever music is used as process, the result is some kind of musical product, such as an improvisation, composition, performance, score, recording, perception, interpretation, and so forth. This musical product is a reflection of everything that happened during the process; it documents everything that has been externalized, worked on, and transformed by the music-maker(s) or listeners. As such, this product of the experience provides a musical image, symbol, metaphor, or projection of each person involved in the process—their problems, resources, feelings, thoughts, solutions, and so forth, while also giving a musical description of the relationships that emerged between the various persons, objects, and events involved in the experience. Thus, an improvisation provides a representation of the improviser and how s/he relates to the world of self, other, and object, just as a composition and performance provides the same kind of representation of the composer or performer. Similarly, the listener's responses to music provide a representation of the listener and how s/he relates to the world of self, other, and object.

Like music-as-process, these musical representations can reflect self, other, object, event, and relationships therein, depending on how they are designed.

- *Music-as-Self-Representation:* An improvisation, composition, or performance which has been recorded or scored serves as a unique manifestation, metaphor, symbol, container, script, or personal myth for the self and various aspects and experiences thereof, involving object, events, or others. Here the music exists as an externalized object of the self which mirrors the self and, as such, is essentially psychological in nature.
- *Music-as-Self/Other-Representation:* An improvisation, composition, or performance which has been recorded or scored serves as a shared but interpersonally unique manifestation, metaphor, symbol, container, script, or myth

for the experiences of and relationship between and self and other. Here the music is a mirroring, externalized object of the self-other, and thus is essentially psychological in nature.

Music-as-representation can be likened to Winnicott's concept of the "transitional object," however, here again it extends beyond the original parameters in the same ways already cited for music-as-process and "transitional space."

Therapist's Role

In this dynamic model, the client, music and therapist are integrally connected to and, in fact, inseparable from the musical process and product. Unlike in other models, the three are not separate entities which can be taken apart and examined scientifically. Rather, the client is a subject relating to music with the therapist, who is also a subject relating to music with the client. Here the emphasis is on personal, subjective meaning, rather than on objective data.

The role of the therapist is to use his or her own subjective self to relate to the client in a therapeutic way, using music either as therapy or in therapy, depending on the roles and responsibilities given to it. To do this, the therapist needs expertise in music, psychology, and psychotherapy, while also having considerable personal experience in using the "self" with "music" as partners in therapy. Meanwhile, the client's main task is to commit to exploring relationships within and between self, music, and therapist.

MUSIC AS COLLECTIVE EXPERIENCE

In addition to having relationships with significant others, every individual is part of many layers of community, from nuclear family to extended family, from friends and colleagues to social network, from town to state and country, and from ethnic and religious groups to society and culture. Each of these layers of community has its own identity as a whole and as part of a larger whole; thus, each community shapes and is shaped by the individual identities, and each community shapes and is shaped by the larger community which contains it.

One of the most important elements that binds these various layers of community together and contributes to each of their collective identities is music. Throughout the history of humankind, music has served as an integral part of rituals that a community creates and shares, it has provided a shared identity of people who belong to a community, and it has provided a container and reflector of the collective psyche of the species.

In this dynamic model, the therapist calls upon collective experiences of music as a basis for therapy with either the individual or the community. Music may be used in three ways: as a ritual, as a collective identity, or as an archetype.

Music as Ritual

Most communities use some form of music activity as a ritual, either by itself or as part of a larger ritual that includes other activities (e.g., the other arts). A ritual is any sociocultural activity that is repeatedly and traditionally carried out by a particular group of people, in a particular and set way, for a particular purpose. Most often, music is an integral part of rituals dealing with medicine, healing, and religion.

In therapy, music can be used as ritual in at least three ways. First, the therapist can create a music ritual as an integral part of the therapeutic process: An example is when certain music activities or pieces are used at certain junctions of a session (e.g., same hello song, following by same sequence of instrumental activities, followed by same good-bye song). Here the music is being used as a therapy ritual specially designed for the client-therapy community. An example is provided by Beer (1990).

Second, the therapist can re-create a ritual practiced by a particular community as part of the therapy process. The most common example of this is the use of shamanic rituals in music therapy (see Moreno, 1988; Winn, Crowe & Moreno, 1989; and Aigen, 1991a). Another example is when the therapist provides clients with music during religious services and other kinds of ceremonies.

Third, the therapist can operate on or utilize a musical custom, tradition, organization, or ritual of a community to induce change. An example is the work of Stige (1993) who worked with an established community music group to accept new members who were mentally retarded.

Music as Collective Identity

Whenever music activity is an integral part of community life, the history and identity of the community becomes integrally linked to the music activities practiced and to the unique repertoire of music that the community creates and adopts over the years. When this happens, each music activity or piece serves as a reminder of the community's heritage. The music of the community thus serves as a reflection of their collective identity.

Therapists often call upon the collective musical identity of their clients as a means of initiating or facilitating the therapy process (see Henderson [1991] and Bright [1993]). For example, when working with elderly clients, therapists often use music that is part of their ethnic or religious heritage to bring them together, to combat their feelings of alienation, to regain the anchor of having roots, and to rebuild a new community and new sense of belonging. Similarly, the musical identities of two different groups or communities can be used as the basis for changing each in relation to the other, as when teenagers and the elderly share their music with one another to create a new level of understanding.

Therapists can also help groups of clients to build their own collective identities. In this approach, rather than calling upon existing identities, the group begins to build its own repertoire of music activities and pieces as a means of expressing and shaping a new collective identity. Here the purpose is not so much to reflect relationships within the group (as in music as subjective experience), but rather to enhance the sense of belonging and community.

Music as Archetype

Music is experienced as an archetypal form or process whenever its meaning is derived from the collective unconscious. Here the music re-enacts or reflects human interior experiences that are universal, that is, experiences that emanate from the inherited, collective psyche of the species. Archetypal music experiences as defined here may be referential or nonreferential. When they are referential, the music refers to, expresses, or depicts myths and various parts thereof (e.g., the hero, the hero's journey, the dragon, the dragon fight), all of which have to some degree reached verbal levels of consciousnesss; when they are nonreferential, the music reenacts energy forms that precede and underlie myth, as indigenously nonverbal experiences of the human condition (e.g., conflict, balance, tension, harmony) that come into consciousness through reenactment.

Therapist's Role

In this dynamic model, the therapist is the keeper of roots. The therapist's role is to remember with and remind clients of all that connects them to one another and the many layers of community they share. Here the expertise is more sociological and anthropological than psychological, as the emphasis is always on the history of the group as a context of meaning for the individual, with less attention given to psychological idiosyncracies of individuals within the group. And even when the focus is psychological, the emphasis is on how the collective unconscious shapes the personal unconscious, rather than vice versa.

Here the music serves as both container for the past as well as space for the present, providing the community with opportunities to create, re-create, and preserve the bonds that keep them together and anchor them to their roots. The client's main task is to connect to and place oneself within the communities in which s/he lives.

MUSIC AS AESTHETIC EXPERIENCE

Dynamically speaking, music can be considered a purely aesthetic experience whenever the client or therapist creates or listens to music for its own sake, that is, for no other purpose than the appreciation of music, either as an art object or an artistic process. Here the music experience is not designed prescriptively, according to therapeutic goals or stimulus-response bonds; rather it is incorporated into the therapy process for its own intrinsic value. Hence the dynamic motivation is experiencing music in and of itself, and for its own sake, rather than for the sake of the therapy process or any of its other extrinsic values for the client. For further discussion of these ideas, see Aigen (1991a, 1995), Ansdell (1995), and Aldridge (1996).

It is important to realize that even when music is used only for its intrinsic value, the experience can still be of considerable extrinsic value. In other words, aesthetic experience, even when pursued for its own sake, still has therapeutic implications. Art is therapy, even when not intentionally undertaken for that purpose. Thus, providing the client with purely aesthetic experiences still facilitates and enhances the therapeutic process. Salas (1990) explains

> Beyond finding new ways to express feelings, beyond achieving a new sense of competence and self-worth, beyond discovering an organized self, the client—playing or listening—is experiencing an ontological coherence coded in the music's beauty. Blocked in the search for meaning by impairments, whether circumstantial, organic or psychological, the client can find intimations of universal order and purpose in music. Healing takes place within the aesthetic experience itself (p. 9).

According to Salas, what makes this so is that every individual continually seeks ontological meaning and beauty in life, and that music provides both. Music imparts ontological meaning on two levels: from within—as a rich texture of sounds in various relationships within one another; and from without—as part of a larger pattern of human life and as a manifestation of the larger order of the entire universe. Beauty is implicated in that it "is no more or less than a phenomenon of universal order" that we experience "as an affirmation of ontological meaning" (p. 4). "Beauty is the quality of integrity of form that echoes, to a greater or lesser degree, the grace and elegance of the patterns of existence" (p. 4).

It is also important to realize that music can be an aesthetic experience, regardless of whether the process and product meet conventional standards of artistry established by professional musicians and critics. See the chapter on music for a discussion of this issue.

Music as Art Object

Music is experienced as an art object whenever the focus is on the piece of music itself (e.g., the improvisation, composition, or performance) for its aesthetic value or beauty as a work of art. This is possible not only when listening to music; it also happens when improvising, composing, and performing and the focus is on striving to make the product a thing of artistic beauty. Hence it is the art work created that is aesthetically fulfilling, with comparatively less concern over whether the process of creating it has been an artistic one.

Music as Artistic Process

Music is experienced as an artistic process whenever the focus is on the sheer aesthetic pleasure derived from the act of music-making or music listening itself. Here aesthetic values and beauty are pursued and achieved while improvising, composing, re-creating, or listening to music, in the creative process itself. Hence it is the act of creating art as it is being created that is aesthetically fulfilling, with comparatively less concern over the artistic value of the resulting product.

Therapist's Role

In this model, the therapist needs to be an accomplished musician capable of infusing the client's music experiences with artistry, beauty, and aesthetic meaning. The therapist may also serve as a teacher, as clients often need some form of instruction or practice to develop the musical skills needed to find personal meaning and fulfillment within the music.

MUSIC AS TRANSPERSONAL EXPERIENCE

As the postmodern world has begun to rediscover the centrality of soul and spirit to the human experience, there has been an increasing interest in the spiritual values of music. The idea that music provides access to soul and spirit is not a new one in philosophy, music, or religion, but its acceptance within the music therapy community has been more recent. Certainly, the work of Nordoff-Robbins (1977), and Bonny (1978) have been moving forces toward that end.

Unfortunately, space does not permit an in-depth discussion of this dynamic model of music therapy, except to say that transpersonal experiences can be of two types: with music being the vehicle leading to the transpersonal realm, and music being an integral part of the transpersonal space itself.

Music as Transpersonal Vehicle

Making or listening to music is a vehicle to the transpersonal when it helps the individual access and enter the transpersonal realm which, when reached, is not integrally related to the music experience. Essentially, the music experience serves as a bridge between ordinary consciousness of ordinary reality to nonordinary and expanded consciousness of the infinite. An example of this is the use of music-making or music listening to facilitate meditative states or rituals (e.g., shamanic journeys) involving music that lead to transpersonal or spiritual worlds. In both cases, the music is not within the expanded consciousness that evolves, nor is it an integral part of the experience of the infinite.

Music as Transpersonal Space

Making or listening to music provides a transpersonal space when the individual has a peak or unitive experience that suspends ordinary boundaries between self/music or self/other to form a new larger, expanded whole. When this occurs, the music is not a mirror of the self, the music is the self on the way to becoming Self; similarly, the music is no longer a mirror of the other or the self-other relationship, rather the three components (self, other, and music) become indistinguishably one as part of the greater Self. Here the expanded consciousness includes the music as an integral but indistinguishable part of the infinite. This type of experience occurs in Guided Imagery and Music (GIM), when the client is ready and the conditions are conducive to transpersonal work.

Therapist's Role

The therapist in this model has to know how to work with clients while they are in nonordinary states of consciousness, while also being knowledgeable about transpersonal work, both personally as a client, as well as professionally as a therapist. The role of the therapist is essentially facilitative and nondirective. In fact, the titles "therapist" and "client" are less appropriate here, as the client is actively doing the healing and transformative work, while the therapist is serving as supportive witness and eventually a bridge for the client to return to ordinary reality.

Chapter Sixteen

CHANGE

As we reach the final word in our definition, it becomes clear that the ultimate aim of music therapy is to induce some kind of change in the client. The very purpose of engaging the client in music experiences and the relationships that emerge through them is to effect change. But what kinds of change take place, and how do these changes qualify as therapy?

In music therapy, the client may undergo changes that are musical and nonmusical. When music is used *as* therapy, the most noticeable changes are more likely to be musical in nature; when music is used *in* therapy, the most noticeable changes are more likely to be nonmusical in nature. Since in both cases the goal is to affect nonmusical areas of the client's life, nonmusical changes are often more obvious indicators that therapy has taken place than musical ones.

Because music involves and affects so many facets of the human being, and because its clinical applications are so diverse, music therapy can be used to achieve a broad spectrum of therapeutic changes. The following are areas most commonly targeted:

- *Physiology:* Heart rate, blood pressure, respiration, galvanic skin response, pupil dilation, brain waves, muscular responses, electromyography, gastric motility, temperature, hormonal levels, glandular secretions, neurological functions, immune responses, and vibrational structure of organs.
- *Psychophysiology:* Pain, levels of arousal, levels of consciousness, state of tension or relaxation, level of energy or fatigue, biofeedback, imagery of body and its functions.
- *Sensorimotor development*: Reflexive responses and their coordination, sensorimotor schemes (viz., control, integration, and internalization of visual, auditory, tactile and kinesthetic functions); fine and gross motor coordination.

- *Perception:* Apprehension of figure-ground, part-whole, and same-different relationships, discrimination of differences, conservation of sameness.
- *Cognition:* Breadth, depth and length of attention, short- and long-term retention, learning skills, knowledge, thought processes, attitudes, beliefs cognitive style, constructs.
- *Behavior:* Patterns, activity level, efficiency, or reinforcement contingencies for behaviors, work productivity, safety, and morale.
- *Music:* Preferences, vocal range and technique, instrumental technique, practice habits, repertoire, ensemble skills, rhythmic, melodic, and formal tendencies when performing, improvising, or composing.
- *Emotions:* Range, variability, appropriateness, and congruence of feelings, reactivity, expressivity, vitality, defenses, impulsivity, anxiety, aggressiveness, depression, motivation, imagery, fantasies, symbols, and so forth.
- *Communication:* Receptive and expressive skills in speech, language, and other nonverbal modalities, including music, dance, drama, poetry, and art.
- *Interpersonal:* Awareness, sensitivity, intimacy, and tolerance of others, interactional skills, role behaviors, relationship patterns and styles, and so forth.
- *Creativity:* Fluidity, originality, inventiveness, and artistry.

Of course, human beings are continually making and undergoing these kinds of changes every moment of each day, some for the better and some for the worse. Which of these can be considered therapeutic in nature? Two fundamental criteria can be used. The first is that the change improves the health status of the client; the second is that the change can be attributed to the therapeutic process.

HEALTH-ENHANCING CHANGE

One of the basic premises of music therapy is that because music experience involves and affects so many facets of the human being, every musical change that a client makes is indicative of a nonmusical change of some kind. When a client who has attentional deficits learns how to concentrate within a musical context, that ability or skill has potential application for many other aspects of the client's life; similarly, when a client releases emotions when making or listening to music, those emotions are not defined only in musical terms, nor is the release a strictly musical process. Thus, every change that a client makes within a music experience is either generalizable to nonmusical areas because of the interdependence in all areas of human functioning, or the musical change already signifies or demonstrates that a nonmusical change has taken place.

While these two notions occupy much attention in music therapy research and theory, an even more basic question needs to be answered: notwithstanding whether the change is musical or nonmusical, is the change health-enhancing? The following types of changes are generally regarded as health-enhancing or therapeutic in nature. Notice that some stem from a "pathogenic" orientation to health, while others stem from a "salutogenic" or "holarchical" orientation, as defined in the previous chapter on health. Notice also that each one is more appropriate for certain kinds of health problems than others, and especially within music therapy.

- *Preventive:* The changes in therapy help the client to decrease health risks or build resistances against health problems.
- *Curative:* The changes in therapy counteract, alter, or eliminate the etiology of a health problem.
- *Reconstructive:* The changes in therapy help the client to deconstruct and then reconstruct parts of self or life so that previous health conditions are not present.
- *Allopathic:* The changes in therapy counteract, alter, or eliminate the symptoms or effects of a health problem.

- *Homeopathic:* The changes in therapy re-create the health condition in a way that stimulates the client's natural healing processes to operate more efficiently.
- *Supportive:* The changes in therapy give the client the support system and insight needed to fight or live with a health condition.
- *Habilitative:* The changes in therapy help the client gain or compensate for capabilities that should be developing but are not developing because of a health condition.
- *Rehabilitative:* The changes in therapy help the client regain or compensate for capabilities that were lost as the result of a health condition.
- *Palliative:* The changes in therapy improve the client's quality of life while coping with or succumbing to a health condition.

THERAPY-INDUCED CHANGE

Once it is determined that the changes in the client are health-enhancing, the next question is whether the changes can be attributed to the therapy process. This is often difficult to determine because therapy always takes place within the context of a client's complete life experience at the time, which may include other forms of therapy as well as other important life events or changes. Four conditions are necessary to conclude that therapy has induced changes in the client's health. First, the changes required help of some kind. Essentially this means that any changes that clients are able to make on their own, without help, or as the result of normal maturation, growth, or healing, cannot be considered therapy-induced. Second, the help needed could only have been provided by a qualified therapist within the context of a therapist-client relationship. Thus, the client did not need any kind of help, or help that anyone could provide, but specifically needed a therapist. Third, the help provided consisted of intervention of a therapeutic nature. The therapist acted upon the client in a way that specifically mitigated those forces in the client's life responsible for health. And finally, the changes made by the client can be attributed to the specific interventions made by the therapist.

Chapter Seventeen

DEFINING AREAS AND LEVELS
OF PRACTICE

Music therapy is incredibly diverse. It is presently being used in many different clinical settings, to address a variety of health concerns, with myriad client populations. Its goals and methods vary from one setting and client to another, and from one music therapist to the next, depending on the therapist's theoretical orientation and training. This diversity has important implications for defining music therapy because a definition, by its very nature, has to make room for the many variations of practice that rightfully belong within its borders while also providing limits for identifying those variations that extend beyond its borders. One way to do this is to organize and classify the various practices according to similarities and differences, and in so doing, to establish criteria for comparing and delimiting them. Toward this end, the clinical literature in music therapy was surveyed and the various practices of music therapy were defined and differentiated. The present chapter is a result of that survey; its purpose is to present an overview of the various areas and levels of practice identified, and to thereby provide a context for understanding the definitions found in the next chapter.

AREAS OF PRACTICE

An *area* of practice is defined by what the primary clinical focus is, or what is in the foreground of concern for the client, therapist, and clinical agency. Of particular relevance are:

- The priority health concern of the client. When a client enters an agency or program, it is because of a particular health concern; when clients seek the services of a music therapist, it is always for a particular purpose; and when professionals refer clients to music therapy, it is usually to accomplish something specific. All of these motivations for seeking help shape what the clinical focus or foreground of therapy is, and because of this, they usually shape the therapeutic contract, determine the types of services to be provided, and indicate the conditions under which therapy should terminate.

• The priority health concern for the agency serving the client. Most clinical agencies focus on a particular client population or health concern, and define their mission accordingly. Thus, when a music therapy program is a service provided by an agency, it already has a specific health focus. The foreground of music therapy in a nursing home is quite different from that in a school or psychiatric hospital.

• The goal of the music therapist. Notwithstanding the client's reason for being in music therapy, or the mission of the agency serving the client, every music therapist conceptualizes the goals of therapy differently, usually according to his/her theoretical orientation and methodology. Therapists who use improvisational methods within a psychodynamic orientation have a different clinical focus than those using receptive methods within a behavioral orientation.

• The nature of the client-therapist relationship. The roles of client and therapist, their titles, and the nature of their relationship all reflect a clinical focus. In a school setting, client and therapist are likely to call one another student and teacher; in a hospital, the titles are likely to be patient and therapist. These titles imply certain roles and responsibilities, and with them, certain parameters for their relationship. A therapist in a hospital setting would address certain aspects of a client's life that a teacher would dare not address in a school setting.

Based on these criteria, six main areas of music therapy have been identified: didactic, medical, healing, psychotherapeutic, recreational, and ecological. An overview of each will be given in this chapter, then in later chapters, specific practices within each area will be described in detail.

Didactic

Didactic practices are those focused on helping clients gain knowledge, behaviors, and skills needed for functional, independent living and social adaptation. In all of these practices, some form of learning is in the foreground of the therapeutic process. This includes all applications of music therapy in classrooms and private studios, as well as in other settings (general or psychiatric hospitals, nursing homes) where the main goals of the program are essentially educational in nature.

Practices in this area vary according to the area of learning emphasized (e.g., musical or nonmusical), the therapeutic value of the learning, the extent to which the goals and methods can be individualized to meet specific client problems and needs, and the nature of the client-therapist relationship.

Five different orientations to learning are taken within this area of practice, with varying emphasis given to musical versus nonmusical learning. They are:

- to develop musical knowledge and skills for their own sake, as an integral part of functional living and social adaptation;
- to develop musical knowledge and skills that involve or generalize to nonmusical areas of functioning;
- to use music and related activities as an aid in nonmusical learning;
- to use music learning as a context for therapy;
- to use music therapy experiences to educate, train, and supervise students and professionals.

Medical

The medical area includes all applications of music or music therapy where the primary focus is on helping the client to improve, restore, or maintain *physical* health. This includes all those approaches that focus on biomedical illness as the main target of change, as well as those that also operate on psychosocial and ecological factors which influence biomedical illness and wellness. Typical settings are hospitals, clinics, rehabilitation centers, hospices, and nursing homes.

Practices in this area vary according to the differential roles given to music and the client-therapist relationship, the medical significance of the goals, the length of treatment, and the clinical setting.

Healing

The healing area includes all uses of the universal properties of vibration, sound, and music for the purposes of restoring harmony within the individual and between the individual and the universe. A central notion is that music is a vibrational manifestation of the order, balance and harmony inherent in the universe, and that because of this, music can be used to restore such qualities to any part of the universe that is disordered, unbalanced, or unharmonious through disease or illness.

Because of their reliance on vibrational energy forms, all healing practices focus on what Wilber (1995) calls "exterior collective" relationships between individuals and the universe. Exterior relationships are essentially physical and behavioral in nature, however, a basic assumption is that as the body comes into harmony, the psyche and spirit will follow, as all three are interrelated forms within the energy field. Thus, the initial focus on the exterior collective can extend to interior relationships within the individual and between the individual and other sociocultural layers; nevertheless, what distinguishes healing practices from ecological ones is that healing starts from the exterior collective and moves to more interior concerns, while the ecological starts from the interior collective and moves to more exterior concerns.

Healing differs from therapy in one fundamentally significant way: in therapy, the agent of change is the client, the therapist, or the music that they make or hear together; in healing, the agent of change is the universal energy forms found in music, and its component sounds and vibrations.

Practices within the area vary according to: the role responsibilities given to client, music, and therapist, the extent to which the practice involves music (as contrasted to sound and vibrations), whether the practice focuses on only one area of health (e.g., body only) rather than the synergistic relationships between various areas of health, and whether the target is an individual or an environment or context.

Psychotherapeutic

The psychotherapeutic area includes all applications of music or music therapy where the primary focus is on helping clients to find meaning and fulfillment. This includes all those individual and group approaches that focus on the individual's emotions, self-contentment, insights, relationships, and spirituality as the main targets of change, as well as those which address medical and didactic factors related to these issues. Typical settings are psychiatric hospitals, counseling centers, and private practice.

Practices in this area vary according to the breadth and depth of treatment, the role of music, and the theoretical orientation of the therapist (e.g., psychodynamic, behavioral, etc.).

Recreational

The recreational area includes all applications of music or music therapy where the primary focus is on personal enjoyment, diversion, or engagement in social and cultural activity. This includes both institutional, community, and individual programs aimed at helping individuals engage in leisure time and social activities that will enhance the quality of life.

Practices in this area vary according to the degree of relevance a particular recreational pursuit has to the client's health needs (e.g., an art pursuit, a personal pastime, social contact, participation in the community), as well as the length and continuity of treatment.

Ecological

The ecological area of practice includes all applications of music and music therapy where the primary focus is on promoting health within and between various layers of the sociocultural community and between any community and its physical environment. This includes all work which focuses on the family, workplace, community, society, culture, or the attitudes that any group has toward the physical environment, either because the health of the ecological unit itself is at risk and therefore in need of intervention, or because the unit in some way causes or contributes to the health problems of its members. Also included are any efforts to form, build, or sustain communities through music therapy.

All ecological practices focus on "interior" relationships between the individual and the various collective contexts in which the individual lives (see Wilber, 1995). Interior relationships are based on the ideas, attitudes, values, feelings, behaviors, meanings, and traditions of individuals within various layers of community, and ultimately the relationship of all communities to the human species at large. Of course, these "interior" concerns can affect "exterior" relationships between groups of people and their physical environments. Nevertheless, what defines the ecological area is that the focus of change is first and foremost interior in nature. This stands in contrast to healing practices, which focus first and foremost on the exterior or physical relationships between the individual and the universe, and then as indicated, on the implications these have for interior matters. Thus, for example, while healing practices are concerned with the energetic relationship between individuals, groups and their physical environment, ecological practices are concerned with the attitudes and values groups have toward their physical environment.

Practices in this area vary according to whether the focus is on the environment as client, or the environment of a client. Thus, the aim may be to improve the health of the environment itself, or to alter those factors in the environment which contribute to the client's health problem while also helping the client to deal with them. Since practices in this area are quite different from those in the other areas, criteria for determining levels are also different. Of greatest significance are the breadth of focus and the degree of change resulting from the interventions.

LEVELS OF PRACTICE

Overview

Each *area* consists of clinical practices that vary according to *level* of therapy. A *level* describes the breadth, depth, and significance of therapeutic intervention and change accomplished through music and music therapy. More will be said of specific criteria determining levels of therapy, but first it is necessary to give a brief overview of the four levels identified in a survey of the literature. They are:

- *Auxiliary Level:* all functional uses of music or any of its components for nontherapeutic but related purposes.
- *Augmentative Level:* any practice in which music or music therapy is used to enhance the efforts of other treatment modalities, and to make supportive contributions to the client's overall treatment plan.
- *Intensive Level:* any practice in which music therapy takes a central and independent role in addressing priority goals in the client's treatment plan, and as a result, induces significant changes in the client's current situation.
- *Primary Level:* any practice in which music therapy takes an indispensable or singular role in meeting the main therapeutic needs of the client, and as a result, induces pervasive changes in the client and the client's life.

Other writers who have defined similar levels of practice include Wolberg (1967), Wheeler (1983, 1988); and Maranto (1993). The present author has also offered other versions (Bruscia, 1987b, 1989a), and has related these levels of practice to the content of education and training at the undergraduate and graduate levels (Bruscia, 1989b).

Criteria

The following criteria were used to identify the above four levels of practice, and ultimately, to classify the various practices within each of the areas described above.

Relevance to Primary Health Needs. The first criterion used to determine level of therapy is the relevance of the practice to the client's health status or primary therapeutic needs. Does the practice deal with health needs? Are its goals therapeutic in nature? Is the focus peripheral, supportive, or central to the client's primary health needs?

When a practice is not concerned with health concerns or therapeutic needs, it falls outside the boundaries of music therapy. When the goals are peripheral or supportive to the client's overall therapeutic program, or when they address secondary health problems or less intense therapeutic needs, the practice is more likely to be at the auxiliary or augmentative level. When the goals are of central relevance, or when they address health problems or needs of primary significance, the practice is more likely to be at the intensive or primary level. Thus, the more severe, urgent, or significant the health problems or therapeutic needs of the client, and the more responsibility taken by music therapy in addressing them, the more intensive the level of therapy is likely to be.

Clinical Independence. When music therapy shares responsibility for priority goals with other modalities, or when it focuses on limited aspects of the client's total treatment plan, the practice is more likely to be at the augmentative level. When music therapy takes major or sole responsibility for key areas in the client's program, addressing a broad spectrum of health problems and therapeutic needs, it is more likely to be at an intensive or primary level.

Role Relationships. Music therapy always involves a client, a therapist, and music, working together to induce change, through specific role relationships. Thus, when any of these three elements is absent, or not given an appropriate role, the practice falls outside of the boundaries of music therapy. For example, when the individual being helped is not defined as a "client," or when music is used alone, without the help of someone defined as a "therapist," the work cannot be considered music therapy per se, and is therefore considered to be at the auxiliary level. When role relationships other than client-therapist (e.g., student-teacher) are involved, or when the client-therapist relationship effects change through indirect rather than direct means, the practice is more likely to be at the augmentative level. When all role requirements of client and therapist are met, and when the relationship itself provides a direct means of effecting therapeutic change—equal to the role of the music—the practice is more likely to be at the intensive or primary level.

Level of Music Experience. A major factor determining the boundaries of music therapy is the extent to which the client's experience involves music, as defined in Chapter 11. In terms of the present levels, those practices that depend primarily on premusical, paramusical, or nonmusical experiences (see Chapter 12) are usually auxiliary to music therapy, but not part of the discipline itself; whereas those practices that depend primarily on musical and extramusical experiences are more likely to be augmentative, intensive, or primary.

Comprehensiveness of Treatment. Related to all of the above criteria is the breadth of the therapeutic process, or the extent to which the therapist and music can address most, if not all, of the client's health concerns. A major factor in determining this is whether music is used *as* therapy or *in* therapy. The issue here is how adaptable the music therapist is in addressing the full spectrum of health problems or needs that a client presents. Does the therapist use only music, or does s/he exploit the full range of experiences and relationships that arise from the music? Does the therapist use other modalities and methods when indicated? Or in more basic terms, to what extent is music therapy client-centered and/or music-centered?

When music is used *as* therapy, the therapist focuses on the specific needs of the client that can best be addressed by the music itself. When music is used *in* therapy, the therapist focuses on the full spectrum of needs presented by the client, and selects that particular component of music therapy (e.g., music, the therapist, the relationships) that best addresses those needs which are considered priority. This does not imply that music *in* therapy is always an intensive or primary level of therapy and that music *as* therapy is always augmentative. Although this is common, the reverse may also occur. Sometimes a priority need can best be addressed by music *as* therapy, and sometimes it is best addressed by music *in* therapy. Here again the ultimate determinant is the nature of the client's needs, and the extent to which either music *as* or *in* therapy can address them.

In terms of the levels, when the therapist stays within the established boundaries of his/her modality and method, and addresses only some of the client's needs (i.e., those that fit within the boundaries of the modality and method), the practice is augmentative; when the therapist stays within the modality and method, but is able to address most or all of the client's needs, the practice is intensive or primary. Similarly, when the therapist extends or goes beyond the modality, but only addresses some of the client's needs, the practice is auxiliary or augmentative; and when the therapist uses the full range of the modality and method, and extends them to address broad therapeutic concerns, the practice is intensive or primary. In Piagetian terms, the augmentative therapist *assimilates* the client's needs into his/her modality and method, while the intensive or primary therapist *accommodates* his/her modality to the client's needs.

Depth of Therapeutic Process. The level of therapy depends not only upon breadth, but also upon the depth of treatment. How far does the intervention process go, and how long does it take? When a practice does not involve a systematic process of intervention over a sufficient period of time, it falls outside of the boundaries of music therapy. When a practice involves occasional or infrequent sessions, or if it extends for only a brief period of time, or when the interventions deal with manifest problems and needs, the practice is more likely to be augmentative. When a practice involves frequent and regular sessions over a long period, and when the interventions address both latent and manifest problems and needs, the practice is more likely to be intensive or primary.

Degree of Therapeutic Change. An ultimate determinant of the level of therapy is the degree of therapeutic change to be made by the client. Does the practice aim at inducing any kind of change? If so, is the change therapeutic, as defined in the previous chapter? Does the practice lead to overt and/or covert therapeutic changes? What specific aspects of the client's problems are addressed—the symptoms, the disorder, the causes, or the resultant difficulties? Are changes made at the conscious or unconscious level? To what extent do the changes involve structural reorganization, adaptation, or manipulation of the environment? Do these changes make the client more independent in resolving or coping with the problem, or is change dependent in some way on the treatment conditions?

Wheeler (1983, 1988) has offered a classification of music therapy practices using degree of change as the criterion. Based on Wolberg (1967), she identified three levels of psychotherapeutic practice for adult psychiatric patients: 1) activity music therapy (the use of music-based activities to achieve adaptive behavior goals); 2) insight music therapy with reeducative goals (the use of music and other psychotherapeutic methods to help the client understand and resolve problems at the conscious level); and 3) insight music therapy with reconstructive goals (the use of music and other psychotherapeutic methods to resolve unconscious conflicts and thereby promote reorganization of the client's personality).

Nature of These Levels

A few final points need to be made about how all of the above criteria affect levels of practice. First, every criterion may not be relevant to every area of practice. That is, a criterion may be relevant in determining levels of practice in one area (e.g., educational) but not another (e.g., healing). As will be seen in the chapters that follow, when determining levels of therapy, different criteria apply to different areas of practice. Thus, the area of practice shapes the levels within it.

Second, one criterion affects another. That is, the relevance of music therapy to the client's needs determines how much clinical independence it will have, which in turn affects the depth of interventions and the degree of client change. Similar interactions can be found between how intrinsically musical the client's experiences are, and whether music is used *as* therapy or *in* therapy.

Third, as with the areas of practice, these levels frequently overlap. One often finds music therapists who work at different levels of therapy with the same client population, either because of stages in the therapeutic process or differences in the type of therapeutic problem being addressed.

In the four sections that follow, each level of therapy is discussed in light of the above criteria.

Auxiliary Level

The auxiliary level includes any application of music (or any of its components) for nonmusical purposes which does not qualify as therapy, either in goal, content, method, or relationship between provider and consumer. Either individuals receiving the service do not qualify as "clients," or the service provider does not act in the capacity of a therapist, or the interventions are not part of a therapeutic process leading to change. This level also includes those practices that use premusical, paramusical or nonmusical experiences for clinical purposes rather than musical or extramusical ones.

Auxiliary practices are peripheral to music therapy in that they do not meet the criteria established, either for music experience or for therapy; nevertheless, they often provide the foundations for many areas of clinical work.

Augmentative Level

The augmentative level includes all those practices within the discipline wherein music therapy augments the education, development, healing, or therapy of individuals who meet the criteria for "client" given in the previous chapter. In this context, "augment" means to add something unique, either to the individual's own efforts at therapeutic change, or to services, programs, or treatment modalities that are also being provided to the individual. Of course, the unique addition is music.

In this category, music is frequently used *as* therapy, and the role of the therapist is often delimited by the setting and the specific functions given to music therein. Typically, the therapist's main functions are to enhance and facilitate the direct effects of music experience on the client. The client-therapist relationship is therefore primarily a musical or activity one, and in most cases, it is not used as the main vehicle or agent of healing or therapy.

On the other hand, because music is used to augment other therapeutic efforts, the role of music may be stretched on occasion to accommodate the particular area of practice and the goals therein. Thus, for example, music activity therapy may be extended to incorporate nonmusical activities; or the contingent use of music may be extended to include nonmusical reinforcers. Nevertheless, a criterion for this level is that the practice relies in large part upon musical and extramusical experiences, and employs premusical, nonmusical, or paramusical experiences only as indicated.

Similarly, the role of the music therapist at this level frequently includes the role functions of other professionals (e.g., teacher, minister, or other type of therapist). Generally, this is determined by what goals have been established as priority within the area of practice or clinical setting.

Music therapy at the augmentative level frequently accommodates the goals of other disciplines, and plays a supportive yet important role. Usually that role involves enhancing, elaborating, expanding, reinforcing, or preparing for what other therapists are striving to accomplish with the client.

In terms of other classifications, this level corresponds to Wheeler's "activity" level (1983) and Wolberg's "supportive level" (1977) with respect to psychotherapy. In synthesizing the two, Wheeler ascribes the following characteristics to this level: 1) the achievement of goals through activities rather than verbalized insight; 2) the suppression of feelings and impulses in favor of developing adaptive behaviors; 3) a focus on behaviors rather than covert processes or causal links; 4) the utilization of client resources; 5) a positive relationship with the therapist who takes a highly directive role in leading the session; and 6) a minimal need for the therapist to have insight into his/her own feelings.

It also corresponds to the "adjunctive" level as previously described by the author (Bruscia, 1987b). Augmentative was chosen as the term here rather than adjunctive because of differences in connotation. Adjunctive often connotes that the practice is nonessential or supplementary. The augmentative level includes supportive services that are integral and important, and often irreplaceable.

Intensive Level

The intensive level includes all those practices within the discipline wherein the music therapist works in tandem with other treatment modalities as an equal partner or as the major therapist. As mentioned earlier, the essential differences between augmentative and intensive practices can best be described in Piagetian terms of *accommodation* (adapting existing structures to meet new demands) and *assimilation* (adapting new demands to fit into existing structures). When used as an augmentative modality, music therapy *accommodates* the goals of other treatment modalities, and thereby *assimilates* the client's needs into the framework of music. When used as an intensive or primary modality, music therapy *assimilates* the goals of other treatment modalities into itself in order to *accommodate* the client's needs.

In terms of Wheeler's and Wolberg's classifications, this corresponds to the "reeducative" level of therapy, in which the client undergoes intensive supportive treatment aimed at learning new ways of solving problems and thereby achieving a higher level of functioning, but not making changes which are reconstructive in nature. Maranto (1993) calls this level "specific."

Generally, music is used *in* therapy more often than *as* therapy, and the role of the therapist is determined in large part by the client's needs. The therapist serves as an equal or dominant partner with music in the intervention process. Music is typically used to establish or enhance the client-therapist relationship, which is more therapeutic than musical in nature. That is, at the intensive level, the client is likely to relate to the music therapist as therapist more than musician, and verbal communication is likely to be an important dimension of the client-therapist relationship. All varieties of music experience may be used, with particular emphasis given to musical and extramusical experiences.

Because this level is geared to address a broad spectrum of client needs, assessment and treatment procedures in one practice often overlap with practices in other areas. Thus, it is at this level that overlaps are often found between didactic, psychotherapeutic, medical, and healing practices. The reason for such overlaps are that there is more of a tendency to view the client's needs holistically, while also giving the therapist greater responsibility for meeting them.

Primary Level

At the primary level, music therapy takes an indispensable or singular role in meeting the main therapeutic needs of the client, and as a result, induces pervasive changes in the client and the client's life. The client undergoes the most intense and comprehensive treatment aimed at altering basic structures within the client and between the client and the environment, thereby addressing core causes of the client's health condition. In Wheeler's and Wolberg's classifications, this level is called "reconstructive," while in Maranto's, it is called "comprehensive."

Music therapy at this level nearly always involves the integration of one area of practice with another (e.g., healing and medical, didactic and psychotherapeutic). As such, the areas of music therapy begin to merge so that the full resources of the discipline can be applied to meet the client's needs.

Thus, two criteria must be met for any practice to qualify as primary music therapy: 1) when the work in one area of practice has the depth needed to induce changes in the client that are fundamental, deep and pervasive and 2) when the work has sufficient breadth so that the goals and processes of the original area of practice have been extended to include another area of practice. Thus, primary therapy has both depth and breadth in both process and change.

Music is used both *as* therapy and *in* therapy; and the therapeutic benefits of both client-music and client-therapist relationships are fully exploited. All levels of music experience, as well as other therapeutic modalities are used as indicated.

OVERVIEW

In summary, an area of practice is defined by the clinical focus of the client, therapist, and clinical agency; a level of practice is defined by the breadth, depth, significance, and autonomy of treatment and outcome, along with the role of music. With these definitions and criteria established, we can now examine specific practices within the various areas and levels. Table 2 provides an overview of auxiliary, augmentative, intensive, and primary levels of practice in didactic, medical, healing, psychotherapeutic, recreational, and ecological areas of music therapy. The next six chapters are devoted to a more detailed description of each practice.

Table 2.

AREAS AND LEVELS OF PRACTICE

	AUXILIARY	AUGMENTATIVE
DIDACTIC	Special Music Education Developmental Music Adaptive Music Instruction Therapeutic Music Instruction Functional Music Music Therapy Demonstrations Music Therapy Consultations	MT in Special Education Arts in Special Education Instructional Music Therapy Behavioral MT Music Activity Therapy Expressive Activity Therapy Experiential MT Training
MEDICAL	Therapeutic Music Music Therapy Consultations	Music in Medicine Music in Palliative Care
HEALING	Sound Healing	Music Healing
PSYCHO-THERAPY	Psychotherapeutic Music	Supportive Psychotherapy Music in Pastoral Counseling
RECREATION	Therapeutic Music Recreation	Recreational Music Therapy Therapeutic Music Play
ECOLOGICAL	Functional Music Ceremonial Music Inspirational Music Music Therapy Activism	Arts Outreach Organizational Music Therapy Healing Music Rituals MT Sensitivity Training

Table 2 (Continued).

	INTENSIVE	PRIMARY
DIDACTIC	Developmental Music Therapy Instructional Music Psychotherapy Supervisory Music Psychotherapy	Combinations with other areas at Intensive Level
MEDICAL	Music as Medicine Music Therapy and Medicine Arts Therapy and Medicine Rehabilitative Music Therapy Palliative Music Therapy	Combinations with other areas at Intensive Level
HEALING	Music Therapy in Healing	Combinations with other areas at Intensive Level
PSYCHO- THERAPY	Insight Music Psychotherapy Transformative Music Psychotherapy Music in Arts Psychotherapy Expressive Psychotherapy Instructional Music Psychotherapy Supervisor Music Psychotherapy	Combinations with other areas at Intensive Level
RECREATION	Music and Play Therapy	Combinations with other areas at Intensive Level
ECOLOGICAL	Family Music Therapy Community Music Therapy	Combinations with other areas at Intensive Level

Chapter Eighteen

DIDACTIC PRACTICES

Didactic practices are those focused on helping clients gain knowledge, behaviors, and skills needed for functional, independent living, and social adaptation. In all of these practices, learning is in the foreground of the therapeutic process. This includes all applications of music therapy in classrooms and private studios, as well as in other settings (general or psychiatric hospitals, nursing homes) where the main goals of the program are essentially educational in nature.

Practices in this area vary according to the area of learning emphasized (e.g., musical or nonmusical), the therapeutic value of the learning, the extent to which the goals and methods can be individualized to meet specific client problems and needs, and the nature of the client-therapist relationship.

Altogether, five orientations to learning can be taken, depending on the setting and clientele:

- To develop musical knowledge and skills for their own sake, as an integral part of the client's functional living and social adaptation;
- To develop musical knowledge and skills that specifically relate to nonmusical areas of functioning needed by the client;
- To use music and related arts activities as an aid in nonmusical learning;
- To use music learning as a pretext and context for therapy; and
- To use music therapy experiences to education, train, and supervise students and professionals.

DISTINCTIONS

Given the many ways that learning enters into music therapy, the boundaries between education, developmental growth and therapeutic change are easily and frequently blurred. Let us therefore take a closer look at what distinguishes them from one another, so that the various levels of didactic practice can be better understood.

Education and Therapy

Education and therapy are similar in that they both help a person to acquire knowledge and skill. Nevertheless, all education is *not* therapy, and all therapy is *not* education. Several important distinctions can be made.

First and foremost, the goals are different. In education, acquiring knowledge and skill is the primary goal, whereas in therapy it is only a means to achieving health. Thus, education focuses on the acquisition of knowledge and skill for its own sake and benefit, whereas therapy works to address educational deficits or learning problems that directly affect the health or well-being of the person.

Second, in education the subject matter learned is general and is not unique to the individual; in therapy, the subject matter is always uniquely personal or autobiographical. That is, education gives a student knowledge about the world, whereas therapy provides a client with access or insight into his/her own way of being in the world. Education builds skills that all human beings need for adaptation, whereas therapy remediates specific problems that an individual experiences with regard to adaptation.

Third, Bloch (1982) points out that learning in therapy is unique in that it is *both* experiential and self-reflective. It is experiential in that the client experiences various facets of self (e.g., mind, body, behavior) in various ways (e.g., intellectually, perceptually, physically, emotionally). It is self-reflective in that "the patient undergoes some intense experience in the course of a session; he is encouraged to immerse himself thoroughly in it without inhibition or constraint, and, when the intensity of the experience has waned, the self-reflective loop comes into operation. The patient now attempts to stand back somewhat from what he has just gone through in order to try and make sense of the experience" (p. 11–12). This holds true for all types of therapy and healing, including those with educational, medical or psychotherapeutic objectives. The client must undergo the treatment process to achieve health, and then reflect upon it to better understand how to maintain health more independently.

Fourth, the student-teacher relationship is substantially different than a client-therapist relationship—in role responsibilities, level of intimacy, dynamics, and content. A student does not bring health or personal problems to a teacher unless they affect his/her learning in the prescribed subject matter; a client does not bring educational problems to a therapist unless they affect his/her health. A teacher does not probe into the precise nature of a student's health or personal problems, especially if they do not affect the student's performance in the subject matter; a therapist does so, regardless of their educational implications. A teacher causes a student to know a subject or to master a skill; a therapist helps a client to achieve health, sometimes by imparting knowledge or skill.

With regard to music education and music therapy, the distinctions are the same. In music education, music learning is the ultimate goal; in music therapy it is a means to an end. In music education, the goals are aesthetic or musical first, and functional second; in music therapy, the goals are health-related first, and aesthetic or musical second. In music education, emphasis is given to the universally shared world of music; in music therapy, emphasis is given to the person's private world of music. In music education, the student-teacher relationship is limited to musical concerns; in music therapy, the client-therapist relationship addresses health concerns that can be addressed through music.

Therapy and Growth

Another distinction that needs to be made is between therapy and self-improvement, self-actualization, or developmental growth. Two main considerations are relevant. First, in therapy, the primary motivation is to address a health concern; in self-improvement, self-actualization, or developmental growth, the main focus is not always on health. Thus, in the former, there is a health concern, and in the latter there is not.

Second, therapy always involves intervention within a client-therapist relationship. In self-improvement, self-actualization, and developmental growth, there may or may not be intervention by another person, and when there is, the person is not necessarily a therapist.

Thus, any form of self-improvement or growth that does not involve intervention within the context of a client-therapist relationship and all of the role responsibilities therein is not considered a form of therapy.

The importance of these distinctions will be clearer as the various practices related to learning, education, and instruction are examined further. What follows is a description of the various didactic practices within each level of therapy.

AUXILIARY LEVEL

Special Music Education

In *Special Music Education*, the music teacher or therapist uses adaptive or compensatory techniques to facilitate or maximize the *music* learning of students with special needs in a school setting. Specific curricular goals include the learning of general musical concepts and skills and successful participation in musical ensembles.

Special Music Education is appropriate in mainstreamed music classrooms, where the students have special instructional needs but are capable of participating with some success in most of the usual curricular activities. It can also be used in self-contained classrooms when the student's challenges do not preclude the possibility of gaining musical knowledge and skills with special assistance.

As an auxiliary practice, *Special Music Education* is on the boundary between music education and music therapy. The main reason it is not considered music therapy per se is that its goals are instructional rather than therapeutic. Music learning is an end rather than a means to an end. In addition, the relationship that forms between student and teacher does not have therapeutic overtones. In fact, any effort a special music educator would make to address the needs of the students in a therapeutic way would be regarded as inappropriate and intrusive.

Books designed to help teachers bring music to special children include: Nocera (1979), Graham and Beers (1980), Edwards (1981), and Atterbury (1990). Incidentally, these books may not make the distinctions drawn here between the goals of music education and therapy.

Developmental Music

In *Developmental Music*, age-appropriate music experiences are used to stimulate the general developmental growth of infants and preschoolers who have no developmental disabilities or handicaps. Here the emphasis is on normal developmental processes in both musical and nonmusical areas. As such, the goals might be to support the development of sensorimotor, perceptual, or cognitive skills, or to enhance parent-child relationships or emotional growth.

A primary characteristic of *Developmental Music* is that it relies on musical interaction involving the child, parents or significant others, and music leader. An example of this practice includes the work of Allison (1988) who holds neighborhood music sessions for mothers and their children. The purpose is to enhance family relationships while stimulating the child's overall development.

Also included in this category is the use of music in regular pre-school or day care programs.

Developmental Music is to be distinguished from more concentrated efforts to enhance the *musical* development of very young normal children, such as the Suzuki method (Mills & Murphy, 1973), and from more clinically-oriented programs for infants and preschoolers with health challenges, such as those by Witt and Steele (1984) and Monti (1985) which are examples of *Developmental Music Therapy*.

Developmental Music is auxiliary because the children do not have health problems, and because the interventions are not really therapeutic in nature. When *therapeutic* intervention is required because of threats to healthy development, this practice becomes *Developmental Music Therapy*.

Adaptive Music Instruction

In *Adaptive Music Instruction*, the teacher or therapist uses adaptive or compensatory techniques to facilitate or maximize the private music studies of students with disabilities. This practice is similar to *Special Music Education* in goal and orientation, but differs in its focus on the mastery of an instrument or voice within a private setting, rather than on general music learning in a classroom.

Like *Special Music Education*, this is an auxiliary practice that falls outside of music therapy, for the same reasons described above (i.e., delimitation of the goals to music learning, and boundaries of the student-teacher relationship).

Examples of *Adaptive Music Instruction* include methods for teaching guitar to special learners by Krout (1983) and Cassity (1977), the Optacon Music-Reading curriculum for blind students developed by Levinson and Bruscia (1983), and the use of the Pitchmaster in teaching singing skills to hearing-impaired students (Darrow & Cohen, 1991).

Therapeutic Music Instruction

In *Therapeutic Music Instruction*, the private music teacher or therapist works with nonhandicapped students who experience personal obstacles or problems with regard to musical self-expression or the music learning process itself. Here the goal is primarily music learning, and the elimination of personal difficulties are a means to that end.

A good example of this category is Ostwald's (1968) description of the music lesson. In it, he discusses the therapeutic role of the private music teacher as a listener, guide, coach and healer. Other examples include Gregoire et al (1989) and Nichols-Rother (1995).

Therapeutic Music Instruction is an auxiliary practice because of the level of intervention and change involved.

Functional Music

Functional Music is the use of music to influence physical states, behaviors, moods, attitudes, etc. outside of a therapy context, that is, in commercial, industrial, work, educational,or home settings. An example of how it relates to didactic music therapy is the use of music to accelerate learning and enhance educational environments, as exemplified in the "Super-Learning" model (Ostrander & Schroeder, 1979). Halpern (1985) cites several similar examples, all based on the research of Georgi

Lazanov. The basic rationale is that listening to music in the background "is helpful in setting a joyful and relaxed atmosphere that helps produce a revitalizing effect on the individual and stimulate whole brain activity" (Halpern, 1985, p. 119). The music is selected to "balance, harmonize, and synchronize the activities of both halves of the brain." (p. 119).

Other examples of *Functional Music* in didactic areas include Miller and Schyb (1989), and Giles et al (1991).

Music Therapy Demonstrations and Role-Plays

Demonstrations are very useful ways to introduce music therapy to persons outside of the field, and for training and supervising music therapists. For purposes of the present discussion, a "demonstration" involves the teacher or supervisor modeling the role of a therapist in a music therapy experience with the learner participating at an appropriate level. In a demonstration, the learner may be asked to either role-play a particular client population or to participate authentically (i.e., as him/herself). The leader may interrupt the process or experience whenever instructional comments are needed, so that the therapeutic process or experience may be discontinuous.

These experiences are at the auxiliary level and do not qualify as music therapy because: their purpose is strictly educational and not thera-peutic or healing; they do not involve a systematic process of intervention and change over a sufficient period of time; or the client-therapist relationship is role-played rather than real.

Music Therapy Consultations

Music therapists often provide short-term services which are consultative in nature. This may include music therapy assessments of individuals on a referral basis, consultation with other professionals on how to use music therapeutically, workshops and training programs for other professionals, and so forth. *Music Therapy Consultations* may be provided at the auxiliary or augmentative level of practice, depending upon the degree and duration of direct involvement by the music therapist in the client's treatment program; they may also belong to other areas of practice (e.g., psychotherapy, recreational, ecological), depending upon the setting, population, and purpose.

AUGMENTATIVE LEVEL

Music Therapy in Special Education

In *Music Therapy in Special Education*, the teacher or therapist uses music to help special students gain *nonmusical* knowledge and skills that are essential to or part of his/her education. Here music learning is secondary to academic or adaptive goals of special education, or music becomes important precisely because it relates in some way to these goals.

Music Therapy in Special Education is appropriate for self-contained classrooms or music therapy groups that are homogeneous in educational needs. Of course, it can also be used in mainstreamed classrooms when both regular and special students might benefit educationally from musical activities.

This practice falls within the boundaries of music therapy because it addresses educational problems that require therapeutic intervention, or needs that have important implications for the student's overall development. Though usually carried out in groups, the goals are nearly always individualized to accommodate the unique needs of each student. Because this usually requires understanding problems of a personal nature that affect learning, the teacher is likely to take on the role behaviors of a therapist, and a therapist-student relationship may develop.

It is considered augmentative because the music therapist accommodates the goals of another discipline (i.e., special education), and assimilates the client's problems into a musical framework of treatment. Alley (1977) points out how music therapy is content free, and therefore applicable to a broad range of problems occurring within an educational setting: "Music therapy is a service-gap filler, a problem solver, a curriculum support service. Music therapy never falls into the category of 'that's not my job.' The music therapist's role in the educational setting might be simply defined as a specialist to resolve individual problems which negate a student's ability to participate in or benefit from his/her educational opportunities" (p. 54).

Jellison (1983) proposed that curriculum development become "an integral part of music therapy planning and that within this process, a criterion of functional value be considered as the standard for the selection and prioritization of objectives" (p.17). For her, the "functional" value of music therapy is the acquisition of those nonmusic and music skills that will help the student become more independent and less handicapped in various life environments.

Clinical examples of *Music Therapy in Special Education* include the work of Robbins and Robbins (1980), Levin and Levin (1998a, 1998b), (1975), Purvis and Samet (1976), Lathom (1980), Colwell (1994), and Standley and Hughes (1997). Also included are community music programs that support and work closely with schools. Steele, Vaughan and Dolan (1976) describe such a program in Cleveland, where the objectives were to help students with behavioral or school adjustment problems develop more productive social behaviors, while also helping school teachers to work with these children in the classroom setting.

The Arts in Special Education

The Arts in Special Education is similar to *Music Therapy in Special Education;* however, it uses music in conjunction with the other arts to enhances the child's learning in the classroom. Two approaches may be taken. In the first, a music specialist engages the students in interrelated arts activities (e.g., moving or drawing to music, setting poems to music, creating a musical story), emphasizing whichever art experience relates directly to the curricular goal. In the second, a music specialist works with another arts specialist to provide the students with either separate and/or collaborative experiences. That is, the students may have separate sessions for each art, joint sessions containing two separate arts, or one session containing integrated arts experiences co-led by specialists in each art area. For examples, see Anderson et al (1979).

Instructional Music Therapy

In *Instructional Music Therapy*, a private music teacher/therapist, working within the context of a private lesson, uses music learning experiences to address the therapeutic needs of the client. Here music learning is secondary to the accomplishment of therapeutic aims, yet lays the foundation for it. *Instructional Music Therapy* is often done in private practice or community music school settings.

At the augmentative level, the goals of instructional music therapy are mostly adaptive in nature, and may be concerned with a broad spectrum of behaviors and skills.

Examples of *Instructional Music Therapy* include the work of Steele (1977) who takes a behavioral approach to private teaching, and Elliott et al (1982) who developed criteria for selecting musical instruments for private study based on physical rehabilitation needs.

Behavioral Music Therapy

In *Behavioral Music Therapy*, the therapist uses music to increase or modify adaptive (or appropriate) behaviors and to extinguish maladapative (or inappropriate) behaviors. Music may be used as a positive or negative reinforcement, a group contingency, a conditioner of other reinforcers, or a behavioral antecedent or cue for other behaviors (Hanser, 1987). The clients or students may be treated in a classroom, therapy group, or individual setting.

This belongs within music therapy because it is concerned with behaviors that interfere with or thwart learning or educational growth, and because music is used to influence these behaviors. It is augmentative because, in comparison to intensive practices, its goals and methods are more limited in scope. That is, the goals are "pinpointed" to address specific, observable "parts" of the client's overall behavior, with less emphasis given to covert processes and causal factors underlying them.

As for methods, treatment procedures are likewise delimited to the use of music to manage behavior, with less emphasis given to musical experiences that access covert phenomena or nonmusical activities that might bring verbalized insight. While the reinforcing properties of the music and therapist are considered quite important, unobservable aspects of the client-music and the client-therapist relationships are not used as vehicles of therapeutic intervention.

The literature abounds with examples of *Behavioral Music Therapy*. Madsen (1981) outlined an approach for the mentally retarded that includes five basic steps: observe, pinpoint, record, consequate, and evaluate. Steele

(1977) used *Behavioral Music Therapy* in a community music school setting within the context of both individual lessons and group music sessions. A few more examples include the work of Saperston (1980), Wolfe (1980, 1982), Dorow (1975), Eidson (1989), Clair (1991), and Standley (1991).

Behavioral music therapy may also be subsumed under other areas of practice, depending on whether the specific outcome is related to medical, psychotherapeutic, recreational, or ecological concerns. However, it is first and foremost didactic, in that it *always* focuses on learning of some kind, regardless of the outcome of that learning.

Music Activity Therapy

In *Music Activity Therapy*, the therapist uses musical activities or tasks to help the client develop knowledge, skills, or behaviors needed for adaptation. The musical activities are designed or selected so that participation in them requires the client to learn or practice the targeted competence. For example, if a client needs to develop gross motor skills, the musical activity might be to walk in time to improvised or recorded music. Note that this activity requires the targeted skill, and that a host of other skills can also be learned at the same time, including selective attention, vigilance to the task, rhythmic perception, and auditory-motor coordination.

Task analysis and skill analysis are central to the work of the music activity therapist. In task analysis, the activity is broken down into very small behavioral segments or components, each of which can be targeted for practice. For example, playing a hand drum consists of the following segments: looking for the drum, finding it, picking up the drum, holding it in one hand, lifting the other hand, hitting the drum with the lifted hand, and so forth.

In skill analysis, the knowledge or skill requirements of the activity are identified. For example, hitting the hand drum requires pincer grasp, eye-hand coordination, coordinated movement of one hand, steadiness in the other hand, and so forth.

Music may be used *in* therapy or *as* therapy, depending on how intrinsically musical the activities are. Examples of the types of musical activities commonly used can be found in Schulberg (1981), Purvis & Samet (1976), and Nowicki & Trevisan (1978).

The primary focus of *Music Activity Therapy* is to improve adaptive behavior through the acquisition of knowledge and skills in the sensorimotor, perceptual, cognitive, emotional, or social domains. Lord (1971) cites twelve goals of an activity approach covering matters such as: tolerance for instruction and authority, avoidance behaviors in failure situations or social settings, methods of achieving success, attentional skills, self-image, irresponsibility and passivity, interpersonal awareness and responsibility, and emotional skills.

Notwithstanding this breadth of goals, it is nearly always an augmentative form of treatment. The reasons are manifold. First, *Music Activity Therapy* is designed to accommodate and augment the goals and treatment plans of other disciplines, such as speech, occupational, and physical therapies.

Second, when compared to in-depth forms of treatment, it is competence oriented rather than insight-oriented, focusing more on overt changes than covert issues underlying them. As such, *Music Activity Therapy* is more concerned with adaptational needs than personal or emotional needs, which greatly reduces the need for the client to disclose anything of a personal or autobiographical nature. Wheeler (1983) notes that this approach to therapy "may be viewed as one which suppresses the client's impulses in favor of more adaptive behaviors which are structured by the therapist, rather than the exploration of instincts and impulses" (p. 10). In contrast to psychotherapeutic forms of therapy, *Music Activity Therapy* does not emphasize exploring one's personal life, gaining insight into one's own emotional world, having a cathartic release of feelings, or resolving latent conflicts. Essentially, this implies that a music activity therapist assimilates the needs of the client into the boundaries of the method.

Third, the client-therapist relationship is geared to maximize the client's learning or adaptation, and is not used as a medium for resolving psychological conflicts. "Sessions which use music as an activity therapy normally utilize a positive relationship with the therapist, who takes a somewhat authoritarian role in directing the session and helping those involved behave more adaptively. Sessions may at times include advice and information giving. Reassurance is frequently used" (Wheeler, 1983, p. 10).

Expressive Activity Therapy

In *Expressive Activity Therapy*, a therapist uses interrelated arts activities and play to help the client acquire knowledge, skills or behaviors needed for adaptation, educational growth, or leisure. The activities are designed or selected so that participation in them requires the client to learn or practice the targeted competencies, and to derive enjoyment from recreation and play through the arts. When employed by a music therapist, the activities often center around the musical component, however the relationships between the arts modalities are usually regarded as an important part of the experience. Examples include the work of Bitcon (1976), Herman and Smith (1988), and Fischer (1991).

Expressive Activity Therapy incorporates the goals of *Music Activity Therapy, Music Therapy in Special Education,* and *Recreational Music Therapy*, and like these categories, provides an augmentative, supportive form of treatment.

Experiential Music Therapy Training

In *Experiential Music Therapy Training*, students experience the process of music therapy or healing: 1) authentically, 2) as clients, 3) through a planned sequence of experiences over an extended period of time, 4) as an integral part of an education or training program, and (5) for both educational and personal growth purposes. These experiences may be led by professors, supervisors, other students, or outside music therapists. In the present discussion, this practice does not include practicum or internship experiences where the student takes the role of a therapist with real clients.

There are several differences between this level of practice and demonstrations, as described above. Students do not role-play, but rather participate authentically. The experiences are not isolated or disconnected, but rather a planned sequence with specific goals and objectives. Because personal growth of the student is regarded as an important part of training, the goals are geared to address both educational and personal needs of the students.

In those academic or field programs where this type of training is offered, it is most often an augmentative practice. That is, it is not intended to supplant any form of therapy or healing that a student might need. In addition, although the students participate as clients authentically, boundaries or limits are usually placed on the kinds of personal problems they are asked to reveal or explore, and no attempts are made to engage the students in an in-depth therapeutic process. When significant issues are revealed, students are advised to seek counseling or psychotherapy elsewhere while receiving this kind of training.

Several approaches to *Experiential Music Therapy Training* have been developed. Hesser (1985) designed a system where master's degree students participate in a music therapy group on a weekly basis over a period of two years. The groups are led by music therapists in the field (Stephens, 1987). Priestley (1975) uses a method she calls "Intertherapy." It involves trainees working in dyads with a supervisor, practicing music therapy with each other. Each trainee is given an opportunity to be both therapist and client, while the supervising music therapist observes and intervenes as necessary. Bruscia (1987a) describes a method called "Experimental Improvisation Therapy" which employs music and/or dance improvisations as a medium for exploring the dynamics of group leadership. Clark (1987) describes a comprehensive three-level approach to experiential training designed to prepare therapists to use "Guided Imagery and Music."

INTENSIVE LEVEL

Developmental Music Therapy

In contrast to *Music in Special Education* which is geared toward curricular or academic goals, *Developmental Music Therapy* is concerned with a broader spectrum of clinical goals. In addition to addressing educational needs, this practice focuses on assisting clients to accomplish a wide variety of developmental tasks that may have been delayed or thwarted at various periods in the life span. Hence, *Developmental Music*

Therapy is used with handicapped clients of all ages (infants through geriatrics) who are encountering obstacles to developmental growth in any area (e.g., sensorimotor, cognitive, affective, interpersonal). As such, it addresses health problems as previously defined.

Since the developmental process is so intimately linked to personal history, this category of music therapy, unlike *Music Therapy in Special Education*, is concerned with autobiographical material, family background, private emotions, and personality development. It may also be concerned with specific physical or medical problems that affect normal development.

Examples of this category include the work of Alvin (1976, 1978), Nordoff and Robbins (1971, 1977, 1982), Boxill (1985, 1997), Orff (1974, Wigram (1991), Oldfield (1991), Shoemark (1991), and in a medical setting, Barrickman (1989).

It should be noted that despite the similarity in title, this category is different from the work described in a book, entitled *Music in Developmental Therapy* by Purvis and Samet (1976), which in the present classification belongs under *Music Therapy in Special Education* or *Music Activity Therapy*.

Developmental Music Therapy belongs within the intensive category of music therapy because of its broad concern for various therapeutic needs of the client. Here the client's needs are primary, and the goals and procedures are accommodated to meet these needs. The music therapist in this category often works as an equal partner with other specialists, and may use music *as* or *in* therapy, depending on client need and his/her philosophical orientation.

Instructional Music Psychotherapy

Instructional Music Psychotherapy is the use of private music lessons as a context for individual psychotherapy. In terms of Wolberg (1967), the goals are most often reeducative, but they may also be supportive or reconstructive. Aspects of the lesson which have psychotherapeutic implications include: the various musical media used for expressive and communicative purposes, the structure of the learning process, the nature of practice and performance, the client-therapist relationship, etc.

Instructional Music Psychotherapy is an intensive practice because, in contrast to the previous practice, its goals go beyond adaptation to include both overt and covert facets of the client's emotional life. It also uses a broader range of methods and techniques. Music is used *in* therapy and *as* therapy, and the client-therapist relationship is equally if not more important than the client-music relationship.

The best example of this category is Florence Tyson's work (1981) with psychiatric patients in the community. She has developed a method of using private music instruction as a vehicle for psychotherapy. The music lessons are provided upon referral by a psychiatrist and in conjunction with regular psychiatric treatment, usually with a psychodynamic orientation. The patients may study voice or other musical instruments.

Tyson (1982) described the typical voice lesson as follows:

> The music therapy session devoted to singing instruction rarely resembles a singing "lesson." All approaches aim to minimize the arduous discipline involved, and emphasize maximum expressive freedom in the shortest possible time. Most sessions include verbal interactions (as well as musical) and interpretations of musical responses; relatively few sessions consist of all talk or all music, but they may. Vocal exercises are used flexibly, always bearing in mind the patient's tolerance levels; some find greatest satisfaction in the repetitive structure of scale work; others detest it (p. 10).

Shields & Robbins (1980) also describe a case in which private vocal therapy lessons were used in conjunction with verbal psychoanalysis. The process involved an analysis of the patient's voice followed by vocal exercises aimed at resolving the unconscious conflicts revealed.

Supervisory Music Psychotherapy

In *Supervisory Music Psychotherapy*, the supervisor-therapist uses musical experiences and the relationships that develop through them as a means of helping the supervisee to work through personal issues that impact on his/her clinical work as a therapist. In other words, this category is concerned with the use of music therapy to uncover and resolve countertransference issues that therapists experience in their relationships with clients.

Supervisory Music Psychotherapy is an intensive music therapy practice, and because of its depth and scope of concern and its reliance on the client-therapist relationship, it may become a primary form of treatment. Most often however, it works towards re-educative rather than reconstructive goals.

Examples of this practice include those cited above for experiential training (Hesser, 1985; Priestley, 1975; Bruscia, 1987a; Clark, 1987), all of which can be easily adapted for more in-depth work with professionals. In addition, Stephens (1984, 1987) has developed a model specifically designed to use music therapy as a method of professional supervision, and Scheiby (1991) describes music therapy with a student during training.

PRIMARY LEVEL

Didactic practices become a primary level of therapy under two conditions: when the work leads to significant and pervasive changes in the area of learning being addressed, and when the goals and processes extend beyond educational and instructional concerns to include those of other areas of practice (e.g., medical, psychotherapeutic, ecological). In short, primary therapy involves a process of intervention and change characterized by both depth and breadth. It is always reconstructive in nature, and it always involves a holistic approach.

Chapter Nineteen

MEDICAL PRACTICES

The medical area of practice includes all applications of music or music therapy where the primary focus is on helping the client to improve, restore, or maintain physical health. This includes all those approaches that focus on the direct treatment of biomedical illness, disease, or injury, as well as those that address related psychosocial factors. When the focus is biomedical, the goals are to effect changes in the client's physical condition; when the focus is psychosocial, the goals may be to modify those mental, emotional, social, or spiritual factors that contribute to the biomedical problem, or to provide psychosocial forms of support to the client during the course of illness, medical treatment, or convalescence.

A distinction is made here between those practices which seek psychosocial changes in the client as a means to an end, that is, ultimately to ameliorate the biomedical problem, and those practices that seek psychosocial changes in the client as an end in itself, quite apart from any biomedical problems the client might have. The former is considered *medical* musical therapy, the latter is considered music *psychotherapy*. The same distinction applies as well to other areas of music therapy practice; thus, when didactic or recreational goals are taken with medical patients as the end rather than the means to a medical end, the practice is didactic or recreational rather than medical. Thus, medical music therapy does not include *every* type of services provided to medical patients; it includes only those that ultimately seek a change in the client's *physical* health, regardless of whether the immediate focus or goal is biomedical or psychosocial. In general, then, areas of practice in music therapy are not defined solely by the client population, but rather by the clinical goal and outcome.

It should be noted that medical music therapy does not include "Performing Arts Medicine" the field concerned with the medical treatment of occupational health problems of musicians, dancers, artists, etc., (Maranto, 1991), unless of course, music is used in the treatment process (See Rider, 1987, Maranto, 1992b).

Levels of practice within the medical area vary according to:

- the differential roles of music and the client-therapist relationship, that is, whether music is used *as* or *in* medicine or therapy.
- whether the goals of music therapy are of primary or secondary medical significance;
- whether the medical treatment is short- or long-term.
- what the clinical setting is (e.g., hospital, clinic, rehabilitation center, hospice).

Other criteria and levels of medical practice have been identified by Maranto (1992a).

AUXILIARY LEVEL

Therapeutic Music

In *Therapeutic Music*, a person (or client) uses music to maintain his/her own health, to prevent illness or disease, and/or to build up one's resistance against physical health threats of various kinds. The person may do this independently, with consultation from various sources (e.g., experts, books, lectures, workshops), or within an established program which uses music for purposes of health maintenance or prevention of specific medical problems.

Examples include the use of music to: relax the body, reduce stress, manage pain, support physical or therapeutic exercises, monitor autonomic body functions, enhance physical performance, and so forth. It may also include the various uses of programmed music listening in different areas of a hospital (e.g., intensive care units, patient rooms), and musical entertainment provided to patients during their stay in a hospital or rehabilitation center.

Therapeutic Music is an auxiliary practice, because it does not involve or depend upon a process of intervention and change within a client-therapist relationship. Note that it differs from *Functional Music* in its focus on health concerns.

Music Therapy Consultations

Music therapists often provide short-term services which are consultative in nature. This may include music therapy assessments of individuals on a referral basis, consultation with other professionals on how to use music therapeutically, workshops and training programs for other professionals, and so forth. *Music Therapy Consultations* may be provided at the auxiliary or augmentative level of practice, depending upon the degree and duration of direct involvement by the music therapist in the client's treatment program.

Music Therapy Consultations may also be provided in other areas of practice (e.g., psychotherapy, recreational, ecological), depending upon the setting, population, and purpose.

AUGMENTATIVE PRACTICES

Music in Medicine

In *Music in Medicine*, music is used as the primary agent within a supportive client-therapist relationship to facilitate brief medical procedures, and to assist the client before, during or after such procedures. Example include the use of music to:

- reduce anxiety before and during surgery or other medical procedures
- facilitate anesthesia and the regaining of consciousness
- provide diversion and distraction during the procedure
- reduce stress and discomfort during and immediately after the procedure
- enhance the effects of pain medication

- facilitate relaxation during labor and delivery
- assist in the monitoring and control of physiological responses during the procedure

Here music takes precedence over the client-therapist relationship, the role of the music is secondary in significance to the medical procedure, and the treatment and client-therapist relationship are relatively brief. See Standley (1995) and Nolan (1992).

Music in Palliative Care

In *Music in Palliative Care*, the therapist uses music experiences within the context of a supportive relationship: to provide comfort or diversion, to help in managing pain, anxiety or stress, or to improve the quality of life during the final stages before death. This practice is augmentative when the relationship is supportive, but does not have role responsibilities of client and therapist, and when the process is not long or deep enough to produce significant changes in the client.

Examples include the work of Beggs (1991), West (1994), and Lee (1995, 1996).

INTENSIVE PRACTICES

Music as Medicine

In *Music as Medicine*, music is used as the primary agent within a supportive client-therapist relationship to address significant needs of the client throughout over an extended period of time, that is, beyond a single short-term procedure or hospital stay. This may involve working with the client in a variety of settings (hospital, clinic, home, hospice, private practice), with the length of treatment varying according to the nature of the medical condition and the client's needs in relation to it. Examples include the use of music: throughout pregnancy and childbirth, during an extended hospital stay, during after-care, convalescence, or ongoing outpatient services, for any extended period during an illness which does not require hospitalization, as an integral part of burn care, and so forth.

Here music takes precedence over the client-therapist relationship, having considerable significance, either to the client or the treatment process; and the treatment and client-therapist relationship are more long-term.

Examples can be found in Froehlich (1996) and Aldridge (1996).

Music Therapy and Medicine

In *Music Therapy and Medicine*, music and the client-therapist relationship are needed and used equally in order to meet significant needs of the client over an extended period of time. Specifically, the therapist uses music experiences and the relationships that develop through them as a means of addressing the biomedical and/or psychosocial needs of the client in overcoming or managing his/her health problem. The settings and length of treatment are the same as for *Music as Medicine*.

Thus, *Music Therapy and Medicine* includes the goals and methods subsumed under *Music in Medicine* and *Music as Medicine* and goes beyond them to assimilate other areas of practice at the augmentative level. Thus *Music Therapy and Medicine* may also include supportive music psychotherapy, music activity therapy, therapeutic music recreation, or any other augmentative practice that might enhance the treatment or quality of life of the medical patient. In all such cases, however, the goals of the other area of practice are secondary to the medical ones established. Thus, as explained above, when other practices are assimilated into *Music Therapy and Medicine*, they are means to a medical end, rather than end goals in themselves; otherwise, the practice is no longer considered medical.

Standley (1986) cites the following uses of music therapy that belong to this practice: to reduce distress, trauma, and fear of illness and injury, for both patients and their families or loved ones; to work through feelings about death, disability, scarring, etc.; to resolve interpersonal conflicts between the patient and loved ones; to facilitate decision making regarding treatment options; to reduce depression, anxiety, stress, or insomnia due to illness, treatment, or recovery; to facilitate support groups among patients;

and to foster positive, health attitudes. Additional but similar goals are given for AIDS patients by Maranto (1988).

Examples of this practice include the clinical approaches of Bailey (1983, 1984) with cancer patients, Chetta (1981) with preoperative children, Christenberry (1979) with burn patients, Fagen (1982) and McDonnell (1984) with pediatric patients, and Schwankowsky and Guthrie (1982) with various health impairments. Also see examples in Maranto (1994), Aldridge (1996), and Loewy (1997).

In pediatric work, therapists often combine music with play and the other arts, working toward the same goals in a "child life" approach (Froehlich, 1996). Depending upon the extent to which the work is music-centered, the practice may be considered *Music and Play Therapy* or *Arts Therapy and Medicine*.

Arts Therapy and Medicine

This practice has the same goals as Music Therapy and Medicine, and differs only in the additional inclusion of related arts experiences. *Arts Therapy and Medicine* can be practiced in two ways. Either the music therapist works alone engaging the client in an integrated arts activity using music (e.g., song-writing, moving or drawing to music); or the music therapist works with another arts therapist providing the client with either separate and/or collaborative arts therapy experiences. In both cases, the therapist preserves the integrity and his/her own modality by exploiting the uniqueness of the art form and the therapeutic process that flows from it. At the same time, the therapeutic process is coordinated so that the client's experiences in the different art modalities are parallel. For examples, see Froehlich (1996).

Rehabilitative Music Therapy

Rehabilitative Music Therapy is the use of musical experiences and the relationships that develop through them as a means of helping clients who have been debilitated by illness, injury, or trauma to regain previous levels of functioning or adjustment to the extent possible. Its goals are restorative rather than educational or developmental, and it has greater scope and depth than activity therapy because it addresses emotional as well as adaptational needs, including feelings that arise out of the recovery process itself. Here the goals of speech, occupation, and physical therapies are assimilated into a comprehensive music therapy treatment which also includes psychotherapeutic goals.

Music may be used *as* or *in* therapy, and the client-therapist relationship is often used as a vehicle for therapeutic change. As such, rehabilitative music therapy is an intensive form of treatment which may become the primary therapy.

Example include the work of Bright (1972, 1981), Claeys et al (1989), McMaster (1991), Erdonmez (1991), and McIntosh et al (1994).

Palliative Music Therapy

In *Palliative Music Therapy*, the therapist and client work together over a period of time, using music experiences and the relationships that develop through them as a means of examining and working through the issues that arise during the final stages of the dying process. Examples include the work of Munro (1984), Martin (1991), Whittall (1991), Salmon (1994), and Lee (1995, 1996).

PRIMARY LEVEL

Medical practices become a primary level of therapy under two conditions: when the work leads to significant and pervasive changes in the specific health condition being addressed, and when the goals and processes extend beyond the focal concern of medicine to include those of other areas of practice (e.g., psychotherapeutic). In short, primary therapy involves a process of intervention and change characterized by both depth and breadth. It is always reconstructive in nature, and it always involves a holistic approach.

Chapter Twenty

HEALING PRACTICES

The history of using sound and music in healing goes back to ancient times. According to McClellan (1988), the philosophical rationale for these healing practices has been that all of creation is organized and governed by sound or vibrational forms, and that like music, everything in the universe is continually in a state of motion or flux, and continually in the process of becoming its own form. Similar explanations are provided by Berendt (1983), Clynes (1985), and Khan (1983,1991).

Because music and the universe are both organized according to vibrations, music can be used to restore harmony within the individual and between the individual and the universe. Thus, the primary focus is on the vibrational or sonic relationships between matter and energy, individual and universe, all of which are essentially physical or exterior in nature. A basic assumption is that as the body comes into harmony with the universe, the psyche and spirit follow, as all three are integrally related to one another energetically. Healing practices are always ecological in that they rely upon the relationship between the individual and the universe; they are distinguished from *ecological practices* as named here, in that they begin with a focus on the exterior collective, and move to more interior concerns, while the ecological practices begin with an interior focus and move to more exterior concerns.

Healing differs from therapy in one fundamentally significant way: in therapy, the agent of change is the client, the therapist, or the music that they make or hear together; in healing, the agent of change is the universal energy forms found in music, and its component sounds and vibrations. The implications of this are manifold. In therapy, resources from within the setting are utilized to their fullest potentials, whereas in healing, resources beyond the setting are called upon to intervene; thus, in therapy the resources (including the music) are human and dependent upon the specific client and therapist for their potentialities; whereas in healing, the resources are natural, universal, and beyond humans, and thus independent of individual differences in resources or potentials. This is one reason why healing practices usually have a spiritual foundation.

Because the human organism is built to take care of itself, healing is often a natural process. Diseases often run their course despite therapeutic interventions, and damages resulting from a disease frequently heal on their own as the result of an inherent capacity of the organism to restore health. In some instances, healing takes place without conscious efforts, in others it requires an active commitment to heal oneself. Moreover, sometimes a person has the capacity for self-healing without outside help, and sometimes the person needs systematic intervention by another person.

Therapy and healing are indistinguishable whenever one person helps in the healing of another, or whenever healing requires systematic intervention. Therapy and healing are not the same, however, when self-healing takes place without the help or intervention of another person.

A common notion is that in healing, because the process is a "natural" one, the client changes his/her health independently, without the need for help from a healer; whereas in therapy the client changes as the result of the treatment process. This is certainly arguable, as both therapy and healing involve the client in some kind of intentional self-transformation, and both therapy and healing teach and encourage the client to make these self-transformations independently. Furthermore, in healing, the client may need just as much intervention and assistance from the healer as a client does from a therapist. Thus, therapy and healing are similar in that a client can use music to change him/herself with and/or without the help of a therapist, and within or outside of a treatment setting. So the difference between therapy and healing is not linked to whether the agent of change is the client or therapist—both parties take various levels of responsibilities in either area of practice. More important determinants are the role given to music, that is, whether it is used *as* or *in* healing, and the extent to which the healing process depends upon the client, the therapist, the "therapeutic" relationship, or the "therapeutic" process.

Another factor that creates variations in healing practices is whether the primary agent is vibration, sound, music, or combinations thereof. Here again it is important to question what is and what is not music, and thereby decide which practices are and are not part of music therapy. For this reason, a distinction has been made here between vibrational healing, sound healing, and music healing, with vibrational healing and sound healing falling outside the boundaries of music therapy, and only music healing belonging within its boundaries.

So far, two main variables have been used to differentiate the healing practices: the role responsibilities given to client, music, and therapist, and the extent to which the practice involves music. A third variable, as we shall see, is whether the practice has a limited health focus (e.g., on the body only, or on psyche only), and one that seeks synergy between the various areas of health.

Vibrational Healing

Examples of vibrational approaches to healing that fall outside of music therapy include:

- Radionics: the use of electronically generated vibrational frequencies to weaken "molecular bonds of the diseased cells [and] to literally `break up' the disease" (McClellan, 1988, p. 49–50);
- Cymatics: the resonance of vibrational relationships in the body using electronically generated fundamental tones and their harmonics (McClellan, 1988);
- Ultrasonics: scanning the body and its internal organs with electonically generated pulses of high-frequency sound waves for purposes of medical diagnosis (McClellan, 1988);
- Tomatis Method of Ear Training: a method designed by Tomatis (1996) which uses electronic instruments to diagnose and stimulate ear functions, and then uses audiovocal exercises to stabilize the auditory gains, all based on the premise that the ear has a profound impact on listening, language, speech, learning, and the emotions.
- Tuning fork resonance: the person uses one or two tuning forks to resonate various areas of the body, and thereby enhance meditation and healing (Beaulieu, 1987).

These practices are not considered a part of music therapy for several reasons: they require a trained specialist who is most often a physician, medical sound technician, or healer with expertise in vibrations rather than music or music therapy; in these practices, the client relates directly to the vibrations and sounds rather than to the healer; and lastly, the vibrational sound experiences which serve as healing agents are not selected or organized according to musical considerations. Of course, whenever any of these practices incorporates music into the treatment, the practice becomes sound healing at the auxiliary level, as described below.

AUXILIARY LEVEL

Sound Healing

Sound Healing is the use of vibrational frequencies or sounds *combined with* music or any of its elements (e.g., rhythm, melody, harmony) in order to induce healing. (Any use of sound alone, without music, is considered *Vibrational Healing)*.

Sound Healing practices are related to music therapy only insofar as some facet of music is included in the treatment, and only insofar as some level of music decision making is involved; they are clearly not "music" healing because the vibrations and sounds are regarded as the healing agents rather than the music component, and because the vibrations and sounds have not been selected or designed according to musical considerations. In most instances, the relationship between the client and sound has more significance than the client-healer relationship, which of course always has to be supportive; for this reason, the practice is considered auxiliary in nature. In these practices, either the client can engage in sound healing without the help of a therapist, or a therapist is needed to administer the sounds, but the healing effects of the sounds are not dependent upon the client-therapist relationship.

For various examples, see Campbell (1991); examples of specific techniques include:

- Vibroacoustic Therapy: a method developed by Olav Skille (1982, 1989) which involves sending sinusoidal, low frequency sound pressure waves blended with music into the client's body, using loudspeakers which have built into a bed or chair (Skille & Wigram, (1995). The method has also been called a "music bath" and a "low frequency sound massage" (Wigram & Dileo, 1997). Similar methods and devices include The Music Vibration Table (Chesky & Michel, 1991), and the Somatron.

- Mantra Meditations: Garfield (1987) defines mantra "as poetic hymn, prayer, incantation and as the uttering of sacred sounds" (p. 80); it has also been called a "sound thought that is used in contemplation and meditation" (Beaulieu, 1987, p. 103). When a mantra is chanted, it becomes a vocal means of focusing all one's attentional energy, and when sustained over an extended period, it can be used to meditate, to enter an altered state of consciousness, to contemplate something, or to change one's mind-set or mental attitude.

- Drum Trances: One person beats a drum, using a very steady beat or repetitive rhythm, while other use the sound to enter an altered state of consciousness and journey through the imagination, either with a specific imagery focus, or freely (See Drury, 1985).

- Toning: an approach to healing that involves the "conscious elongation of a sound using the breath and voice" (Campbell, 1989, p. 62), or what McClellan (1988) describes as the sustained vocalization of pitch. Gardner-Gordon (1993) is even more specific in defining it as a healing technique that utilizes "the vibratory power of the voice by making long, sustained sounds, without the use of melody, beat, or rhythm . . . using a vowel, a consonant, or a combination of both, without the use of words or specific meaning" (p. 61). This includes vocal sounds of release and comfort such as sighing, groaning, moaning, and humming (Goldman, 1992). It may also involve the conscious production of overtones in the harmonic series (Campbell, 1989), which Goldman (1992) has termed "overtoning." The purpose of toning (and overtoning) may be to: alter cellular structures in the body (Garfield, 1987), activate energy centers or chakras (Gardner-Gordon, 1993), relieve pain (Gardner-Gordon, 1993), induce emotional release (Gardner-Gordon, 1993), release the healing power already within the body (Keyes, 1973), and/or restore harmonic balance and wholeness (Garfield, 1987). The client and/or practitioner may do the toning, nearly always with specific intent or an image of some kind (Keyes, 1973). Toning may also be combined with active body work (Beaulieu, 1987).

- Vocal Harmonics: a technique described by Goldman (1992) which involves two or more persons toning and overtoning until harmony occurs between the various layers of sound.

- Breath and Voice Work: the use of breathing and vocal exercises to free the individual's natural voice, and in the process to remove tensions, energy blocks, and constrictions in mind, body, and spirit.

- Voice Energetics: a method developed by Beaulieu (1987) which studies "the speaking voice and its relationship to a person's life energy. It involves improving auditory abilities as well as voice training and development through use of a five-element voice evaluation and creating vocal intervention strategies for healing" (p. 59). The speed, volume and pitch of the person's speech is related to the five basic timbres of the elements (ether, air, fire, water and earth).

- Healing Gongs: the use of special gongs to produce, tones, overtones, and harmonics to activate and resonate with the individual, to meditate, enter altered states, and image. See Moreno (1989).

When practiced as defined, these examples of sound healing are classified at the auxiliary level, and therefore fall outside of the boundaries of music therapy; however, when practiced with greater reliance on a *music* experience within a systematic process of treatment, any of them may become augmentative and therefore within the boundaries.

AUGMENTATIVE LEVEL

Music Healing

Music Healing is the use of music experiences and the universal energy forms inherent in them to heal mind, body, and spirit. The client may participate in active or receptive music experiences. Active experiences may include singing, playing instruments, improvising, or composing music as well as all those sound-making activities listed under *Sound Healing* (e.g., breathing, vocalizing, toning, chanting) when combined with music. Receptive techniques may include listening, entraining, resonating, imaging, or relaxing to music which has been selected or designed according to its energetic qualities.

What differentiates music from sound healing is that in music healing, the aesthetic properties of the music are as important as its healing energies; thus the healing results from *both* the experience of the music in and for itself, as an aesthetic object, as well as the experience of the universal energy forms within the music. In other words, in music healing, the music experience is much more complete and it is much more at the center of the practice than in sound healing. This way of using music makes music healing an augmentative practice in two ways. First, the purpose, method, and required expertise for music healing is the same as in music therapy. Second, a full music experience has more healing potential than a more limited sound experience, thus the range or degree of change in the client is likely to be greater.

Music healing is not classified as an intensive level of practice because, as in sound healing, the client-music relationship takes precedence over the client-healer relationship, and because the healing does not necessarily involve or depend upon a process of "therapy" wherein client and therapist forge out a relationship through which the client's problems are addressed. Thus, music healing may take place outside of a therapy setting and client-therapist relationship, and still be effective. On the other hand, music healing can and often does take place within a therapy setting and client-therapist relationship. Naturally, when this happens, the setting and the relationship have to be conducive to the music healing; nevertheless, these components are not primary agents or determinants of the music healing process or its ultimate effectiveness.

Music can be used *as* healing or *in* healing. When the universal energy forms are accessed or found directly in the music, and when these forms are applied to the client as the main healing agent, it is music *as* healing. Music *as* healing can be further differentiated according to whether the client uses the healing energies of music alone, without the help of a healer or therapist, or whether the therapist administers the healing energies of music to the client. Examples include:

- Emotional or spiritual healing experiences that take place when the client is creating or listening to music in short-term music therapy or quasi-therapeutic settings (e.g., workshops, retreats).
- Somatic Music Listening: the client listens to music (rather than sound) to activate, resonate or harmonize vibrational structures in the body. The music may be recorded or created live by the therapist.
- Voice Healing: the client sings or improvises songs, and in the process of experiencing the various facets of the voice and music, resonates the body in relation to psyche and spirit.
- Instrument Healing: the client plays or improvises instrumental music, and in the process resonates the body in relation to psyche and spirit.

In contrast, when the music assists the therapist or client in activating universal energies that lie beyond or outside of the music, it is music *in* healing. Examples include:

- Music Rituals: the use of music in the healing rituals of any community (social, religious, cultural). The music is used to access, enhance and facilitates the healing potentials that lie within the group of people or the ritual itself. The ritual may be an already established tradition within the community (May, 1983; McClellan, 1988), or it may be specially created around these traditions (Kenny, 1982).
- Music Trances: the use of music to help a person enter an altered state of consciousness, which in turns provides access to transpersonal realms and the healing potentials therein.

- Music in Shamanism: an ancient healing tradition wherein shamans or "medicine men" use music to assist in the process of healing themselves and others. More specifically, repeated drum rhythms, chants, and songs are used to help the shaman enter and sustain an altered state of consciousness. The altered state enables the shaman to contact and utilize the world of spirits and thereby gain the knowledge and power needed to help or heal the person (Harner, 1982). Examples of how shamanism relates to music therapy and music/sound healing can be found in the works of Kenny (1982), Kovach (1985), Garfield (1987), and Moreno (1988).
- Music in Energetic and Body Work: the use of music in healing methods such as Reiki, Polarity, Therapeutic Touch, Massage Therapy, or Rolfing, where music is given a central role in healing.

INTENSIVE LEVEL

Music Therapy in Healing

Music Therapy in Healing is the use of music experiences *and* the relationships that develop through them to heal the mind, body, and spirit, to induce self-healing, or to promote wellness. Here a person is healed through music experiences (including all levels and components), with the ongoing guidance and support of a therapist or healer, within the context of a client-therapist relationship. The therapist or healer plays an integral role in the healing process, however, rather than "intervene" in the usual sense, the therapist provides a supportive presence to the client and music. The therapist's aim is to assist the client through his/her own natural healing process by providing continual support and guidance in benefiting from the music, and offering their relationship with one another as a vehicle for healing whenever needed. Essentially, the therapist respects the integrity of the self-healing process and the powerful role of music, and avoids imposing anything foreign or nonessential onto that process.

In this category, music is used *as* therapy more than *in* therapy. Often the client-therapist relationship develops within and through their musical relationship, and takes its shape according to the role of music.

An example is "Guided Imagery and Music" (GIM), a method originated by Bonny (1978), which involves imaging to specially designed programs of classical music while in an altered state of consciousness and dialoguing with a trained guide. Bonny (1978) describes the guide as: reflector, resonator, relaxer, encourager, helper, comforter, listener, sharer, observer, and recorder. For a clinical example, see Bruscia (1992).

Another example is "Creative Music Therapy" which was originated by Paul Nordoff and Clive Robbins as a result of their work with handicapped children (1971, 1977, 1982). In this approach, the individual client is engaged in musical improvisation as the chief vehicle for therapeutic healing. A key concept is that the client heals and changes from within, using inner resources, rather than from without, as the result of external interventions. Music serves as the healing agent because it activates the client's inner resources.

> The therapeutic role of music permeates every session. It is through music that the child's inner impulses become transformed into action and thereby available to consciousness. It is through music that the child discovers inmost feelings about him/herself and the world. It is through the music that the child can learn to let go of fear, inhibition, and pathological restrictions which control him/her. It is through music that the child experiences expressive freedom and interresponsiveness, and gradually turns these qualities into intentional ways of being. It is through music that the child builds a relationship with the therapist and learns how to live in the world of others. It is through the music that the child experiences the "new" self and persuades the "old" self to change. It is through music that the child secures his progress and becomes self-confident and independent of the therapist" (Bruscia, 1987a, p. 58).

Nordoff and Robbins gave the music therapist four main functions (Bruscia, 1987a): 1) to accept the client with respect and reverence, 2) to work through various relationships that develop through the music, 3) to create music that will activate the client's inner resources, and 4) to continually develop one's own musical life. For clinical examples, see Robbins and Robbins (1991), and Salas and Gonzalez (1991).

It should be noted, that both GIM and the Nordoff-Robbins approach can be practiced in such a way, that they belong under the category of *Transformative Music Psychotherapy*. In both cases, music experiences are central to the process of change; the differences lie only in: how the client-therapist relationship is construed and utilized; the extent to which music is used as a universal versus subjective experience (see Chapter 15), and the extent to which insight is gained through verbal discourse of the music experience. Given the subtlety of these differences, *Music Therapy in Healing* and *Transformative Music Psychotherapy* overlap considerably, and are in fact, quite similar. For a discussion of the differences and overlaps, see Robbins (1996), Aigen (1996), and Ansdell (1995, 1996).

Chapter Twenty-one

PSYCHOTHERAPEUTIC
PRACTICES

Broadly speaking, music psychotherapy is concerned with helping clients find meaning and fulfillment in their lives. Its goals may be: "greater self-awareness, the resolution of inner conflicts, emotional release, self-expression, changes in emotions and attitudes, improved interpersonal skills, the resolution of interpersonal problems, the development of healthy relationships, the healing of emotional traumas, deeper insight, reality orientation, cognitive restructuring, behavior change, greater meaning and fulfillment in life, or spiritual development" (Bruscia, 1998, p. 1–2). The goals and methods of psychotherapy vary considerably according to the theoretical orientation of the therapist. The orientations most commonly found in music psychotherapy are: psychodynamic, existential-humanistic, Gestalt, cognitive, and behavioral, each of which has many variations. As a result, the emphasis may be on conscious or unconscious motivations, manifest or latent issues, and changes in the client which are covert or overt.

Clients for music psychotherapy may include individuals with psychiatric problems at varying degrees of severity, as well as individuals with a wide range of problems in living which implicate the psyche. Typical settings are psychiatric hospitals and clinics, counseling centers, and private practice. It is important to realize that psychotherapy is not defined by the client population or setting. Specifically, music therapy with psychiatric patients is not necessarily psychotherapeutic; it is so only when the goals and methods are psychotherapeutic in nature. Similarly, psychotherapeutic practices are not limited to clients who have psychiatric diagnoses; all individuals who seek psychological change are candidates for psychotherapy.

Psychotherapy may be practiced in individual, group, or family settings. Of utmost importance in all these settings is the relationship between client and therapist. It is within and through this relationship that the therapy process unfolds, and the client makes the necessary changes. In group and family settings, the multifarious relationships between clients are of equal additional significance.

As originally conceived and traditionally practiced, psychotherapy is essentially a verbal experience: the client and therapist use verbal discourse as the primary means of communicating, developing a relationship, and working towards established goals. In contrast, in music psychotherapy, the client and therapist use music experiences as well as verbal discourse towards these ends, with the relative emphasis varying considerably according to numerous factors. See Smeijsters (1993).

Four approaches to engaging the client in music and words have been identified, ranging on a continuum from exclusively musical to exclusively verbal (Bruscia, 1998). They are:

1) The work is done entirely through the music with no need for verbal discourse.
2) The work is done essentially through the music, with verbal discourse used only to guide, interpret, or enhance the music experience and its relevance to the therapy process.
3) The work is done equally in music and words, either alternately or simultaneously, with music used for its unique nonverbal advantages, and words used to enhance insight.
4) The work is done primarily through verbal discourse, with music used to facilitate or enrich the process.

These four approaches of working with music and words lead to a further important distinction between "transformative" and "insight" orientations. In the transformative (or "experiential') orientation, it is the music experience itself that precipitates therapeutic change—in, of, and by itself. This includes the first and second levels of the above continuum, both of which are examples of music *as* therapy or music healing.

In the insight orientation, it is the verbally mediated awareness gained as the result of the music experience that leads to change, as for example, when a music experience is discussed and analyzed afterward for important discoveries and insights. This orientation includes the third and fourth levels of the above continuum, both of which are examples of music *in* therapy.

Psychotherapy overlaps with the other areas of practice in several ways. It can have didactic overtones when education or instruction serves as the context for the psychotherapeutic process; it can relate to medicine when the client has a biomedical illness, and the psychotherapy is aimed at addressing the psychological challenges accompanying the illness; it can be recreational when any aspect of play or diversion contextualizes the work; and it can be ecological when individual work is combined with treatment of the individual's environment or milieu.

AUXILIARY LEVEL

Psychotherapeutic Music

In *Psychotherapeutic Music* a person uses music to maintain his/her own psychological health, or to enhance personal growth and self-actualization. This may involve performing, learning, composing, improvising, or listening to music, either alone or in groups. These activities are not part of a treatment program, and are pursued outside of a client-therapist relationship. The person may, however, receive ongoing guidance from various sources (e.g., experts, books, lectures, workshops).

Examples include the personal use of music to: examine or release feelings, reduce stress or anxiety, bring solace, dispel loneliness, develop self-esteem, establish rapport or communication with others, enhance cognitive skills, develop one's creativity, or develop spirituality. In the mental domain, the person may use music to sharpen one's attention, memory, or perception, or to develop one's creativity to the fullest. In the physical domain, a person may use music to: relax the body, manage pain, support therapeutic exercises, facilitate psychomotor learning, develop motor skills, monitor autonomic functions, or enhance physical performance in sports activities. For more examples and suggestions, see books by Rolla (1993), Merritt (1996), and Katsh and Merle-Fishman (1998).

Psychotherapeutic Music is an auxiliary practice, and is not considered within the boundaries of music therapy because it does not involve a process of intervention and change within a client-therapist relationship. Notice that it is very similar to *Therapeutic Music*, except that its focus is psychological rather than medical. Also note that it differs from *Functional Music* in its focus on health concerns.

Music Therapy Consultations

Music therapists often provide short-term services which are consultative in nature. This may include music therapy assessments of individuals on a referral basis, consultation with other professionals on how to use music therapeutically, workshops and training programs for other professionals, and so forth. *Music Therapy Consultations* may be provided at the auxiliary or augmentative level of practice, depending upon the degree and duration of direct involvement by the music therapist in the client's treatment program.

Music Therapy Consultations may also be provided in other areas of practice (e.g., medical, recreational, ecological), depending upon the setting, population, and purpose.

AUGMENTATIVE LEVEL

Supportive Music Psychotherapy

In *Supportive Music Psychotherapy*, the therapist uses music experiences to stimulate or support emotional adjustment or growth, relying largely on the client's existing resources. The client-therapist relationship is important in facilitating the music experiences and enhancing their therapeutic value; however, often, because of the length of treatment, the relationship does not develop the depth needed for it to serve as a primary vehicle for client change.

According to Wolberg (1967), the main objective of supportive psychotherapy is to bring or return the client to a psychological equilibrium as rapidly as possible. This may involve ameliorating symptoms, strengthening existing defenses and resources, developing better coping mechanisms, and reducing the effects of external forces. The intent is not to dramatically alter the client's personality, although some characterological changes may result from the work.

Supportive Music Psychotherapy may take place in individual, couple, family or group settings. Its main uses are: 1) short-term recovery programs for acute psychiatric or substance abuse clients; 2) long-term support and maintenance programs for certain chronic psychiatric or incarcerated clients; 3) crisis intervention and counseling for individuals, couples, or families suffering from trauma, illness, or loss; 4) preparation for or respite from more in-depth forms of psychotherapy; and 5) personal encounter workshops. This is considered an augmentative practice because of the level of intervention and change involved, and/or the duration of treatment. Examples are provided by Nolan (1991), Murphy (1991), and Borczon (1997).

Music in Pastoral Counseling

In *Music in Pastoral Counseling*, a minister, music therapist or counselor uses music to help the client gain spiritual insights and to develop a relationship with God that will facilitate emotional adjustment and growth. This falls within the definition of music psychotherapy, because music is used to address emotional-spiritual needs, and because a counselor-client relationship is implied. *Music in Pastoral Counseling* is very similar to *Supportive Music Psychotherapy* in level of intervention and change, and is therefore considered to be at the augmentative level. An example of this practice is the work of Houts (1981), and the religious exercises in Bonny and Savary (1973).

INTENSIVE LEVEL

Insight Music Psychotherapy

In *Insight Music Psychotherapy*, the therapist uses music experiences and the relationships that develop through them as the means of bringing clients greater insights about themselves and their lives, while also inducing the necessary psychological changes therein. The work may be done within individual, dyadic, family, or group settings. According to Wheeler (1988), the main uses of insight-oriented therapy are with "those who are less ill or who evidence less severe personality disorganization, including substance abusers and those with affective disorders, neuroses/ anxiety disorders, situational disorders or personality disorders. Clients with the diagnosis of schizophrenia and those with organic disorders would be expected to respond less favorably . . . " (p. 47). In addition, this practice is quite appropriate for "normal" individuals in the community who want to improve their emotional life, either through individual psychotherapy, group therapy, or sensitivity training.

Insight music psychotherapy is an intensive level of practice. Music is used *in* therapy most frequently, but it can also be used *as* therapy; the client-therapist relationship provides an important vehicle for therapeutic change. Interferences to the therapy process (e.g., resistance, defenses, transference, and countertransference reactions) are acknowledged and resolved depending on the therapist's theoretical orientation. Though the primary focus is how the client's problems are manifested at the conscious level, causes outside of the client's awareness may be explored.

Wheeler (1983) distinguishes between two levels of insight music therapy according to whether the goals are reeducative or reconstructive, which in turn depends upon whether unconscious determinants of the client's problems are accessed and resolved. According to Wolberg (1967), reeducative goals include behavior change, environmental readjustment, goal modification, and/or self-actualization.

> Changes are rarely of sufficient depth to permit a real dissolution of unconscious conflict. Nevertheless, the individual achieves sufficient command of his problem to enable him to check acting-out tendencies; to rectify remediable environmental distortions or to adjust to irremediable ones; to organize his life goals more rationally and to execute them in a facile manner; to consolidate some adaptive defenses and to alter others that are less adaptive (Wolberg, 1967, p. 103).

Hence the most immediate causes of the client's problems may be brought into awareness. In the present classification, reeducative goals are consistent with the "intensive" level of practice.

In contrast, reconstructive goals are to discover unconscious determinants of the client's conflicts, and to make in-depth changes in the client's personality structure. In the present classification, this level is a "primary" form of music therapy.

Insight Music Psychotherapy is practiced within various orientations (e.g., psychodynamic, behavioral). Examples within a psychodynamic orientation include: Bruscia (1991, 1998), Scheiby (1991), Boone (1991), Smith (1991), Pickett (1991), Warja (1994), Priestley (1994), and Austin (1996).

Examples of behavioral approaches include: the use of music-facilitated relaxation and imagery in the reduction of anxiety (Winslow, 1986); an evaluation model of music group psychotherapy based on learning theory and applied behavior analysis (Hanser, 1984), the use of music for stress reduction within a psychotherapy setting (Hanser, 1985), and the treatment of phobias (Eifert et al., 1988).

Transformative Music Psychotherapy

In *Transformative (or Experiential) Music Psychotherapy*, the therapist uses music experiences and the relationships that form through them in order to access, work through, and resolve the client's therapeutic needs; verbal techniques are used only if or when they will enhance the music experience and its therapeutic potential. It is within the music experiences that the client and therapist develop their relationship, and the client makes the necessary changes. The music experience is therapeutically transformative and complete in, of, and by itself, independent of any insight gained through verbal exchange (Bruscia, 1998). Thus, most often, music is used *as* therapy.

Examples include "Guided Imagery and Music" (GIM) (Bonny, 1978), and "Creative Music Therapy (Nordoff & Robbins, 1977), which may also be considered *Music Therapy in Healing*, a very similar practice (See Chapter 20). Also see Clark (1991), Kenny (1991), Lecourt (1991), Bruscia (1992), Friedlander (1994) and Ventre (1994).

Music in Arts Psychotherapy

Music in Arts Psychotherapy is the psychotherapeutic application of music and related arts experiences within a client-therapist relationship. It can be practiced in two ways. In the first, a music therapist engages a client in an integrated arts activity (e.g., song-writing, moving or drawing to music), and makes one art form the primary or focal experience, while using the other art form to support, enhance, or expand upon the primary experience. Thus for example, in song-writing the therapist might focus the client on the music and/or words, depending upon which has more relevance and which has the greater potential for intervention. Examples include Aigen (1991b) and Hibben (1991).

In the second, a music therapist works with another arts therapist (i.e., art, movement/dance, drama, or poetry therapist) providing the client with either separate and/or collaborative arts therapy experiences. That is, the client may have separate sessions for each arts therapy, joint sessions containing two separate arts therapy experiences, or one session containing integrated arts therapy experiences co-led by therapists in each art area. In all cases, the therapist preserves the integrity and his/her own modality by exploiting the uniqueness of the art form and the therapeutic process that flows from it. At the same time, the therapeutic process is coordinated so that the client's experiences in the different art modalities are parallel.

An example of two therapists working with the same group, using music and dance separately, is "Experimental Improvisation Therapy" (Bruscia, 1987a). Examples of an interdisciplinary approach to music in creative arts therapies are found in articles by Free, Tuerk, and Tinkleman (1986), Pulliam et al. (1988), and Clark-Schock (1988).

Instructional Music Psychotherapy

Instructional Music Psychotherapy is the use of private music lessons as a context for individual psychotherapy. In terms of Wolberg (1967), the goals are most often reeducative, but they may also be supportive or reconstructive. Aspects of the lesson which have psychotherapeutic implications include: the various musical media used for expressive and communicative purposes, the structure of the learning process, the nature of practice and performance, the client-therapist relationship, etc.

Instructional Music Psychotherapy is an intensive practice because, unlike supportive therapy, its goals go beyond adaptation to include both overt and covert facets of the client's emotional life. It also uses a broader range of methods and techniques. Music is used *in* therapy and *as* therapy, and the client-therapist relationship is equally if not more important than the client-music relationship. Examples include Tyson (1981, 1982) and Shields and Robbins (1980).

Supervisory Music Psychotherapy

In *Supervisory Music Psychotherapy*, the supervisor-therapist uses music experiences and the relationships that develop through them as a means of helping the supervisee to work through personal issues that impact on his/her clinical work as a therapist. In other words, this category is concerned with the use of music therapy to uncover and resolve countertransference issues that therapists experience in their relationships with clients.

Supervisory Music Psychotherapy is an intensive music therapy practice, and because of its depth and scope of concern and its reliance on the client-therapist relationship, it may become a primary form of treatment. Most often however, it works toward reeducative rather than reconstructive goals.

Examples of this level include those cited above for experiential training (Hesser, 1985; Priestley, 1975; Bruscia, 1987a; Clark, 1987), all of which can be easily adapted for more in-depth work with professionals. In addition, Stephens (1984, 1987) has developed a model specifically designed to use music therapy as a method of professional supervision.

Expressive Psychotherapy

In *Expressive Psychotherapy*, a therapist uses various expressive modalities and the relationships that develop through them as a means of bringing the client insights into his/her emotional life and of stimulating the desired changes therein. The therapist selects the art or sensory modality according to which is most relevant to the client's need for expression, creativity, emotional investigation, or resolution (Knill, 1994). Robbins (1980) explains the rationale for his approach as follows: "In any one session, we can detect in patient-therapist communications both verbal and nonverbal cues that can be examined within the artistic parameters of sight, sound, and motion; that is, in rhythm, pitch, and timbre; in color, texture and form; and in muscular tension, energy, and spatial relation" (p. 13). He goes on:

> The essence of expressive therapy lies in process rather than in technique, for the therapy occurs through the vehicle of psychic play rather than in the actual products of artistic production. Dance, art, music, as well as other expressive modalities, can facilitate this process, but the actual use of a particular art form will depend on the special talents of the therapist and on the particular receptivity to that art form of a given patient. What is crucial, however, is the therapist's availability to hear and attend to the dance, music, and visions of his patient's communications" (p.14).

Evelyn Heimlich developed a method of child psychotherapy called "Paraverbal Therapy". She used "various expressive media (viz., speech, language, music, the components of music, mime, movement, psychodrama, drawing and painting) in unorthodox and nontraditional ways, in order to address the expressive, communicative, and therapeutic needs of the individual from moment to moment" (Bruscia, 1987a, p. 267).

Other examples found in the literature include the work of Naitove (1980, 1984), Grinnell (in Bruscia, 1987a), and Lewis (1987). Moreno (1988) and McNiff (1981, 1988) also advocate an integrated approach to the arts in shamanic healing and psychotherapy.

Expressive Psychotherapy meets all criteria for being an intensive or primary level of treatment.

PRIMARY LEVEL

Music psychotherapy becomes a primary level of therapy under two conditions: when the work leads to significant and pervasive changes in the specific goal areas being addressed, and when the goals and processes extend beyond the focal concern of psychotherapy to include those of other areas of practice (e.g., medical, ecological). In short, primary therapy involves a process of intervention and change characterized by both depth and breadth. It is always reconstructive in nature, and it always involves a holistic approach.

Chapter Twenty-two

RECREATIONAL PRACTICES

This area encompasses all applications of music, music activities, and music therapy where the focus is on diversion, play, recreation, activity, or entertainment. Music activity is broadly defined to include a host of related media and experiences, including the other arts, recreational games, educational exercises, and so forth. The primary aim, whether implemented in institutional or community settings, is to help individuals engage in music or the other arts as leisure time or social activities that will enhance the quality of life, while also serving as a vehicle for therapeutic change.

Levels of practices in this area vary according to how therapeutically oriented the goals are. Those practices which provide recreation for its own sake, to meet the immediate entertainment or leisure needs of clients are regarded as less intense than those which use recreational activities for therapeutic purposes. Related to this is the length and continuity of treatment. Providing occasional music activities which bring clients some personal enjoyment, though extremely important to their immediate needs, is less intense than using music activities in a systematic way, and over an extended period of time to achieve health-related goals.

AUXILIARY LEVEL

Therapeutic Music Recreation

In *Therapeutic Music Recreation*, music activities are provided for entertainment purposes, to enhance the overall quality of life, and to help develop pleasurable leisure-time activities. This category is considered auxiliary because a client-therapist relationship is not essential, and though the benefits are many, the process is not a therapeutic one, involving neither clinical intervention nor significant change.

Therapeutic Music Recreation can be used in schools, hospitals, institutions, community centers, and day programs for impaired or unimpaired individuals of all ages. For a practical guide to planning and implementing music programs for leisure and recreation, see Batcheller and Monsour (1972).

AUGMENTATIVE LEVEL

Recreational Music Therapy

In *Recreational Music Therapy*, the therapist uses music, music learning, and/or related activities to help the client develop recreational skills and to use leisure time as a means of self-fulfillment. This is an augmentative practice because it focuses on the goals of recreation therapy, and because it is a supportive form of therapy, as defined by Wolberg (1967). It can be a very important part of the treatment program when the client"s priority needs relate to leisure time, and when music is the most desirable leisure-time activity for the client.

Therapeutic Music Play

In *Therapeutic Music Play,* the therapist uses music, games, recreational activities, and the arts as brief or occasional form of diversion during a difficult period or situation (e.g., hospitalization) or to facilitate developmental growth or learning (e.g., in a day care or preschool program).

INTENSIVE LEVEL

Music and Play Therapy

In *Music and Play Therapy,* the therapist uses music, games, spontaneous play, and the arts as part of a systematic process aimed at helping a child or group of children explore and work through therapeutic issues. The goals of *Music and Play Therapy* vary according to the setting. When used in a medical setting, the usual focus is on helping the child to understand and cope with his/her illness, hospitalization, or treatment; when used in a psychotherapeutic setting, the focus is on helping the child understand, express, and deal with feelings about self and significant others. Play may include various traditional games (e.g., peek-a-boo) as well as games and activities specially created by child and therapist. It may also include playing with toys, objects, or puppets, storytelling, art, movement, drama, writing, and games of the imagination. Examples in the literature include: Hibben (1991, 1992), Herman (1991), Burke (1991), Bartram (1991), and Agrotou (1993a).

PRIMARY LEVEL

Recreational practices become a primary level of therapy under two conditions: when the work leads to significant and pervasive changes in the client's quality of life, and when the goals and processes extend beyond the focal concern of diversion to include those of other areas of practice (e.g., psychotherapeutic, medical, ecological, didactic). In short, primary therapy involves a process of intervention and change characterized by both depth and breadth. It is always reconstructive in nature, and it always involves a holistic approach.

Chapter Twenty-three

ECOLOGICAL PRACTICES

The ecological area of practice includes all applications of music and music therapy where the primary focus is on promoting health within and between various layers of the sociocultural community and/or physical environment. This includes all work which focuses on the family, workplace, community, society, culture, or physical environment, either because the health of the ecological unit itself is at risk and therefore in need of intervention, or because the unit in some way causes or contributes to the health problems of its members. Also included are any efforts to form, build, or sustain communities through music therapy. Thus, this area of practice expands the notion of "client" to include a community, environment, ecological context, or individual whose health problem is ecological in nature. While the therapist may work to facilitate changes in the individual or the ecological context, the basic premise is that changes in one will ultimately lead to changes in the other. Thus, helping an individual to become healthier is not viewed as a separate enterprise from improving the health of the ecological context within which the individual lives; conversely, helping any ecological context to become healthier is not a separate enterprise from improving the health of its members; and helping individual and ecology to relate to one another harmoniously makes both healthier.

The concept of ecological therapy stems from "systems" theory where all entities are viewed as inextricably linked to one another at various levels of reciprocal influence (Kenny, 1985, 1989), and more recent notions of "holarchization" and its relation to health, as described by Wilber (1995) (see the chapter on "Health").

A distinction is made here between traditional forms of group therapy and ecological forms of group work. In traditional group therapy, members are selected according to common or complementary needs; thus, the group, regardless of its potential cohesiveness, is a constructed rather than a natural ecological unit. A traditional therapy group is therefor not the actual milieu in which the member lives and works, rather it is an artificial, albeit carefully constructed, replica of that milieu. In contrast, an ecological group is a natural community, group, or context that already exists, with an already established or defined membership of individuals who live and work within it.

A second difference is that in traditional group therapy, the aim is to effect therapeutic change in individual members; whereas in ecological group work, the aim is to effect therapeutic change in the ecological system and the individuals that are a part of it. This means that in traditional group therapy, changes in individual members have to be generalized or applied to each member's own ecological context away from the group; in ecological work, no such generalization is necessary. In other words, the client in traditional group therapy is each individual member, rather than the group itself; the client in ecological work is both the individual and the community.

Music is regarded as intrinsically ecological in two ways. First, music itself is an organized holarchy or system, wherein each layer of the music or experience is part of a whole which is part of another whole, ad infinitum, with each part-whole inextricably and reciprocally linked to one another. Second, music permeates every layer of the ecology; it is found within every layer of the physical environment and sociocultural system, and, in fact, serves as a catalyst, container, or unifier within and between the various layers.

Boxill (1997) explains that music therapists have a special role to play in bringing the whole of music to bear on the entire planet, beyond the individual client or group in the treatment room:

> . . . we music therapists have more than even an imperative to heighten and broaden our vistas—to effect an impact globally that reaches far beyond the traditional treatment room. We must look to new ways and possibilities for bringing the essence of music therapy—its profound humanness—to the 'ordinary' people on planet Earth. Our intention is attainable. For *we music therapists have as our therapeutic agent a universal means of human contact, communication, and expression—music.* The potential is unbounded (p. 179).

In a similar vein, Ruud (1988, 1998) suggests that music therapy should be considered a cultural movement as well as a therapeutic treatment modality. The main reason he gives for this is that music and music therapy serve "an important role in improving quality of life . . . it strengthens our emotional awareness, installs a sense of agency, fosters belongingness, and provides meaning and coherence in life" (p. 49). He further explains that this emphasis upon the relationship between health and quality of life is a very unique and important philosophical concept which the arts therapies have contributed to worldviews on health and health care, and that as music therapists we should begin to promulgate this pioneer way of thinking.

Before proceeding to a description of the various levels of ecological practice, a few comments are necessary. First, this area is a relatively new development in the field, consequently many of the practices within it have not been identified, contextualized, or even developed yet. Second, ecological practices are quite different from those in other areas, and this has major implications for determining levels. Not only does therapy extend beyond the treatment room, regardless of setting, it also extends beyond the client-therapist relationship to include many layers of relationship between client and community, therapist and community, members within a community, and between communities. Going even further, the process of intervention itself is different, sometimes not anything like traditional therapy. Thus, treatment setting, client-therapist relationship, and "process" cannot be used as criteria for determining levels of therapy as they have been in other areas of practice. As a result, the levels of therapy identified here may seem inconsistent with other areas of practice, and though a practice is listed under one level, it may easily move to another. Here the criteria of greatest significance are: whether the focus is on the individual, the ecology, or both, and the degree of change resulting from the interventions.

AUXILIARY PRACTICES

Included in this level are all those uses of music that are directed toward large groups of people. The groups are ecological in that they occur within a natural context, or they were intentionally formed as a community. Also included are the various efforts of music therapists as an organized group of professionals.

Functional Music

Functional Music is the use of music to influence physical states, behaviors, moods, attitudes, etc. outside of a therapy context, that is, in commercial, industrial, work, educational, or home settings. According to Radocy and Boyle (1979), this includes the use of music: to increase vigilance, efficiency, productivity, morale, and safety in the workplace; to mitigate tension, fatigue, boredom, melancholy, or loneliness while engaged in any activity; to monitor moods of people in public areas (e.g., hospitals, doctor's offices, airports); to establish an atmosphere conducive to conversation, either in work or recreational settings; to mask unwanted or distracting sounds in the environment; to create moods in commercial establishments that reflect or describe the product being sold; to encourage buying behaviors; to enhance radio and television advertising by making products more desirable and memorable; to facilitate other forms of propaganda; and to enhance the dramatic effects of television and films. For examples, see Harris et al. (1992) and Brodsky (1991).

Ceremonial Music

Ceremonial Music is the use of music to accompany formal affairs such as military or state ceremonies, athletic events, or award ceremonies. In military or state ceremonies, patriotic music is used to inspire feelings of love for country, to commemorate historical events or significant people, and to give significance to specific aspects of the ceremony (Radocy & Boyle, 1979). In sports events, music is used to help the spectators identify with the players or teams, to engender feelings of competition, and to support moments of accomplishment or triumph. In award ceremonies, music is used to accompany processions and the actual conferring of awards or titles. In all cases, music stimulates certain values, feelings, or attitudes in the audience, while also helping to shape their understanding of and participation in the ceremony itself.

Inspirational Music

Inspirational Music is the use of music to stimulate spiritual experiences, to facilitate religious meditation, and to enhance prayer and worship activities. It also includes the use of gospel or sacred music during church services, or what is sometimes called the "music ministry." According to Radocy and Boyle (1979):

> Music in religious services appears to serve several functions: at times it serves as a signal to stimulate the congregation to respond in a certain way. At other times quiet organ interludes are used to help establish a mood of reverence or tranquility. Congregational singing serves to draw people together, while choir anthems appear to lead the worshipers to reflect on the beliefs and values of the religion and its implications for them as individuals. Special religious ceremonies are accompanied by special music. Certainly weddings, funerals, and special religious days are made more meaningful by music designed to enhance the significance of the occasion (p. 243).

Music Therapy Activism

In its short history as a profession, music therapy has played a significant role in various social, cultural, and political movements, using the unique perspectives and skills inherent in its focus on music and the ability of its members to network and organize themselves to effect change. Examples include the various efforts that music therapists have made to support and shape deinstitutionalization, mainstreaming, inclusion, and the ongoing changes in health care. A particularly notable example of group legislative action is the testimony given by music therapists to the U.S. Senate in its special hearings on "Music and Aging." Both professional music therapy associations in the USA demonstrated the importance of music to the elderly, not only as treatment modality but also as a means of enhancing their quality of life (see *Music Therapy Perspectives, 10 (1),* 1992).

An even broader initiative has been taken by Boxill (1989) who founded "Music Therapists for Peace."

As a worldwide network of music therapists, we are exploring, and *applying*, new ways of consciously using the unique powers of music and music-making: to create harmonious relationships among peoples of all conditions and levels of society; to utilize our special strategies and techniques in helping people resolve conflicts through nonverbal means of communication; to provide means for making more peaceful contact on individual and group bases—for peaceful living (p. 135).

Another example of this practice is given by Routhier (1988).

AUGMENTATIVE LEVEL

This level is characterized by systematic, sustained efforts to use music to improve relations between individuals and the ecological contexts in which they live or work.

Arts Outreach Programs

Arts Outreach Programs are defined here as any sustained effort to help persons with health problems be consumers of the arts in the mainstream of their culture, that is, like any other member of the community. This may consist of helping persons who are impaired or institutionalized attend and participate in public or community events in the arts, or bringing artists and performances into institutions or homes where residents cannot leave. An outstanding example of such programs is "Hospital Audiences" founded by Michael Jon Spencer in New York City, and duplicated by many others around the country. Another approach is to organize and promote the artistic efforts of people who have health problems or impairments. An example of this is "The Very Special Arts Festivals" of the John F. Kennedy Center for Performing Arts, sponsored around the country through public schools and community organizations. One can also find many music groups in the community made up of persons with various handicaps and impairments. For other examples, see Bunt (1994), and Educational Facilities Laboratory (1995).

These practices are considered augmentative when they are implemented over an extended period, when they have permeated various facets of the community, and when they lead to changes in both the individual and community, not only with regard to attitude, but also with regard to policy and custom.

Organizational Music Therapy

Although relatively undeveloped, *Organizational Music Therapy* is the potential application of music for staff development and support (O'Neill, 1995), and to improve relations in work settings and professional groups. Like "Organizational Psychology," this practice could involve consultation, assessment, or intervention.

Healing Music Rituals

Healing Music Rituals includes all those forms of therapy and healing which utilize music and rituals which are indigenous to the clients or which form an important part of our collective past. The purpose is to rediscover the wisdoms of previous healing practices, most of which relied heavily upon music, while also reconnecting clients to their collective and personal roots. Three main approaches are taken: using music rituals which are indigenous to the client's specific community or culture; using traditional healing rituals (e.g., music in shamanism); and creating special music rituals to address the individual and ecological needs of the clients. For examples, see Kenny (1982), Moreno (1988), Beer (1990), Aigen (1991a), and Agrotou (1993a).

This practice may also be implemented at the intensive level, depending upon the breadth and depth of the therapeutic process and change.

Music Therapy in Sensitivity Training

Music Therapy in Sensitivity Training is a group method which uses music to explore relations between groups of people. The purpose may be to understand and accept differences in race, culture, religion, gender, or sexual orientation. The setting may be a traditional music therapy group in an institution where such differences are pronounced, or a community workshop designed to resolve a specific relational problem. When the groups have indigenous musics, their respective music repertoires and traditions are utilized to facilitate communication and insight between the groups.

A good example of this practice is the use of music in intergenerational programs aimed at fostering communication and understanding between various age groups (Gardstrom, 1993; Darrow et al., 1994; Frego, 1995; and Bowers, 1998). Couture (1993) used music to explore cultural differences. Similarly, Katz (1993) organized a "Peace Train Tour" in which a multi-cultural, multi-racial youth choir performed indigenous music throughout South Africa during the dismantling of apartheid.

This practice may also be implemented at the intensive level, depending upon the breadth and depth of the therapeutic process and change.

INTENSIVE LEVEL

Whereas the auxiliary level focuses on larger groups and communities, and the augmentative level focuses on relations between disenfranchised individuals and their communities, this level approaches ecological work through traditional individual and group music therapy settings. Two main approaches are taken: incorporating ecological aims and values into the client's music therapy, or combining traditional forms of therapy with community work.

Family Music Therapy

In *Family Music Therapy*, the therapist works to improve relationships between members of a family, and in the process improves the health of the family as an ecological unit. A distinction is made here between individual therapy which involves family members and true family therapy. When therapy involves family members for the purpose of helping the individual rather than the family make the necessary therapeutic changes, it is considered individual therapy; when therapy is aimed at helping every family member make the necessary changes in relation to one another, it is considered family therapy.

Families most often seek therapy when they are disrupted by a serious health problem of some kind. Sometimes a child is born with a severe physical or mental impairment, or a parent becomes seriously ill; sometimes, a member of the family has psychological problems which affect relationships between all members of the family, and the family falls apart. Depending on the nature of the problem or disruption, *Family Music Therapy* may be implemented within a medical or psychotherapeutic context. Frequently then, it begins with a focus on one member of the family, and then extends to other members until it includes the whole family unit. Examples include the work of Hibben (1992), Oldfield (1993), and Slinka and Magill (1986).

Community Music Therapy

In *Community Music Therapy*, the therapist works with clients in traditional individual or group music therapy settings, while also working with the community. The purpose is twofold: to prepare the client to participate in community functions and become a valued member of the community; and to prepare the community to accept and embrace the clients by helping its members understand and interact with the clients. Thus, *Community Music Therapy* combines the *Arts Outreach Program* with traditional forms of music therapy (e.g., didactic, psychotherapeutic, recreational).

A pioneering example is the work of Stige (1993) who integrated a group of individuals with mental handicaps into the community, using concepts such as "combined posts" and "period-collaboration." When music therapists have "combined posts" they work in different systems within the community (e.g., community music group, an institution for the mentally handicapped), and they use their connections to establish social networks between the two groups. In period collaboration, "a group of handicapped musicians work out musical products together with a choir, a brass band or another musical organisation in the community. In this process the social interaction between the musicians is seen as very important" (p. 26). Stige's project culminated in a concert which integrated the two groups of musicians.

Also included in *Community Music Therapy* are all those follow-up or after-care programs which use music to facilitate integration of the client back into his/her life community following institutionalization or hospitalization (Langdon et al., 1989). Unlike traditional therapy which focuses only on the client's adaptation and assimilation into the community, *Community Music Therapy* also works to help the community adapt and accommodate to the client.

PRIMARY LEVEL

Ecological practices become primary when they lead to significant and enduring changes in the individual or community, and when the goals and processes extend across several areas of practice (e.g., psychotherapy, recreation, didactic)

Chapter Twenty-four

DEFINING RESEARCH
AND THEORY[1]

Now that music therapy practice has been defined and described in detail, we are ready to look at the other two elements of the discipline, research and theory. Practice, research, and theory differ from one another in purpose and process, yet are integrally linked to one another. As different forms of knowledge, they organize and are organized by one another, and together they constitute the state of the art we call music therapy. The purpose of this chapter is to define research and theory, and to differentiate them from clinical practice.

DEFINING RESEARCH

Research is a systematic, self-monitored inquiry which leads to a discovery or new insight, which when documented and disseminated contributes to or modifies existing knowledge or practice. Each section of this definition warrants further elaboration.

- To be systematic, the researcher must have a focus or question, and formulate an organized and appropriate method of studying it.
- To be self-monitored, the researcher must continually observe and manage all factors which affect the ethical and scholarly integrity of the inquiry.

---

[1] This chapter is an adaptation and expansion of a previous work by the author, entitled "The Boundaries of Music Therapy Research." In B. Wheeler (Ed.) (1995), *Music Therapy Research: Quantitative and Qualitative Perspectives*, pp. 17-27. Gilsum, NH: Barcelona Publishers.

- To be an inquiry, the researcher must not only gather and organize information, but also reflect upon it to gain new insights. As such, research always goes beyond mere data collection to include both reflection and discovery. The reflection may be accomplished through various forms of data analysis (e.g., statistical, logical, aesthetic); the discovery may be in the form of new knowledge, explanations, under-standings, perspectives, conceptions, meanings, innovations, or levels of awareness.

- To make a contribution to knowledge or practice, research findings must be documented and disseminated in some way, otherwise it is merely personal knowledge which has not been communicated. Thus, research is, by nature, public and collective, rather than private and individual. This does not mean that all research must be published writings, rather it means that the outcomes of research, whatever the format, must be documented in a way that is communicable to others.

With these criteria it is now possible to establish boundaries for what is considered research and what is not. The first set of boundaries needed is between research, practice, and theory; then boundaries are needed to distinguish research from writing and creative activity.

DIFFERENTIATING
RESEARCH AND PRACTICE

Research is different from practice in very significant ways. (NOTE: For purposes of brevity, the present discussion deals only with the difference between research and practice within the *discipline* rather than in the profession, as further detailed in the next chapter).

The most obvious difference between research and practice is that practice involves "doing" something (e.g., working directly with clients), whereas research involves "studying" what is being done. Unfortunately, this simple distinction gets easily muddled whenever one begins to study what one is doing while it is being done! It is quite easy to confuse research with practice whenever therapists study their own clinical work. Three different perspectives are involved in "clinical" or "action" research: working directly with the client, observing one's work with the client as it is happening to further inform the clinical work, and studying these observations of one's clinical work for research purposes. In clinical work, there is action and reflection, and in research there is an added perspective or "metareflection."

But even when there are these kinds of overlaps in practice and research, very important distinctions need to be made. First and foremost, the goals are different. Research is aimed at increasing or modifying the knowledge base in music therapy; in contrast, clinical practice is aimed at helping clients achieve health. Of course, the more we know about music therapy the better we can help clients, but this difference in goal and orientation has considerable significance in the immediate clinical situation. Consider the difference between determining the method of intervention or clinical response according to what a client is presenting at the moment or what a client needs therapeutically, versus determining the method or responding to a client according to what the goals of the research study are or according to the protocol for clinical treatment established beforehand. Naturally, every clinical researcher tries to integrate these two purposes or keep them consistent with one another, but this is not always possible.

Also consider how in research, knowledge is gathered for its own sake, whereas in clinical work, knowledge is gathered for the client's sake. This point is especially helpful in differentiating research from clinical assessment and evaluation. All three are concerned with gathering information, but the former is concerned with how the data will add to our knowledge base, and the latter are concerned with how the data can help the client or therapeutic process. Thus, the use of knowledge is quite different. In research, the purpose is to extend, generalize, transfer or apply the findings to comparable clients and contexts, thus moving from specific data on specific clients to more general knowledge. In clinical work, the purpose is to utilize the data gathered primarily in reference to a specific client and context.

Another important difference involves roles and beneficiaries. Research reverses the roles of helper and helped found in clinical practice. In research, the client is helping the researcher to accomplish the researcher's goals; in clinical work, the "therapist" is there to help the client achieve the client's goals.

Related to the beneficiary issue, there is a difference in who consumes and uses the knowledge gained in research versus practice. Typically, research findings are shared with one's profession, which consists of colleagues and any interested parties. Thus, the first beneficiary of research knowledge is the professional world, which then uses it for the benefit of their clients; nevertheless, it is important to point out that in most cases, these consumers have no direct involvement (or investment) in the client who served as the research subject or participant. In clinical practice, the data are communicated only to the clients or to co-therapists who are working directly with the clients. Thus, whereas research discoveries are nearly always made public, clinical information is always kept confidential.

Because music therapy involves an art form, there is another boundary issue that must be considered. What is the difference between creative work and research? Research is not creative activity for its own sake, nor is it creative activity within clinical practice without systematic inquiry and discovery. Thus for example, distinctions must be made in music therapy between: writing songs for use in therapy without doing systematic inquiry (i.e., creative activity); using the songs in actual therapy sessions without collecting any data (i.e., clinical work [treatment]); documenting how certain clients responded to the songs (i.e., clinical work [assessment and evaluation]); collecting and synthesizing data on how clients respond to the songs (i.e., research [assessment and evaluation]); and collecting and synthesizing data on how to use the songs in therapy (i.e., research [treatment]).

DEFINING THEORY

Before comparing research with theory, we have to define what a "theory" is. There are many definitions, depending on the field. The one provided here is the writer's elaboration of definitions found in Webster's dictionary (Merriam, 1974), in Reber's dictionary of psychology (1985), and in the discussion of theory by Hall and Lindzey (1957).

A theory is a set of interrelated principles or constructs which have been created by a theorist in order to: a) describe and organize a particular domain in a comprehensive and coherent manner; b) explain or understand related facts, empirical data, and phenomena within the domain; and c) offer a conceptual framework for decision making in future theory, research and practice.

Notice that a theory is not a single finding or construct, it is a *set* of principles which are logically related to one another. Unlike a research study which yields discoveries about a very specific and limited phenomenon, a true theory has application for an entire phenomenal field. It is meant to provide a comprehensive framework for describing and organizing all phenomena within a domain, showing how they are interrelated. In practical terms, a theory links together related research findings, relates a set of similar clinical ideas or strategies, or synthesizes facts derived from both research and clinical practice. Thus theory goes beyond research and practice to provide a fuller and more articulate foundation for either or both endeavors.

Besides linking and relating facts to one another, theoretical principles or constructs are supposed to explain or provide a better understanding of the facts. A theory must go beyond description and organization of information to yield new insights. These new explanations, understandings, or insights may increase knowledge, call into question what is already known or assumed, or modify existing ways of thinking. In this way, a theory is very much like a research study.

Another important aspect of a theory is that it is *created* by an individual. The principles and constructs of a theory are in actuality one person's logical "construction" (or some would say "reconstruction") of empirical and/or clinical "realities;" they are personal but nevertheless rational "interpretations" of facts discovered through research and practice. Because of this, many believe that it is moot to ask whether any theory is true or false—it can only be useful or not useful, heuristic or not heuristic, depending upon whether its constructs are able to efficiently and economically account for the empirical or clinical information, and thereby provide guidance in solving related problems or making decisions.

A theory always refers to a specific area of interest, and in music therapy, we have three domains, each containing many different areas of interest for theorists. Theories within the *disciplinary* domain deal with research and practice on the many facets of client assessment, treatment, and evaluation, or how a therapist uses music to help clients achieve health. Theories within the *professional* domain deal with research and practice on music therapists, education and training, employment practices, etc. In addition, there are many *foundational* domains, including theories of music, theories of therapy, or other clinical theories.

One can create a theory in many different ways, depending upon the objective. The following are some of the main methods of theory-building.

- Explication: A theory is developed by classifying, organizing, differentiating, and redefining concepts, practices, and terms found in music therapy theory, practice, and research. This very book provides an example of this type of theory-building. Other examples include the definition of sixty-four improvisational techniques (Bruscia, 1987), and levels of structure in music therapy (Hadsell, 1993).

- Integration: A theory is developed by relating music therapy to another field. This is typically done through a process of accommodation and/or assimilation. In accommodation, phenomena in music therapy are fit into theories or constructs in other fields, and in the process, some aspect of music therapy is expanded, limited, revisioned, or modified to accommodate the other field. In assimilation, theories or constructs outside the field are modified to fit into music therapy. Here the external model is expanded, limited, revisioned or modified to accommodate music therapy phenomena. Theories which integrate music therapy with other fields can vary greatly according to the relative emphasis given to accommodation and assimilation. Examples of this type of theory include: Ruud (1980), Kenny (1985), Broucek (1987), Eagle (1991), Lehtonen (1993), Wrangsjo (1994), Summer (1995), Ruud (1980), Rugenstein (!996), and certain chapters in Priestley (1994), Bruscia (1987a), and Bruscia (1998).

- Philosophical Criticism: The theory is developed based on philosophical criticism of existing theory, practice, or research. Such criticism may include: the uncovering and evaluation of underlying assumptions (Aigen, 1995); the identification of inconsistencies and faulty reasoning; or the presentation of suppporting and/or challenging arguments. An example is Aigen (1991a).

- Empirical Analysis: A theory is developed based on the analysis of data of some kind. The data may exist already, or they may be gathered through any form of empirical research. In the quantitative paradigm, an empirical theory is an attempt to *explain* a body of research, or make deductions from it. Examples include Standley (1986) and Maranto (1996). In the qualitative paradigm, an empirical theory is an attempt to *describe* a phenemona based on some form of systematic observation or inquiry. Examples include: Bruscia (1995), Amir (1996a), Forinash (1992), and Aigen (1996).

- Speculation: The theory is based on an expert's reasoned opinion, direct experience with the phenomenon, and intuitive observations. Examples include: Gaston (1968), Sears (1968), Kenny (1982, 1989), Forinash & Robbins (1991), and Amir (1996b).

- Revisioning: The theory consists of new conceptual schemes, propositions and terminology, all created by the theorist to describe or explain music therapy phenomena in a way that breaks from past traditions, or takes them even further. Examples include: Broucek (1987), Kenny (1989), Aldridge (1989, 1996), Bruscia (1991), and Ruud (1998).

- Symbolization: The theory relies upon symbols, metaphors, or stories to describe and conceptualize any aspect of music therapy. Examples include Kenny (1982, 1988), Bruscia (1996) and Bruscia (in press).

It should be noted that these methods of theory-building can be, and often are combined within the same theory; thus, the examples given above may belong in more than one category.

DIFFERENTIATING
THEORY AND RESEARCH

In the previous discussion on what a theory is, certain differences have already been cited between theory and research. Theory has a much broader scope than research. Whereas a theory can deal with a larger realm, having many topics and subtopics, research has to have very narrow limits placed on its purpose and focus. A theory can also combine and include many research studies and models of practice. Thus, we can say that the purpose of theory is to enlarge our perspectives on what we know, while the purpose of research is to establish what we know by describing and explaining what occurred or what was observed. Theory, then, is a way of thinking or conceptualizing about something; it attempts to put existing research and practice into a broader perspective that will expand their meaning and significance. Another way of saying this is that theory and research relate to "facts" differently. A theory tells us how to make sense out of the facts, research tells us what the facts are. And this brings us to a very important issue.

The relationship between theory and research is very much influenced by one's orientation toward facts: the quantitative (positivistic) paradigm, or the qualitative (nonpositivistic) paradigm. Since the differences between these paradigms will be discussed at length elsewhere in the book, only a few comments need to be made here. The most important one is that these two camps have a difference of opinion on what a "fact" is. Quantitative researchers believe that facts are objective truths that are discovered through systematic inquiry by "disinterested" scientists; qualitative researchers believe that "facts" are merely "constructions" of the researcher or "co-constructions" of researcher and participants based on focused interactions. Needless to say, since "facts" are what a theory seeks to explain or explicate, a "theory" is also conceived differently. Quantitative researchers believe that research and theory continually add to an existing repository of knowledge or truths; qualitative researchers believe that research and theory increases our understanding of existing "constructions" and therefore leads to "reconstructions" that are more relevant and build more consensus among interested parties (Guba & Lincoln, 1994).

What these differences suggest is that there is a clearer boundary between theory and research within the quantitative paradigm than within the qualitative paradigm. For qualitative researchers, so long as there is data, a focus, and systematic inquiry, doing research is theorizing (i.e., constructing and reconstructing), and theorizing is part of doing research. Because of this close connection, other boundary issues arise.

Theory and research are often confused with writing about one's clinical work or ideas. The following boundaries may help to clarify the differences between these endeavors:

- Theory and research do not include expository writings which present discoveries or insights based on the writer's general experiences, but which are not based on a specific body of empirical or clinical data. This includes opinion statements, self-descriptions, and speculations which do not refer to existing research or practice. Thus, to be research, there must be systematic inquiry and discovery, or in more concrete terms, data collection, analysis, and interpretation. Research is not an act of wisdom or introspection. Its purpose is not to present what is already known, but to discover what is not known. And to be theory, there must be a set of interrelated principles which organize and clarify what is known through research or practice.

- Theory and research do not include expository writings which present unfocused or unorganized clinical data without any attempt to arrive at a discovery or insight that have any implications beyond themselves. Included are clinical logs, records, or reports which do not present conclusions based on the data.

- Theory and research do not include inquiries or speculations which were not self-monitored. Included are writings which are presented as "research" but which give no indication that the investigator has taken sufficient steps to insure the integrity of the data or findings, and writings that present principles or constructs but which are not clearly linked to any empirical or clinical data.

SUMMARY

Research is a systematic, self-monitored inquiry which leads to a discovery or new insight, which when documented and disseminated contributes to or modifies existing knowledge or practice. Research differs from clinical practice in: the need for metareflection on the data, goals, roles, beneficiaries, use of knowledge, and consumers. Research is not creative activity for its own sake, nor is it creativity within a clinical situation which is not accompanied by systematic, self-monitored inquiry.

A theory is a set of interrelated principles or constructs which have been created by a theorist to describe, organize, explain, and explicate empirical facts and phenomena within a particular domain, and thereby provide a conceptual framework for decision-making. Research and theory have the same goal—to increase knowledge and understanding of music therapy; however, a theory goes beyond research in dealing with a much broader domain of knowledge and in offering a fuller and more articulate conception of it. There is a clearer distinction made between theory and research in the quantitative paradigm than in the qualitative paradigm. Theory and research do not include expository or clinical writings which do not have a data base, or which lack systematic, self-monitored methods of inquiry. Music therapy theories may be based on research and/or clinical practice, and may deal with discipline, profession, or foundational topics.

Chapter Twenty-five

TOPICS OF RESEARCH[1]

As pointed out in the very first chapter, music therapy is both discipline and profession. As a discipline, it is an organized body of knowledge and practices essentially concerned with the process by which therapists use music to help client promote health. As a profession, music therapy is an organized group of people who share, utilize, and advance this body of knowledge and practices through their work as clinicians, supervisors, theorists, researchers, administrators, and educators.

Given this distinction, the topics of research for these two aspects of music therapy are quite different. Whereas discipline research is concerned with how music therapists interact with clients using music for therapeutic purposes, profession research is concerned with how music therapists interact with one another and with other professionals, along with the socioeconomic, political, and educational conditions affecting the discipline of music therapy. Notice that while discipline research is essentially client-centered, profession research is essentially therapist-centered.

TOPICS ON THE DISCIPLINE

Research on the discipline of music therapy deals with three broad topical areas: assessment, treatment, and evaluation. Assessment studies are those aimed at gaining insights about individual clients or client populations served by music therapy—their conditions, problems, resources, experiences and therapeutic needs. To belong within the

---

[1] This chapter is an excerpt from a previous work by the author entitled, "The Boundaries of Music Therapy Research." In B. Wheeler (Ed.) (1995), *Music Therapy Research: Quantitative and Qualitative Perspectives*, pp. 17–27. Gilsum NH: Barcelona Publishers.

boundaries of music therapy, assessment studies must meet four criteria: the use of clients (as defined previously) as subjects or participants; the use of music as the primary source, method, or context for data collection; interpretation of the data in terms of both their musical and clinical significance; and the formulation of conclusions which relate specifically to the nature of the client, population, and/or condition. Put another way, a music therapy assessment study reveals how clients listen to, make, experience or otherwise respond to music under various conditions, and relates these data to their conditions, problems, resources, experiences, and therapeutic needs. Studies regarded as outside these parameters include those on the musical functioning of subjects who are not clients (as defined previously), and those on the functioning of clients outside of a musical or music therapy context.

    In contrast to assessment studies which pertain to the client and/or the client's condition, treatment studies focus on clinical interventions, or the methods used by a music therapist to induce change in the client. Included are topics such as the role of music in therapy, the specific role of the various musical elements, how clients respond to different types of music or musical experiences, the therapist's contribution to the therapeutic process, the way a particular method or technique is utilized with specific populations or problems, the effects of environmental conditions or interpersonal settings on the therapeutic process, the client-therapist relationship, the client-music relationship, the dynamics of therapy, etc. Studies regarded as outside of these boundaries are those which do not use music as a treatment modality (e.g., the use of dance in building gross motor skills), and those which do not focus on health concerns or clinical problems (e.g., the effects of background music on sales).

    While treatment studies focus on methods of therapist intervention, evaluation studies focus on the resulting process of change in the client. As such, evaluation research is concerned with the outcomes or effects of music therapy. These outcomes may be either musical and/or nonmusical changes or accomplishments made by the client. Essentially, evaluation research poses two basic questions: Were the methods used in music therapy effective? And, did the client and his/her condition improve as result of these methods? Of course, evaluation studies can deal with a wide range of related topics such as the sequence of changes made by clients during music therapy, a client's experience of his/her own change, and products resulting from therapy which reflect such changes (e.g., songs or improvisations created by the client). Studies which do not fall within these topical boundaries are those that deal with treatment methods other than music therapy, and those that focus on changes in the client which are not considered therapeutic in nature.

TOPICS ON THE PROFESSION

Research on the profession covers a wide spectrum of interrelated topics, such as:

- *Employment practices:* where music therapists work; trends in employment opportunities; job titles, salaries and benefits, reimbursement; job duties and tasks in various settings; qualification requirements for employment; how music therapy services fit into various health-care systems and institutions; policies and procedures for the provision of music therapy services; role of a music therapy administrator; accountability issues in music therapy; etc.
- *Music therapists:* personality profiles of professionals and students; attitudes toward various matters related to clinical practice, employment, etc; values and orientations; motivation and burn-out; professional self-esteem and identity issues; demographic information; existing levels of education and competence, etc.
- *Professional education and training:* academic requirements and curricula in music therapy at various levels; field training and internship requirements; methods of teaching and supervising, and their effectiveness; etc.
- *Professional standards:* standards for clinical practice in music therapy; rules governing the ethical conduct of music therapists; ethical issues and problems in practice, research, and theory; competency standards and procedural requirements for becoming registered or certified in the field; relevance of these standards and requirements to job analyses;

accreditation and approval standards for academic and clinical training programs, etc.

- *Legislation and public relations:* how laws and regulations on the city, state, and federal level impact on music therapy; licensing issues; political and cultural factors in the advancement of music therapy; how music therapy relates to other disciplines and professions; cooperative ventures with other professionals or organizations; etc.

- *History and culture:* historical accounts of the discipline or profession of music therapy; organizational history; biographies of music therapists; cultural aspects of music therapy practice; meta-analyses and descriptions of the research literature, etc.

FOUNDATIONAL RESEARCH TOPICS

Because music therapy is so interdisciplinary in nature, there are many areas of research which overlap or relate to the above topics, but do not, strictly speaking, fall within the boundaries of music therapy. Such research can be considered "foundational" because though not always completely generalizable to clinical problems in music therapy, the findings often provide empirical support for related concepts or notions. For example, the following are foundational topics for the discipline of music therapy:

- Research studies on music which do not pertain to client populations (as defined earlier), their conditions, problems, needs, experiences, etc., or the process of therapy. Such studies instead belong under the the categories of psychology or physiology of music, sociology or anthropology of music, acoustics or psychoacoustics, music learning, music education, etc., all of which are regarded as foundations for music therapy.

- Research studies on clients and/or therapy which do not pertain to music. This includes studies on the problems and needs of client populations without reference to music, and studies on various forms of therapy which do not employ music.

Similarly, foundational topics for the profession include any study which pertains to health care, other health professions and professionals, and any socioeconomic, political, or cultural factors which impact on them.

SUMMARY

Discipline research is any systematic, self-monitored inquiry which leads to a discovery regarding how a therapist uses music to help clients achieve health. Included are studies on assessment, treatment, and evaluation. To fall within the boundaries of discipline research, the topic must include these four elements: the client, the therapist, the musical experience, and the therapeutic process. Topics considered foundational to discipline research include those studies which deal with any one of these elements, with the more relevant studies dealing with two or three of them.

Profession research is any systematic, self-monitored inquiry which leads to a discovery regarding music therapists, professional standards, education and training, employment, history, and public relations, and conditions affecting the discipline of music therapy. Topics considered foundational to profession research include those studies which deal with any of these topics, but in relation to a profession other than music therapy.

Chapter Twenty-six

DEFINING QUANTITATIVE
AND
QUALITATIVE RESEARCH[1]

Quantitative and qualitative research represent two completely different and mutually exclusive world views about the nature of truth, reality, and the possibilities of knowing either. Quantitative researchers subscribe to the "positivist" view, and qualitative researchers subscribe to a number of different views, which we will simply call "nonpositivist."

Positivists believe that absolute truth and reality exist in the form of immutable laws and mechanisms of nature. Research can reveal the truth and the way things *really* are by discovering time- and context-free generalizations. A primary purpose is to explain phenomena in terms of cause-effect relationships. Generalizations about these relationships are more meaningful than idiographic statements. The discoveries of science are additive, thus each research finding adds a fact to a general repository of human knowledge about the real world.

Nonpositivists believe that truth and reality exist in the form of multiple, intangible mental constructions, which are influenced by individuals and social experiences. Research reveals not whether these constructions are true or real, but whether they are "more or less informed and/or sophisticated" (p. 111). All discoveries are bound to the time and context of the inquiry; idiographic statements are more meaningful than generalizations. It is not possible to separate cause and effect, as all entities are in a constant state of reciprocal influence. Science does not add to

---

[1] This chapter is taken from a previous work by the author entitled, "Differences between Quantitative and Qualitative Research Paradigms: Implications for Music Therapy." In B. Wheeler (Ed.) (1995), *Music Therapy Research: Quantitative and Qualitative Perspectives,* pp. 65–76. Gilsum, NH: Barcelona Publishers.

previous knowledge of reality, but rather reconstructs previous constructions of it.

Positivists believe that the researcher and subject are independent entities, and that with the proper methodological precautions, the researcher can make the subject an "object" of investigation without being biased. For positivists, the best way to study other human beings is to be as objective as possible. All research must be value-free.

Nonpositivists believe that researcher and "participant" are linked together through their relationship, and that together they create their own truth and reality. Methodological precautions cannot remove the reciprocal influences of this relationship. Thus the way to study other human beings is to be as human as possible within a relationship. All research is value-bound.

QUANTITATIVE RESEARCH

Quantitative research is essentially concerned with three variables: stimulus, organismic, and response. Stimulus variables are those pertaining to input or any aspect of the physical or psychological environment that elicits or arouses a response, including treatments or interventions. Organismic (or subject) variables are those pertaining to persons, including any physical, emotional, behavioral, or social characteristic or trait. Response variables are those pertaining to output or any type of reaction that subjects make to the input. These are important to mention here because they will provide the principal focuses or topics for quantitative research.

Although quantitative studies pose myriad kinds of questions, both simple and compound, the following are prototypical (though not all-inclusive):

- Incidence: What is the frequency or prevalence of a particular phenomenon?
- Measurement: What is the most accurate and reliable way of measuring a particular variable?
- Correlation: How does one variable fluctuate in relation to another?

- Factoring: What factors are common or unique among different variables?
- Development: How does a variable change as a function of time or growth?
- Comparison: Are there any differences between two or more sets of variables?
- Treatment: Does a variable change as the result of a particular treatment?
- Interaction: Are the differences between two variables the result of another variable?

Quantitative research usually begins by operationally defining the phenomena of interest. The purpose of an operational definition is to reduce each part of the phenomenon to "variables" which can be observed and measured. The word "reduce" is used because as the result of an operational definition, covert aspects of the phenomena are reduced to overt events that accompany them, and subjective insights of the researcher are controlled, discounted, or regarded as only secondary in significance to objective evidence. Once the phenomena have been defined in quantifiable terms, the study is then designed so that: "extraneous" variables will be eliminated or controlled, "independent" variables will be systematically manipulated or controlled, and "dependent" variables will be accurately observed and measured. In "descriptive" studies, the design involves gathering data about the present, with little or no intervention by the researcher; in "experimental" studies, the design involves administering some form of intervention or treatment to subjects in order to determine the effects. Subjects for both types of studies are selected so that they constitute a representative sample of the populations being studied, thereby allowing generalization from the research subjects to larger populations. Hypotheses are formulated prior to data collection regarding the likelihood that cause-effect or predictive relationships exist between the variables. Data are collected using uniform or standardized procedures and materials, and efforts are made to ensure reliability of the measures. The data are then analyzed through various levels of statistical treatment (e.g., central tendencies and normal distributions, correlation and regression, analysis of variance, etc.), and as a result, the hypotheses are proved or disproved on the basis of statistical probability. Probability statements give numerical intervals of confidence (e.g., .05 or .01) for accepting or rejecting the hypotheses as true or false. Essentially, this reveals whether the predictive or causal relationship under investigation really exists or whether it can be attributed to chance.

QUALITATIVE RESEARCH

In contrast to the quantitative focus on stimulus, organismic, or response variables, qualitative studies focus on entire phenomena which have not been reduced to specific variables. There are four broad categories of foci for qualitative research: 1) events (behaviors, interactions, incidents, contextual conditions); 2) experiences (how persons apprehend, perceive, feel, and think about an event, person, or thing); 3) materials (objects that result from events or experiences); and 4) persons.

A qualitative study might focus on one or more of these phenomena and subcategories within them, depending on the purpose of the inquiry. In contrast to quantitative research, where detailed research questions and hypotheses are formulated beforehand, the qualitative researcher establishes a broad purpose for the inquiry. The following goals are typical:

- Holistic description: the elaboration and construction of an entire phenomenal field, with attention to its context.
- Description of essence: the identification of those properties of a phenomenon that give it its essential meaning.
- Analysis: the identification, classification, and explanation of patterns, recurrences, themes, and regularities that can be observed in a phenomenon.
- Theory building: the development of propositions, constructs, and principles which describe and give insight into the phenomenon.
- Interpretation: the explication of deep or latent structures, or layers of meaning embedded in a phenomenon.
- Re-creation: the reconstruction of a phenomenon through the use of symbols, metaphors, images, art, music, dance, drama, etc.

- Critique: a critical evaluation of the data, phenomenon, or research study itself.
- Self-exploration: the researcher's analysis and interpretation of his/her own event processes, experiences, or materials.

Qualitative research begins by establishing a broad focus for the inquiry which is refined as the study progresses. No attempts are made to identify or define all of the variables deemed important, to operationally define the variables, or to formulate specific hypotheses regarding research outcomes. The intent is to examine the phenomenon openly and as it is— without manipulation, control, or interference by the researcher, yet within an interpersonal context.

After a focus has been established, the next step is to identify instances of the phenomenon or "cases." A case may be an individual client or group, a therapist, a treatment program or method, a therapeutic event, a form of musical experience, etc. In some instances, one case is sufficient to accomplish the research goal; in others, more than one case may be selected. Samples of cases may be selected to maintain homogeneity or to maximize heterogeneity, to find extreme or deviant cases or to focus on typical or critical cases, and to confirm or disconfirm previous findings or existing data. The purpose of sampling several cases is to gain a wholistic picture of the phenomenon in all its variation; it is not to find a representative sample of a population so that generalizations can be made. Instead, each case is regarded as a unique whole, as well as a unique part of a larger whole.

The most commonly used methods of data collections in qualitative research are naturalistic observation, interview, and the study of artifacts. Specific procedures are kept open-ended, so that different techniques and approaches can be developed as needed, according to what and how the phenomenon presents itself. There are, however, two major considerations. First, the researcher attempts to study the phenomenon in its natural setting, not in an artificial or laboratory setting. This "ecological" approach allows the researcher to study the phenomenon within its own context, where its essential features and meanings can be most easily apprehended. Hence, there is no clear separation of stimulus and response or cause and effect. The phenomenon and its context are inseparable and reciprocal in influence.

Second, whenever necessary and appropriate, the researcher may have direct contact and involvement with the subjects or phenomena under investigation. Thus, the researcher may be both participant and observer. This active engagement gives the researcher the first-hand experiences and empathy needed to understand the subjects or phenomena from an inside perspective.

In qualitative research, data are interpreted using inductive rather than deductive reasoning. That is, rather than trying to prove or disprove hypotheses formulated before data collection, the qualitative researcher allows working hypotheses to emerge with the data. Thus, inductive analysis is an explication of whatever realities present themselves, whereas deductive analysis is a directed search for specific facts or truths.

Chapter Twenty-seven

IMPLICATIONS

In the previous chapters, problems in defining music and therapy were identified, a working definition of music therapy was presented in detail, and distinctions were made between areas and levels of practice, and between various approaches to research and theory. The purpose of this chapter is to examine what implications all of this has for both the discipline and profession of music therapy. In what ways might the information in this book influence music therapy theory, practice and research? How might the book affect education, training, and credentialing in the field?

FOR THE DISCIPLINE

Music therapy is too diverse and complex in clinical practice to be defined or contained by a single approach, model, method, setting, population, practitioner, or training program. Furthermore, it cannot be delimited or defined only in terms of a single area or level of practice. Thus, for example, didactic music therapy is not the entire discipline, nor is any other area of practice (e.g., medical, psychotherapeutic); similarly, a particular level of practice (i.e., augmentative, intensive, or primary) is not the entire discipline. Each area and level of practice is only a part of the whole, and should not be mistaken for the whole of music therapy. Another way of saying this is that music therapy practice has a collective identity that both includes and goes beyond the individual identities of all practitioners.

Similarly, music therapy is too diverse and complex to be embraced by a single theory of music, a single theory of therapy, a single theory of music therapy, or a single method of theorizing. And the same holds for research. Practice and theory are too diverse and complex to be served or contained by a single approach to research. Both quantitative and qualitative paradigms are needed to address the full range of questions and problems that inhere in the discipline.

Practice, theory, and research are interdependent and equally important; however, ultimately, each serves a different purpose. Music therapy is first and foremost a discipline of practice, with the specific purpose of helping clients to promote health. The purpose of research and theory is to enhance our knowledge about clinical practice, and thereby facilitate its aims.

FOR THE PROFESSION

Given the diversity and complexity of music therapy, it is impossible to prepare music therapists to practice all areas and levels within the confines of an undergraduate degree. Thus, different areas and levels of practice should be taught at the undergraduate and graduate levels, and credentials in the field should reflect these differences in competence. In terms of the present classification, the undergraduate degree (and graduate equivalency curriculum) should introduce students to *all* areas of practice, while preparing them to practice each area only at the augmentative level. The credential earned upon completion of entry level training should reflect this delimitation in preparation. The master's degree in music therapy should prepare students to practice one or more areas at the intensive level, while also imparting basic skills in research and theory. An advanced credential should be created to reflect this level of competence. A doctoral degree in music therapy, separate from any other discipline, is needed in the field. Its purpose would be to prepare students to practice at the primary level, while also imparting advanced skills in research and theory.

Professional associations in music therapy have a responsibility to represent and promote *all* areas and levels of music therapy, or to state their delimitations in this regard in all published materials. The identity of music therapy that any association projects should be consistent with clinical practice, theory, and research, rather than with any professional image demanded in the current marketplace. In other words, the profession of music therapy has to define itself according to the discipline, rather than according to its socioeconomic or political environment.

Similarly, music therapists have to define themselves in terms of where they fit within the discipline, that is, according to the specific areas and levels of music therapy they practice, and their orientations with regard to research and theory. It is time for us to recognize that we cannot be masters of the entire discipline—music therapy has grown far too much for that to be possible. We are all specialists in a vast and diverse field. Thus, music therapy can no longer be defined in terms of what I do, or in terms of what you do—it is what we all do, and it is constantly growing.

Appendix

DEFINITIONS OF MUSIC THERAPY

Agrotou: "Music therapy is the use of predominantly improvised music as a vehicle for transference and countertransference. Improvised music, created by the patient, therapist, or both, reflects the state of the patient-therapist relationship at any given moment. Music addresses the affective state of the patient in the 'here and now' of the therapeutic relationship, and also what this represents in his fantasy world and own psychic history" (1993, p. 184).

Alley: "Music therapy in the schools is the functional use of music to accomplish specific pupil progress in an academic, social, motor, or language area. Music therapy for the special child deals with inappropriate behaviors or disabilities and functions as a related service, a supportive service that assists a handicapped child to benefit from special education" (1979, p.118).

Alvin: "Music therapy is the controlled use of music in the treatment, rehabilitation, education and training of children and adults suffering from physical, mental, or emotional disorder" (1975, p. 4).

Association for Professional Music Therapists in Great Britain: "Music therapy is a form of treatment whereby a mutual relationship is set up between patient and therapist, enabling changes to occur in the condition of the patient and therapy to take place. The therapist works with a variety of patients, both children and adults, who may have emotional, physical, mental or psychological handicaps. By using music creatively in a clinical setting, the therapist seeks to establish an interaction, a shared musical experience and activitiy leading to the pursuit of the therapeutic goals determined by the patient's pathology" (Association pamphlet entitled "A Career in Music Therapy").

Australian Association for Music Therapy: Music therapy is "the planned use of music to achieve therapeutic aims with children and adults who have special needs because of social, emotional, physical, or intellectual problems" (Association pamphlet).

Austrian Association of Professional Music Therapists: Music therapy is a medically prescribed method of treatment which is carried out by persons with appropriate training. It is a diagnosis-specific therapeutic method which attempts to effectively influence psychical process through acoustic and musical stimuli. It is based on the experience and knowledge of the effects of music on the emotions of physically and mentally ill persons" (Association brochure, 1986; Maranto, 1993, p. 64).

Bang: "Music therapy is the controlled application of specially organised music activities with the intention of furthering the development and cure during the treatment, education, and rehabilitation of children and adults with motor, sensory, or emotional handicaps . . . The aim of the music therapist is centered on the client, and is not starting from the music" (1986, p. 20).

Barcellos: "Music therapy is the use of music and/or its integral elements as an intermediate object of a relationship that permits the development of a therapeutic process, mobilizing bio-psychosocial reactions in the individual for the purpose of minimizing his specific problems and facilitating his integration/reintegration into a normal social environment" (1982, p. 2–3).

Benenzon: "From a scientific point of view, music therapy is a branch of science that deals with the study and investigation of the sound-man complex, whether the sound is musical or not, so as to discover the diagnostic elements and the therapeutic methods inherent in it. From a therapeutic point of view, music therapy is a para-medical discipline that uses sound, music, and movement to produce regressive effects and to open channels of communication that will enable us to start the process of training and recovering the patient for society" (1981, p. 3).

Bonny: Music therapy is "the systematic application of music as directed by the music therapist to bring about changes in the emotional and/or physical health of the person. As such, its functional rather than aesthetic and entertainment aspects are emphasized" (1986, p. 4).

Boxill: "Music therapy is an amalgam of music and therapy. When music, as an agent of change, is used to establish a therapeutic relationship, to nurture a person's growth and development, to assist in self-actualization, the process is music therapy. Broadly defined, music therapy is the use of music as a therapeutic tool for the restoration, maintenance, and improvement of psychological, mental, and physiological health and for the habilitation, rehabilitation, and maintenance of behavioral, developmental, physical, and social skills—all within the context of a client-therapist relationship" (1985, p. 5).

Bright: "Music therapy is the planned use of music to improve the functioning in his environment of an individual or a group of clients who have social, intellectual, physical or emotional needs of a special nature. Music therapy is carried out by a trained music therapist working in the context of a clinical team" (1981, p. 1).

Bruscia: "Music therapy is an interpersonal process involving therapist(s) and client(s) in certain role relationships and in a variety of musical experiences, all designed to help the client find the resources needed to resolve problems and increase the potential for wellness" (1984b).

"Music therapy is an interpersonal process wherein musical experiences are used to improve, maintain, or restore the well-being of the client" (1986, p. 1).

"Music therapy is a goal-directed process in which the therapist helps the client to improve, maintain, or restore a state of well-being, using musical experiences and the relationships that develop through them as dynamic forces of change" (1987a, p. 5).

"Music therapy is an interpersonal process in which the therapist uses music and all of its facets—physical, emotional, mental, social, aesthetic, and spiritual—to help clients to improve, restore or maintain health" (1991, p. 5).

Bunt: Music therapy is "the use of organised sounds and music within an evolving relationship between client and therapist to support and encourage physical, mental, social and emotional well-being" (1994, p. 8).

Canadian Association for Music Therapy: Music therapy is "the use of music to aid the physical, psychological and emotional integration of the individual, and in the treatment of illness or disability. It can be applied to all age groups, in a variety of treatment settings. Music has a non-verbal quality but offers a wide opportunity for verbal and vocal expression. As a member of a therapeutic team, the professional Music Therapist participated in the assessment of client needs, the formulation of an approach and programme for the individual client, and then carries out specific musical activities to reach the goals. Regular evaluations assess and ensure programme effectiveness. The nature of music therapy emphasizes a creative approach in work with handicapped individuals. Music therapy provides a viable and humanistic approach that recognizes and develops the often untapped inner resources of the client. Music therapists wish to help the individual to move towards an improved self-concept, and in the broadest sense, to develop each human being to their own greatest potential" (From brochure entitled "About Music Therapy").

Carter: "Music therapy is the scientific application of music or music activities to attain therapeutic goals. Music therapy also can be defined as the structured use of music to bring about desired changes in behavior" (1982, p. 5).

Codding: "Music therapy is the scientific application of music and the therapist's skills to bring about desirable changes in human behavior . . . The structure provided by the therapeutic environment, and the relationship between therapist and child, child and peers, facilitates the learning of necessary life skills. Children may learn skills which facilitate the effective emotional, social, communicative, [social,] and academic functioning over time" (1982, p. 22).

Colon: Music therapy is "the scientific study which engages in the investigation and analysis of the sonorous musical complex world every human being has internally, with the objective of obtaining positive changes in his conduct" (Bruscia, 1984a, p. 15).

"Music therapy is a scientific technique which investigates, explores and analyzes the musical feelings and emotions that emerge from the deepest intrapsychic dynamics of the human being with the goal of modifying these behaviors" (Colon, 1993, p. 490).

Costa: "Music therapy is a self-expressive therapy which uses music in the latent sense, as an intermediary object, in the relationship between music therapist and patient, and which uses the bio-psycho-social aspects of the individual, opening new channels of communication which help that individual to recuperate and integrate dynamically with himself and his social group" (Maranto, 1993, p. 104-105).

DeBacker & Peuskens: Anthroposophic music therapy is "a process of working harmoniously with the person through music. This harmony begins at the individual's current level of development; its goal is to the lead the individual farther along on his or her own developmental path. This is done receptive as well as actively, with the music often acting as a catalyst (1993, p. 90).

Del Campo: "Music therapy is the scientific application of sound, music and movement, which through listening, training, and the execution of instrumental sounds, contribute to the integration of cognitive, affective and motor aspects, developing the conscience and strengthening the creative process. The goals of music therapy are: 1) to facilitate the communication process, 2) to promote individual expression and 3) to improve social integration" (1993. p. 547).

DiFranco & Perilli: "Music therapy is a discipline which utilizes the sound-music language within the patient-therapist relationship in a systematic process of intervention. A characteristic of music therapy in Italy is its multidisciplinary context wherein its basic elements (patient, therapist, sound) are viewed from a medical perspective (its diagnostic potential), a psychological perspective (its evaluative potential) or a musical perspective (its potential for utilization of sound language for and in the professional relationship)" (1993, p. 322).

Doyle: Music therapy is "the use of music within a specific environment to inspire, liberate, and nurture the discovery process of each individual. In the involvement with music, individuals draw forth their imaginations, make choices and realize dreams" (1989, p. 81).

Fleshman & Fryear: Music therapy is the use of music "in a therapeutic environment, to influence changes in the patient's feelings and behavior" (1981).

French Association for Music Therapy: Music therapy is "the use of sounds and music in a psychotherapeutic relation" (Bruscia, 1984a, p.16)

Gomes & Leite: "Music therapy, as viewed by its practitioners in Portugal, is a model of intervention within the fields of mental health and special education; it involves the use of music as an intrinsic element within a tri-polar system including music, client and therapist/educator. Music provides an activity and/or the content of an activity that is adapted to the functioning level of the client and directed by the therapist/educator to the achievement of nonmusical goals" (1993, p. 480).

Guaraldi: Music therapy is the use of "active and passive musical activities in order to relieve and resocialize adults or children with various kinds of handicaps which limit their relational or social experiences . . ." (Bruscia, 1984a, p. 17).

Hadsell: Music therapy is "the use of the unique properties and potential of music in a therapeutic situation for the purpose of changing human behavior so that the individual affected will be more able to function as a worthwhile member of today's as well as tomorrow's society" (1974, p. 114).

Hesser: "Music therapy is the conscious use of the power of sound and music for therapy and healing . . . The music therapist's work is to tap the unique potential of sound and music for the health and well-being of the clients. The music therapist is an artist who sensitively and creativly moves with and guides the process of music therapy" (1995, p. 46).

Jondittir: "Music therapy is the structured use of music, sound and movement to obtain therapeutic goals aimed at the restoration, maintenance, and development of mental, physical, and emotional health. In a systematic manner, a specially trained individual uses the properties and unique potentials of music and sound, and the relationship that develops through musical experiences to alter human behavior, to assist the individual to use his fullest potential, to communicate his uniqueness and to increase his well-being" (1993, p. 280).

Kortegaard & Pedersen: "In Denmark, there is no recognized definition of music therapy . . . A very broad definition . . . may be provided however: music therapy is the use of music in the treatment/development of resources, wherein the music is an essential factor in the therapeutic relationship. The role of function of the music can vary from relationship to relationship" (1993, p. 198).

Kenny: "Music therapy is a process and form which combines the healing aspects of music with the issues of human need for the benefit of the individual and hence society. The music therapist serves as a resource person and guide, providing musical experiences which direct clients towards health and well-being" (1982, p.7).

Lecourt: Music therapy is the "use of sound (including noise) and music (receptive or creative, pre-recorded or live) within a therapist-patient relationship for psychotherapeutic or re-educative purposes" (1993, p. 222).

Lehtonen: In Finland, music therapy could be defined as "a curative process between music, music therapist and one or more clients; its purpose is to promote the client's health. The most important part of this process is the social interaction between the personalities of the music therapist and his/her clients. Music promotes communication by activating different kinds of psychic phenomena and by bringing new material into the communication process . . . the individual is able to express and feel experiences which are nonverbal and nondiscursive, such as bodily rhythms and unconscious and traumatic experiences which are anchored in the early childhood of the individual (1993, p. 212).

Mid-Atlantic Music Therapy Region: National Association for Music Therapy: "Music therapy is the structured use of music as a creative process to develop and maintain maximum human potential. Music therapy is used successfully in areas of social, motor, communication skill development, academic achievement, and behavioral management. Utilizing re-educative goals music therapy aids in fostering optimum functioning through a variety of experiences" (From brochure entitled "Music Therapy for Mental Health").

Munro & Mount: "Music therapy is the controlled use of music, its elements and their influences on the human being to aid in the physiologic, psychologic, and emotional integration of the individual during the treatment of an illness or disability" (1978, p. 1029).

National Association for Music Therapy: Music therapy is "the use of music in the accomplishment of therapeutic aims: the restoration, maintenance, and improvement of mental and physical health. It is the systematic application of music, as directed by the music therapist in a therapeutic environment, to bring about desirable changes in behavior. Such changes enable the individual undergoing therapy to experience a greater understanding of himself and the world about him, thereby achieving a more appropriate adjustment to society. As a member of the therapeutic team the professional music therapist participates in the analysis of individual problems and in the projection of general treatment aims before planning and carrying out specific music activities. Periodic evaluations are made to determine the effectiveness of the procedures employed" (From brochure entitled "A Career in Music Therapy," 1980).

"Music therapy is the specialized use of music in the service of persons with needs in mental health, physical health, habilitation, rehabilitation, or special education...the purpose is to help individuals attain and maintain their maximum levels of functioning." (From NAMT *Standards of Clinical Practice*, 1983).

"Music therapy is the scientific application of the art of music to accomplish therapeutic aims. It is the use of music and of the therapist's self to influence changes in behavior (From brochure entitled "Music Therapy as a Career," 1960).

Natanson: "Music therapy is a planned activity which aims at re-humanizing contemporary life-style through the many facets of the musical experience, to protect and restore the client's health, and to improve both the environment and social relationships therein. In this definition, 'planned' refers to 'deliberate action with established function, course and goals.' The restoration and protection of health refers to 'acting in the areas of prophylaxis, therapy, and rehabilitation.' By 'health' the author implies not only the lack of illness, but also the feelings of well-being in physical, psychological and social domains" (Maranto, 1993, p. 460).

National Coalition of Arts Therapies Associations: "Music therapy is the use of music as a creative and structured therapeutic tool to improve and maintain skills in communication, socialization, motor development and functioning, sensory usage and the cognitive and affective domains" (NCATA brochure).

New Zealand Society for Music Therapy: "Music is a powerful and useful tool in establishing communication with children and adults in supporting learning and re-learning in intellectual, physical, social and emotional areas of need. This includes the use of music for preventative and rehabilitative purposes. Music so used in a variety of settings whether with individuals or groups is MUSIC THERAPY" (Bruscia, 1984a, p. 16).

"Music therapy is the planned use of music to support identified need where there is physical, intellectual, social or emotional dysfunction . . . Music therapy is based on the humanity of music, involving body, mind, and spirit. Music therapy is the bridge to communication" (Maranto, 1993, p. 424).

Nishihata: The Japanese Institute for Music Therapy defines music therapy as "a discipline dedicated to improving the quality of life, through the skillful use of music and its traditional medical interventions as designed by a music therapist, as a tool to restore, maintain and improve a client's mental, physical, emotional health and welfare" (Maranto, 1993, p. 342).

Odell: "Music therapy in the field of mental health is the use of music to allow an alternative means of communication and expression where words are not necessarily the most effective way to fulfill therapeutic aims for the client. These aims are worked towards through a developing relationship between client and therapist with practical music-making as the primary medium . . . Some common aims in music therapy are: encouraging motivation, providing a forum for exploration of feelings, developing social skills, self awareness and awareness of others, and stimulation of movement through improvisation and spontaneous music-making" (1988, p. 52).

Orff: "Orff Music Therapy is a multi-sensory therapy. The use of musical material - phonetic-rhythmic speech, free and metric rhythm, melos in speech and singing, the handling of instruments—is organised in such a way that it addresses itself to all the senses . . . " (1980, p. 9).

Paul: "Music therapy is a behavioral science and an aesthetic experience which uses music as a tool to bring about positive changes in human behavior. These changes include educational as well as rehabilitative, social, or emotional changes" (1982, p. 3).

Peters: Music therapy is "the prescribed, structured use of music or music activities under the direction of specially trained personnel (i.e., music therapists) to influence changes in maladaptive conditions or behavior patterns, thereby helping clients achieve therapeutic goals" (1987, p. 5).

Plach: Group Music Therapy is "the use of music or music activities as a stimulus for promoting new behaviors in and exploring predetermined individual or group goals in a group setting" (1980, p. 4). The four advantages of using music are its ability to: evoke feeling, provide a vehicle for expression, stimulate verbalizations, and provide a common starting place.

Polit: "Humanistic Music Therapy refers to the psychotherapeutic space wherein the personal and transpersonal development of the person through sound and music is facilitated, using an approach emphasizing respect, acceptance, empathy and congruence. Implicit in the holistic model is the interrelationship between sound and the whole human being, i.e., physical, mental, emotional, and spiritual components" (1993, p. 366).

Priestley: "Analytical Music Therapy is the symbolic use of improvised music by the music therapist and client to explore the client's inner life and provide the proclivity for growth. It is not a music lesson, psychoanalysis, or a magic therapy that enables the therapist or patient to transcend all problems; rather it is a form of treatment like with its own limitations and contraindications" (1980, p. 6–7).

Prinou: In Greece, music therapy is defined in various ways, such as: "the use of music as a therapeutic instrument...a psychotherapeutic activity involving music and often verbal activities to increase self-awareness through the sub-conscious, ultimately guiding the patient to behavior which meets his needs...an educational and psychotherapeutic tool used to discover the undeveloped capacities and intellectual status of the patient and to facilitate more rational thinking. Through both educational and psychotherapeutic interventions, the patient's personality is addressed...in the definition of the Greek association, both music and therapy are defined because each as a specific function with music therapy. Therapy is supported by sounds and music of all kinds: 1) to alleviate the patient's pain both physically and psychologically, 2) to bring the patient into a more harmonic relationship with himself and his environment, and 3) to give him, through musical education, a greater personal self-awareness and a discovery of his hidden capabilities" (1993, p. 240–241).

Rudenberg: Music therapy is "the use of music and music-related activities under the supervision of professionally trained individuals (i.e., music therapist) to assist a client or patient in attaining a prescribed therapeutic goal" (1982, p. 1).

Schmolz: " . . . taking the psychopathology and the personality level of the patient into consideration, music therapy aims at transforming and/or influencing certain aspects of the personality with goal directed musical means, within a multiple medical and/or special educational treatment plan. This integrated music therapy (it is never carried out on its own) thus enriches nonverbal therapeutic possibilities, both in individual and in group music therapy" (Bruscia, 1984a, p. 17).

Schomer: "Music therapy may be defined as the application of music to produce a condition of well-being in an individual" (1973, p. 95).

Sekeles: Music therapy is "the direct use of sound and music in order: to support diagnostic observation by specific tools of the media; to facilitate meaningful changes in the human organism and to improve physiological and psychological states; to develop music expression, which presumably, is essential for healthy life" (Bruscia, 1985, p. 10).

"A profession which utilizes the inherent therapeutic potential found in the basic components of music (frequency, duration, intensity, timbre) and in music as a complex art-form in order to preserve the patient's healthy capabilities, to promote beneficial change and development, and to enable the achievement of a better quality of life" (Maranto, 1993, p. 306).

Silva: "Music therapy is the collection of techniques and procedures which use sound, musical or otherwise, as a means to facilitate relationships, allowing the growth of the patient as a person while modifying emotional, mental and physical aspects of that person" (Maranto, 1993, p. 104).

South African Institute: Music therapy is "the planned use of music to give therapeutic effects" (Bruscia, 1984a, p. 18).

Southeastern Pennsylvania Music Therapy Supervisors: "Music therapy is the process by which the elements of musical experience are applied in a purposive and systematic way to establish, improve, and modify specific cognitive, emotional, physical, and social functions crucial to the development of the atypical individual" (From "Standards of Practice").

Steele: "Music therapy, as it is practiced at the Settlement, is the structuring of music learning and participation experiences, in order to modify inappropriate behavioral patterns and ineffective learning processes. Music is used in therapy as a reinforcer, as an extra-auditory cue, as a music learning experience, and to set the occasion for modifying nonmusical behavior" (1977, pp. 102–103).

Swedish Association for Music Therapy: Music therapy is "the use of music in educational and therapeutic settings in order to offer individuals with psychic, physical, and social handicaps possibilities to development" (Bruscia 1984a, p. 17).

Uruguayan Association for Music Therapy: Music therapy is "a paramedical career of scientific principles which comprises not only therapeutic aspects but also diagnostic and prophylaxis. In this process we have the patient and the music therapist in a determined situation with a fixed structure and in which there exists a dynamic integration by means of a sound stimuli. The music therapist, working with the group, uses musical sound stimuli to stimulate patients with physical, psychical, or psychosomatic problems, and observes the inertic changes in what he does, says, and expresses through other means. The patient answers the therapist's sound stimuli and reacts at the organic, emotional, behavioural, communicative, and movement levels of social integration. The music therapist's role is to employ a sound stimulus to stimulate the answers of a given situation which will tend to produce changes in the behaviour of the patient which will make him able to integrate with his own environment" (Bruscia 1984a, p. 15).

World Federation of Music Therapy: "Music therapy is the use of music and/or its musical elements (sound, rhythm, melody, and harmony) by a music therapist, and client or group, in a process designed to facilitate and promote communication, relationship, learning, mobilization, expression and organization (physical, emotional, mental, social and cognitive) in order to develop potentials and develop or restore functions of the individual so that he or she can achieve better intra- and interpersonal integration and, consequently a better quality of life" (Ruud, 1998, p. 53).

Yamamatsu: "Psychotherapy by music—music therapy should primarily be a part of educational activity not of medical service: it aims at discovery and cultivation of the client's potentialities, not at the cure of disease. In other words it should try to bring free self-expression from the clients" (Bruscia, 1984a, p. 15).

References

Agrotou, A. (1993a). Spontaneous Ritualised Play in Music Therapy: A Technical and Theoretical Analysis. In M. Heal & T. Wigram (Eds.), *Music Therapy in Health and Education.* (pp. 175–192). London: Jessica Kingsley Publishers.

Agrotou, A. (1993b). Music Therapy in Cyprus. In C. Maranto (Ed.), *Music Therapy: International Perspectives* (pp. 183–196). Pipersville PA: Jeffrey Books.

Aigen, K. (1990). Echoes of Silence. *Music Therapy: Journal of the American Association for Music Therapy, 9 (1),* 44–61.

Aigen, K. (1991a). The Voice of the Forest: A Conception of Music for Music Therapy. *Music Therapy: Journal of the American Association for Music Therapy, 10 (1),* 77–98.

Aigen, K. (1991b). Creative Fantasy, Music, and Lyric Improvisation with a Gifted, Acting-out Boy. In K. Bruscia (Ed.), *Case Studies in Music Therapy,* (pp. 109–126). Gilsum, NH: Barcelona Publishers.

Aigen, K. (1991c). The Roots of Music Therapy. Towards an Indigenous Research Paradigm. Unpublished doctoral dissertation, New York University (University Microfilms No. 9134717).

Aigen, K. (1995a). An Aesthetic Foundation of Clinical Theory: An Underlying Basis of Creative Music Therapy. In C. Kenny (Ed.), *Listening, Playing, Creating: Essays on the Power of Sound.* (pp. 233–257). Albany, NY: State University of New York.

Aigen, K. (1995b). Philosophical Inquiry. In B. Wheeler (Ed.), *Music Therapy Research: Quantitative and Qualitative Perspectives* (pp. 447–484). Gilsum, NH: Barcelona Publishers.

Aigen, K. (1996a). *Being in Music: Foundations of Nordoff-Robbins Music Therapy.* St. Louis, MO: MMB Music.

Aigen, K. (1996b, April). Thoughts on Nordoff-Robbins Music Therapy, Music Psychotherapy, and Psychotherapy. *International Association of Nordoff-Robbins Music Therapists Newsletter,* 8–12.

Aigen, K. (1998). *Paths of Development in Nordoff-Robbins Music Therapy.* Gilsum NH: Barcelona Publishers.

Aldridge, D. (1989). A Phenomenological Comparison of the Organization of Music and the Self. *The Arts in Psychotherapy, 16 (1),* 91–97.

Aldridge, D. (1996). *Music Therapy Research and Practice in Medicine.* London: Jessica Kingsley Publishers.

Alley, J. (1977). Education for the Severely Handicapped: The Role of Music Therapy. *Journal of Music Therapy, 14* (2), 50–59.

Alley, J. (1979). Music in the IEP: Therapy-education. *Journal of Music Therapy,16 (3),* 111–127.

Allison, D. (1988). Personal Communication.

Allison, D. (1991). Music Therapy at Childbirth. In K. Bruscia (Ed.), *Case Studies in Music Therapy* (pp. 529–546). Gilsum, NH: Barcelona Publishers.

Alvin, J. (1975). *Music Therapy* (Revised Paperback Edition). London: John Clare Books.

Alvin, J. (1976). *Music for the Handicapped Child.* New York: Oxford University Press.

Alvin, J. (1978). *Music Therapy for the Autistic Child.* New York: Oxford University Press.

Anderson, F., Colchado, J., & McAnally, P. (1979) *Art for the Handicapped.* Normal IL: Illinois State University.

Amir, D. (1996a). Experiencing Music Therapy: Meaningful Moments in the Music Therapy Process. In M. Langenberg, K. Aigen, & J. Frommer (Eds.), *Qualitative Music Therapy Research: Beginning Dialogues,*(pp. 109–130). Gilsum, NH: Barcelona Publishers.

Amir, D. (1996b). Music Therapy—Holistic Model. *Music Therapy: Journal of the American Association for Music Therapy 14 (1),* 44–60.

Ansdell, G. (1995). *Music for Life: Aspects of Creative Music Therapy with Adult Clients.* London: Jessica Kingsley Publishers.

Ansdell, G. (1996, April). An Open Letter to Ken Aigen. *International Association of Nordoff-Robbins Music Therapists Newsletter* (pp. 5–7). New York: International Association for Nordoff-Robbins Music Therapists.

Antonovsky, A. (1987). *Unraveling the Mystery of Health: How People Manage Stress and Stay Well.* San Francisco: Jossey-Bass Publishers.

Association for Professional Music Therapists in Great Britain (APMT) (1982). *A Career in Music Therapy.* Cambridge, England: Author.

Austin, D. (1996). The Role of Improvised Music in Psychodynamic Music Therapy. *Music Therapy: Journal of the American Association for Music Therapy 14 (1),* 29–43.

Australian Music Therapy Association (AMTA). (1984). Music Therapy Definition. In K. Bruscia (Ed.), *International Newsletter of Music Therapy* (Volume 2, p. 16). New York: American Association for Music Therapy.

Austrian Association of Professional Music Therapists (1986). Brochure on Music Therapy.

Bailey, L. (1983). The Effects of Live Music versus Tape-recorded Music on Hospitalized Cancer Patients. *Music Therapy: Journal of the American Association for Music Therapy, 3 (1),* 17–28.

Bailey. L. (1984). The Use of Songs in Music Therapy with Cancer Patients and Their Families. *Music Therapy: Journal of the American Association for Music Therapy, 4 (1)*, 5–17.

Bang, C. (1986). A World of Sound and Music. Music Therapy and Musical Speech Therapy with Hearing-impaired and Multiple-handicapped Children. In E. Ruud (Ed.), *Music and Health* (pp. 19–36). Oslo, Norway: Norsk Musikforlag.

Barcellos, L. (1982). Music as a Therapeutic Element. Paper presented at the First International Symposium on Music and Man. New York University, June 1982, New York City.

Barrickman, J. (1990). A Developmental Music Therapy Approach for Preschool Hospitalized Children. *Music Therapy Perspectives, 7*, 10–16.

Bartram, P. (1991). Improvisation and Play in the Therapeutic Engagement of a Five year old Boy with Physical and Interpersonal Problems. In K. Bruscia (Ed.), *Case Studies in Music Therapy* (pp. 137–152). Gilsum, NH: Barcelona Publishers.

Batcheller, J. & Monsour, S. (1983). *Music in Recreation and Leisure* (2nd Edition). Dubuque, IA: W.C. Brown.

Bateson, G. (1980). *Mind and Nature: A Necessary Unity.* Fort Collins: Fontana.

Beaulieu, J. (1987). *Music and Sound in the Healing Arts.* Barrytown, NY: Station Hill Press.

Beer, L. (1990). Music Therapy: Sounding Your Myth. *Music Therapy: Journal of the American Association for Music Therapy, 9 (1)*, 35–43.

Beggs, C. (1991). Life Review with a Palliative Care Patient. In K. Bruscia (Ed.), *Case Studies in Music Therapy,* (pp. 611–616). Gilsum, NH: Barcelona Publishers.

Benenzon, R. (1981). *Music Therapy Manual.* Springfield, IL: Charles C Thomas Publishers.

Berendt, J. (1983). *Nada Brahma: The World is Sound.* Rochester VT: Destiny Books.

Bitcon, C. (1976). *Alike and Different: The Clinical and Educational Uses of Orff-Schulwerk.* Santa Ana, CA: Rosha Press.

Bloch, S. (1982). *What is Psychotherapy?* New York: Oxford University.

Bohm, D. (1980). *Wholeness and the Implicate Order.* London: Routledtge & Kegan Paul.

Bonny, H. (1978). *Facilitating GIM Sessions.* (First Monograph). Salina, KS: Bonny Foundation for Music-centered Therapies.

Bonny, H. (1986). Music and Healing. *Music Therapy: Journal of the American Association for Music Therapy, 6A (1)*, 3–12.

Bonny, H., & Savary, L. (1973). *Music and Your Mind.* New York: Harper Row.

Boone, P. (1991). Composition, Improvisation, and Poetry in the Psychiatric Treatment of a Forensic Patient. In K. Bruscia (Ed.), *Case Studies in Music Therapy,* (pp. 433–450). Gilsum, NH: Barcelona Publishers.

Borczon, R. (1997). *Music Therapy: Group Vignettes.* Gilsum NH: Barcelona Publishers.

Bowers, J. (1998). Effects of an Intergenerational Choir for Community-based Seniors and College Students on Age-Related Attitudes. *Journal of Music Therapy 35 (1),* 2–18.

Boxill, E. (1985). *Music Therapy for the Developmentally Disabled.* Rockville, MD: Aspen Systems.

Boxill, E. (1988). Continuing Notes: Worldwide Networking for Peace. *Music Therapy: Journal of the American Association for Music Therapy, 7 (1),* 80–81.

Boxill, E. (1989). Continuing Notes: Having Courage to Act. *Music Therapy: Journal of the American Association for Music Therapy 8 (1),* 133–136.

Boxill, E. (1997). *The Miracle of Music Therapy.* Gilsum NH: Barcelona Publishers.

Briggs, C. (1991). A Model for Understanding Musical Development. *Music Therapy: Journal of the American Association for Music Therapy, 10 (1),* 1–21.

Bright, R. (1972). *Music in Geriatric Care.* New York: Musicgraphics.

Bright, R. (1981). *Practical Planning in Music Therapy for the Aged.* New York: Musicgraphics.

Bright, R. (1993). Cultural Aspects of Music in Therapy. In M. Heal & T. Wigram (Eds.), *Music Therapy in Health and Education* (pp.193–207). London: Jessica Kingsley Publishers.

Brodsky, W. (1991). A Personal Perspective of the Power of Music and Mass Communication, Prior to and During the Gulf War Crisis in Israel: Implications for Music Therapy. *Music Therapy: Journal of the American Association for Music Therapy 10 (1),* 99–113.

Broucek, M. (1987). Beyond Healing to "Whole-ing:" A Voice for the Deinstitutionalization of Music Therapy. *Music Therapy: Journal of the American Association for Music Therapy Music Therapy 6 (2),* 50–58.

Bruscia, K. (1984a). *International Newsletter of Music Therapy.* (Volume 2). New York: American Association for Music Therapy.

Bruscia, K. (1984b). Are We Losing Our Identity as MUSIC Therapists? Paper presented at the annual conference of the Mid-Atlantic Region of the National Association for Music Therapy, April 5, 1984, Philadelphia, PA.

Bruscia, K. (Ed.) (1985). *International Newsletter of Music Therapy.* (Volume 3). Springfield NJ: American Association for Music Therapy.

Bruscia, K. (1986a). *Music Therapy Brief.* Philadelphia: Temple University, Esther Boyer College of Music.

Bruscia, K. (1986b). Advanced Competencies in Music Therapy. *Music Therapy: Journal of the American Association for Music Therapy 6A (1),* 57–67.

Bruscia, K. (1987a). *Improvisational Models of Music Therapy.* Springfield, IL: Charles C Thomas Publishers.

Bruscia, K. (1987b). Professional Identity Issues in Music Therapy Education. In C. Maranto & K. Bruscia (Eds.) *Perspectives on Music Therapy Education and Training.* Philadelphia, PA: Temple University, Esther Boyer College of Music.

Bruscia, K. (1988a). Songs in Psychotherapy. Proceedings of the Fourteenth National Conference of the Australian Music Therapy Association, (pp. 1–4). Melbourne, Australia.

Bruscia, K. (1988b). Perspectives: Standards for Clinical Assessment in the Arts Therapies. *The Arts in Psychotherapy, 15 (1),* 5–10.

Bruscia, K. (1989). *Defining Music Therapy.* Gilsum NH: Barcelona Publishers.

Bruscia, K. (Ed.) (1991a). *Case Studies in Music Therapy.* Gilsum NH: Barcelona Publishers.

Bruscia, K. (1991b). Musical Origins: Developmental Foundations for Therapy. *Proceedings of the Eighteenth Annual Conference of the Canadian Association for Music Therapy* (pp. 2–10). Regina, Canada: Canadian Association for Music Therapy.

Bruscia, K. (1992). Visits from the Other Side: Healing Persons with AIDS though Guided Imagery and Music. In D. Campbell (Ed.), *Music and Miracles* (pp. 195–207). Wheaton IL: Quest Books.

Bruscia, K. (1995). Modes of Consciousness in Guided Imagery and Music (GIM): A Therapist's Experience of the Guiding Process. In C. Kenny (Ed.), *Listening, Playing, Creating: Essays on the Power of Sound* (pp. 163–197). Albany, NY: State University of New York.

Bruscia, K. (1996a). Authenticity Issues in Qualitative Research. In M. Langenberg, K. Aigen, & J. Frommer (Eds.), *Qualitative Music Therapy Research: Beginning Dialogues,*(pp. 81–108). Gilsum, NH: Barcelona Publishers.

Bruscia, K. (1996b). Daedalus and the Labyrinth: A Mythical Research Fantasy. In M. Langenberg, K. Aigen, & J. Frommer (Eds.), *Qualitative Music Therapy Research: Beginning Dialogues,*(pp. 205–212). Gilsum, NH: Barcelona Publishers.

Bruscia, K. (Ed.) 1998). *The Dynamics of Music Psychotherapy.* Gilsum NH: Barcelona Publishers.

Bruscia, K. (in press). Standards of Integrity for Qualitative Music Therapy Research. *Journal of Music Therapy.*

Bruscia, K., Hesser, B., & Boxill, E. (1981). Essential Competencies for the Practice of Music Therapy. *Music Therapy: Journal of the American Association for Music Therapy 1 (1),* 43–49.

Bruscia, K. & Maranto, C. (1985). The Projective Musical Stories of Child Molesters and Rapists. Paper presented at the first conference of the National Coalition of Arts Therapy Associations, November 5, 1985, New York City.

Bunt, L. (1994). *Music Therapy: An Art beyond Words.* New York: Routledge.

Burke, K. (1991). Music Therapy in Working Through a Pre-schooler's Grief. In K. Bruscia (Ed.), *Case Studies in Music Therapy* (pp. 127–136). Gilsum, NH: Barcelona Publishers.

Campbell, D. (1989). *The Roar of Silence: Healing Powers of Breath, Tone and Music.* Wheaton, IL: Quest Books.

Campbell, D. (1991). *Music: Physician for Times to Come.* Wheaton IL: Quest Books.

Canadian Association for Music Therapy (CAMT) (No date). *About Music Therapy.* Association pamphlet.

Carter, S. (1982). *Music Therapy for Handicapped Children: Mentally Retarded.* Washington, DC: National Association for Music Therapy.

Cassity, M. (1977). Nontraditional Guitar Techniques for the Educable and Trainable Mentally Retarded Residents in Music Therapy Activities. *Journal of Music Therapy, 14 (1),* 39–42.

Chesky, K. & Michel, D. (1991). The Music Vibration table (MVT): Developing a Technology and Conceptual Model for Pain Relief. *Music Therapy Perspectives 9(1),* 32–38.

Chetta, H. (1981). The Effect of Music and Desensitization on Preoperative Anxiety in Children. *Journal of Music Therapy, 18 (2),* 74–87.

Christenberry, E. (1979). The Use Music Therapy with Burn Patients. *Journal of Music Therapy, 16 (3),* 138–148.

Claeys, M., Miller, A., Dalloul-Rampersad, R., Kollar, M. (1989). The Role of Music and Music Therapy in the Rehabilitation of Traumatically Brain Injured Clients. *Music Therapy Perspectives, 6,* 71–77.

Clair, A. (1991). Music Therapy for a Severely Regressed Person with a Probable Diagnosis of Alzheimer's Disease. In K. Bruscia (Ed.), *Case Studies in Music Therapy* (pp. 571–580). Gilsum, NH: Barcelona Publishers.

Clark, M. (1987). The Institute for Music and Imagery Training Program for Guided Imagery and Music. In C. Maranto and K. Bruscia (Eds.) *Perspectives on Music Therapy Education and Training* (pp. 191–194). Philadelphia: Temple University, Esther Boyer College of Music.

Clark, M. (1991). Emergence of the Adult Self in Guided Imagery and Music (GIM) Therapy. In K. Bruscia (Ed.), *Case Studies in Music Therapy* (pp. 321–332). Gilsum, NH: Barcelona Publishers.

Clark-Schock, K., Turner, Y., & Bovee, T. (1988). A Multidisciplinary Psychiatric Assessment: The Introductory Group. *The Arts in Psychotherapy, 15 (1)*, 79–82.

Clynes, M. (1985). On Music and Healing. In R. Spintge & R. Droh, *Music in Medicine: 2nd International Symposium* (pp. 3–23). Basel, Switzerland: Editones "Roche."

Codding, P. (1982). *Music Therapy for Handicapped Children: Visually Impaired.* Washington, DC: National Association for Music Therapy.

Colon, R. (1984). Music Therapy Definition. In K. Bruscia (Ed.), *International Newsletter of Music Therapy* (Volume 2, pp. 15–16). New York: American Association for Music Therapy.

Colwell, C. (1994). Therapeutic Applications of Music in the Whole Language Kindergarten. *Journal of Music Therapy 31 (4)*, 238–247.

Couture, J., Severence, E., Kyler-Hutchinson, P. (1993). Cultural Sensitivity and the Therapeutic Process: The Use of Music to Help Accept Differences. Paper presented at the Joint North American Conference of Music Therapy, Toronto, Ontario (Abstract of Sessions, p. 149).

Darrow, A., & Cohen, N. (1991). The Effect of Programmed Pitch Practice and Private Instruction on the Vocal Reproduction Accuracy of Hearing-Impaired Children: Two Case Studies. In K. Bruscia (Ed.), *Case Studies in Music Therapy* (pp. 191–206). Gilsum, NH: Barcelona Publishers.

Darrow, A., Johnson, C., & Ollenberger, M. (1994). The Effect of Participation in an Intergenerational Choir on Teens' and Older Persons' Cross-Age Attitudes. *Journal of Music Therapy 31 (2)*, 119–134. ˜

DeBacker, J., & Peuskens, J. (1993). Music Therapy in Belgium. In C. Maranto (Ed.), *Music Therapy: International Perspectives* (pp. 89–102). Pipersville PA: Jeffrey Books.

Decuir, A. (1991). Trends in Music and Family Therapy. *Arts in Psychotherapy, 18 (3)*, 195–200.

DelCampo, P. (1993). Music Therapy in Spain (Part Two). In C. Maranto (Ed.), *Music Therapy: International Perspectives* (pp. 546–556). Pipersville PA: Jeffrey Books.

Diamond, J. (1981). *The Life Energy in Music. (Volume 1).* Valley Cottage, NY: Archaeus Press.

Diamond J. (1983). *The Life Energy in Music. (Volume 3).* Valley Cottage, NY: Archaeus Press.

Diaz de Chumaceiro, C. (1998a). Unconsciously Induced Song Recall: A Historical Perspective. In K. Bruscia (Ed.), *The Dynamics of Music Psychotherapy*, (pp. 335-364). Gilsum, NH: Barcelona Publishers

Diaz de Chumaceiro, C. (1998b). Consciously Induced Song Recall: Transference-Countertransference Implications. In K. Bruscia (Ed.), *The Dynamics of Music Psychotherapy*, (pp. 365-386). Gilsum, NH: Barcelona Publishers.

DiFranco, G., & Perilli, G. (1993). Music Therapy in Italy. In C. Maranto (Ed.), *Music Therapy: International Perspectives* (pp. 321–339). Pipersville PA: Jeffrey Books.

Dorow, L. (1975). Conditioning Music and Approval as New Reinforcers for Imitative Behavior with the Severely Retarded. *Journal of music therapy, 12 (1)*, 30–40.

Doyle, P. (1989). The Past, Present and Future: Like the Circle, It is all One. *Music Therapy Perspectives, 6*, 78–81.

Drury, N. (1985). *Music for Inner Space*. San Leandro CA: Prism Press.

Eagle, C. (1978). *Music Psychology Index*. Fort Worth, TX: Institute for Therapeutics Research.

Eagle, C. (1991). Steps to a Theory of Quantum Therapy. *Music Therapy Perspectives, 9*, 56–60.

Eagle, C. & Harsh, J. (1988). Elements of Pain and Music: The Aio Connection. *Music Therapy: Journal of the American Association for Music Therapy, 7(1)*, 15-27.

Educational Facilities Laboratories (1975). *Arts and the Handicapped: An Issue of Access*. New York: Author.

Edwards, E. (1981). *Making Music with the Hearing Impaired*. South Waterford, ME: Merriam Eddy.

Eidson, C. (1989). The Effect of Behavioral Music Therapy on the Generalization of Interpersonal Skills from Sessions to the Classroom by Emotionally Handicapped Middle School Students. *Journal of Music Therapy 26 (4)*, 206–221.

Eifert, G., Craill, L., Carey, E., & O'Connor, C. (1988). Affect Modification through Evaluative Conditioning with Music. *Behavioral Research Therapy, 26 (1)*, 1–10.

Elliott, B., et al (1982). *Guide to the Selection of Musical Instruments with Respect to Physical Ability and Disability*. Philadelphia, PA: Kardon Institute.

Ellis, A. (1981). The Use of Rational Humorous Songs in Psychotherapy. *Academy of Psychotherapists, 16 (4)*, 29–36.

Erdonmez, C. (1991). Rehabilitation of Piano Performance Skills Following a Left Cerebral Vascular Accident. In K. Bruscia (Ed.), *Case Studies in Music Therapy* (pp. 561–570). Gilsum, NH: Barcelona Publishers.

Fagen, T. (1982). Music Therapy in the Treatment of Anxiety and Fear in Terminal Pediatric Patients. *Music Therapy: Journal of the American Association for Music Therapy, 2 (1)*, 13–24.

Fischer, R. (1991). Original Song Drawings in the Treatment of a Developmentally Disabled, Autistic Adult. In K. Bruscia (Ed.), *Case Studies in Music Therapy* (pp. 359–372). Gilsum, NH: Barcelona Publishers.

Fleshman, B., & Fryear, J. (1981). *The Arts in Therapy*. Chicago: Nelson-Hall.

Forinash, M., & Robbins, C. (1991). A Time Paradigm: Time as a Multilevel Phenomenon in Music Therapy. *Music Therapy: Journal of the American Association for Music Therapy, 10 (1)*, 46–57).

Forinash, M. (1992). A Phenomenological Analysis of Nordoff-Robbins Approach to Music Therapy: The Lived Experience of Clinical Improvisation. *Music Therapy: Journal of the American Association for Music Therapy, 11 (1)*, 120–141.

Free, K., Tuerk, J., & Tinkleman, J. (1986). Expression of Transitional Relatedness in Art, Music, and Verbal Psychotherapies. *The Arts in Psychotherapy, 13 (3)*, 197–214.

Frego, R. (1995). Uniting the Generations with Music Programs. *Music Educators Journal 81(6)*, 17–19.

French Association for Music Therapy (FAMT). (1984). Music Therapy Definition. In K. Bruscia (Ed.), *International Newsletter of Music Therapy*. (Volume 2, p. 16). New York: American Association for Music Therapy.

Friedlander, L. (1994). Group Music Psychotherapy in an Inpatient Psychiatric Setting for Children: A Developmental Approach. *Music Therapy Perspectives, 12 (2)*, 92–103.

Froehlich, M. (1996). *Music Therapy with Hospitalized Children: A Creative Arts Child Life Approach.* Cherry Hill NJ: Jeffrey Books.

Gardner-Gordon, J. (1993). *The Healing Voice: Traditional and Contemporary Toning, Chanting and Singing*. Freedom CA: The Crossings Press.

Gardstrom, S. (1993). Partners: Intergenerational Music Therapy. *Music Therapy Perspectives, 11 (2)*, 66–67.

Garfield, L. (1987). *Sound Medicine: Healing with Music, Voice and Song*. Berkeley, CA: Celestial Arts.

Gaston, E. (1962). Commentary on Impressional and Expressional Music Therapists. *Bulletin of the National Association for Music Therapy, 11 (1)*, 1–3.

Gaston, E. (1968). Man and Music. In E. Gaston (Ed.), *Music in Therapy* (pp. 7–29). New York: MacMillan.

Giles, M., Cogan, D., & Cox, C. (1991). A Music and Art Program to Promote Emotional Health in Elementary School Children. *Journal of Music Therapy, 28 (3)*, 135–148.

Goldberg, F., Hoss, T., & Chesna, T. (1988). Music and Imagery as Psychotherapy with a Brain Damaged Patient: A Case Study. *Music Therapy Perspectives, 5*, 41–45.

Goldman, J. (1992). *Healing Sounds: The Power of Harmonics*. Rockport MA: Element, Inc.

Gomes, G., & Leite, T. (1993). Music Therapy in Portugal. In C. Maranto (Ed.), *Music Therapy: International Perspectives* (pp. 479–488). Pipersville PA: Jeffrey Books.

Graham, R. & Beers, A. (1980). *Teaching Music to the Exceptional Child*. Englewood Cliffs, NJ: Prentice Hall.

Gregoire, M., Hughes, J., Robbins, B., & Voorneveld, R. (1989). Music Therapy with the Gifted? A Trial Program. *Music Therapy Perspectives 7*, 23–27.

Guaraldi, G. (1984). Music Therapy Definition. In K. Bruscia (Ed.), *International Newsletter of Music Therapy* (Volume 2, p. 16). New York: American Association for Music Therapy.

Guba, E., & Lincoln, Y. (1994). Competing Paradigms in Qualitative Research. In N. Denzin and Y. Lincoln (Eds.), *Handbook of Qualitative Research* (pp. 105–117). Thousand Oaks CA: Sage Publications

Hadsell, N. (1974). A Sociological Theory and Approach to Music Therapy with Adult Psychiatric Patients. *Journal of Music Therapy, 11 (3)*, 113–124.

Hadsell, N. (1993). Levels of External Structure in Music Therapy. *Music Therapy Perspectives, 3*, 61–64).

Hahnemann University (1984). *Looking Ahead, Planning Together: The Creative Arts in Therapy as an Integral Part of Treatment for the 90's*. Philadelphia: Author.

Hall, C., & Lindzey, G. (1957). *Theories of Personality*. New York: John Wiley & Sons.

Halpern, S. (1978). *Tuning the Human Instrument*. Belmont, CA: Spectrum Research Institute.

Halpern, S. (1985). *Sound Health: The Music and Sounds that Make Us Whole*. San Francisco: Harper & Row Publishers.

Hamel, P. (1979). *Through Music to the Self*. Boulder, CO: Shambhala.

Hanser, S. (1984). Music Group Psychotherapy: An Evaluation Model. *Music Therapy Perspectives, 1 (4)*, 14–16.

Hanser, S. (1985). Music Therapy and Stress Reduction Research. *Journal of Music Therapy, 22 (4)*, 193–206.

Hanser, S. (1987). *Music Therapist's Handbook*. St. Louis: Warren H. Green.

Harris, C., Bradley, R., & Titus, S. (1992). A Comparison of the Effects of Hard Rock and Easy Listening on the Frequency of Observed Inappropriate Behaviors: Control of Environmental Antecedents in a Large Public Area. *Journal of Music Therapy 29 (1)*, 6–17.

Harner, M. (1982). *The Way of the Shaman*. New York: Bantam Books.

Heimlich, E. (1984). Metaphoric Use of Song Lyrics as Paraverbal Communication. *Child Psychiatry and Human Development, 14 (2)*, 67–75.

Henderson, H. (1991). Improvised Song Stories in the Treatment of a Thirteen Year-old Sexually Abused Girl from the Xhosa Tribe in South Africa. In K. Bruscia (Ed.), *Case Studies in Music Therapy* (pp. 207–218). Gilsum, NH: Barcelona Publishers.

Herman, F. (1991). The Boy that Nobody Wanted: Creative Experiences for a Boy with Severe Emotional Problems. In K. Bruscia (Ed.), *Case Studies in Music Therapy* (pp. 99–108). Gilsum, NH: Barcelona Publishers.

Herman, F. & Smith, J. (1988). *Accentuate the Positive: Expressive Arts for Children with Disabilities*. Toronto: Jimani Publications.

Hesser, B. (1985). Advanced Clinical Training in Music Therapy. *Music Therapy: Journal of the American Association for Music Therapy, 5 (1)*, 66–73.

Hesser, B. (1995). The Power of Sound and Music in Therapy and Healing. In C. Kenny (Ed.), *Listening, Playing, Creating: Essays on the Power of Sound.* (pp. 43–50). Albany, NY: State University of New York.

Hibben, J. (1991). Group Music Therapy with a Classroom of 6-8 Year-old Hyperactive Learning-disabled Children. In K. Bruscia (Ed.), *Case Studies in Music Therapy* (pp. 175–190). Gilsum, NH: Barcelona Publishers.

Hibben, J. (1992). Music Therapy in the Treatment of Families with Young Children. *Music Therapy: Journal of the American Association for Music Therapy,11 (1)*, 28–44.

Hongshi, M. (1988). Music Therapy in China. Paper presented at the annual conference of the National Association for Music Therapy. Atlanta, GA.

Houts, D. (1981). The Structured Use of Music in Pastoral Psychotherapy. *Journal of Pastoral Care, 35 (3)*, 194–203.

Jarvis, J. (1988). Guided Imagery and Music (GIM) as a Primary Psychotherapeutic Approach. *Music Therapy Perspectives, 5*, 69–72.

Jellison, J. (1983). Functional Value as Criterion for Selection and Prioritization of Nonmusic and Music Educational Objectives in Music Therapy. *Music Therapy Perspectives, 1 (2)*, 17–22.

Jondittir, V. (1993). Music Therapy in Iceland. In C. Maranto (Ed.), *Music Therapy: International Perspectives* (pp. 279–303). Pipersville PA: Jeffrey Books.

Kahn, H. (1983). *The Music of Life*. New Lebanon NY: Omega Press.

Kahn, H. (1991). Healing with Sound and Music. In D. Campbell (Ed.), *Music: Physician for Times to Come* (pp. 317–329). Wheaton, IL: Quest Books.

Katsh, S., & Merle-Fishman C. (1998). *The Music Within You*. Gilsum, NH: Barcelona Publishers.

Katz, S. (1993). The Peace Train Tour Souvenir Cassette (Audio-tape). Durban South Africa: Unity Productions.

Kenny, C. (1982). *The Mythic Artery: The Magic of Music Therapy*. Atascadero, CA: Ridgeview Publishing Co.

Kenny, C. (1985). Music: A Whole Systems Approach. *Music Therapy: Journal of the American Association for Music Therapy 5 (1)*, 3-11.

Kenny, C. (1988). A Song of Peace: Dare We to Dream? *Music Therapy: Journal of the American Association for Music Therapy 7 (1)*, 51–55.

Kenny, C. (1989). *The Field of Play: A Guide for the Theory and Practice of Music Therapy*. Atascadero CA: Ridgeview Publishing.

Kenny, C. (1991). The Use of Musical Space with an Adult in Psychotherapy. In K. Bruscia (Ed.), *Case Studies in Music Therapy* (pp. 333–346). Gilsum, NH: Barcelona Publishers.

Keyes, L. (1973). *Toning: The Creative Power of the Voice*. Marina del Rey, CA: DeVorss & Co.

Knill, P. (1994). Multiplicity as Tradition: Theories for Interdisciplinary Arts Therapies—An Overview. *The Arts in Psychotherapy, 21 (5)*, (pp. 319–328).

Kovach, A. (1985). Shamanism and Guided Imagery and Music: A Comparison. *Journal of Music Therapy, 22 (3)*, 154–167.

Kortegaard, H., & Pedersen, I. (1993). Music Therapy in Denmark, In C. Maranto (Ed.), *Music Therapy: International Perspectives* (pp. 197–209). Pipersville PA: Jeffrey Books.

Krout, R. (1983). *Teaching Basic Guitar Skills to Special Learners*. St. Louis: MMB Music.

Langdon, G., Pearson, J., Stastny, P., Thorning, H. (1989). The Integration of Music Therapy into a Treatment Approach in the Transition of Adult Psychiatric Patients from Institution to Community. *Music Therapy: Journal of the American Association for Music Therapy 8 (1)*, 92–107.

Langenberg, M., Aigen, K., & Frommer, J. (1996). *Qualitative Music Therapy Research: Beginning Dialogues*. Gilsum NH: Barcelona Publishers.

Lathom, W. (1980). *The Role of Music Therapy in the Education of Handicapped Children and Youth*. Washington, DC: National Association for Music Therapy.

Lecourt, E. (1991). Off-beat Music Therapy. In K. Bruscia (Ed.), *Case Studies in Music Therapy* (pp. 73–98). Gilsum, NH: Barcelona Publishers.

Lee, C. (1995). *Lonely Waters: Proceedings of the International Conference, "Music Therapy in Palliative Care."* Oxford England: Sobell House.

Lee, C. (1996). *Music at the Edge.* New York: Routledge.

Lehtonen, K. (1993a). Music Therapy in Finland. In C. Maranto (Ed.), *Music Therapy: International Perspectives* (pp. 211–220). Pipersville PA: Jeffrey Books.

Lehtonen, K. (1993b). Reflections on Music Therapy and Developmental Psychology. *Nordisk Tidsskrift for Musikkterapi, 2 (1),* 3–12.

Leonard, G. (1978). *The Silent Pulse.* New York: E. P. Dutton.

Levin, H., & Levin, G. (1998a). *Learning through Music.* Gilsum, NH: Barcelona Publishers.

Levin, H., & Levin, G. (1998b). *Learning through Songs.* Gilsum, NH: Barcelona Publishers.

Levinson, S., & Bruscia, K. (1983). Optacon Music-reading: A Curriculum for Teaching Blind Students. Unpublished manuscript.

Lewis, P. (1987). The Expressive Arts Therapies in the Choreography of Object Relations. *The Arts in Psychotherapy, 14 (4),* 321–332.

Lingerman, H. (1983). *The Healing Energies of Music.* Wheaton, IL: Theosophical Publishing House.

Loewy, J. (1997). *Music Therapy and Pediatric Pain.* Cherry Hill NJ: Jeffrey Books.

Loveszy, R. (1991). The Use of Latin Music, Puppetry, and Visualization in Reducing the Physical and Emotional Pain of a Child with Severe Burns. In K. Bruscia (Ed.), *Case Studies in Music Therapy* (pp. 153–162). Gilsum, NH: Barcelona Publishers.

Lord, W. (1971). Communication of Activity Therapy Rationale. *Journal of Music Therapy, 8 (1),* 68–71.

Madsen, C. (1981). *Music Therapy: A Behavioral Guide for the Mentally Retarded.* Washington, DC: National Association for Music Therapy.

Maranto, C. (1992a). A Comprehensive Definition of Music Therapy within an Integrative Model for Music Medicine. In R. Spintge & R. Droh (Eds.), *Music Medicine* (pp. 19–29). St. Louis MO: MMB Music.

Maranto, C. (1992b). Music Therapy in the Treatment of Performance Anxiety in Musicians. In R. Spintge & R. Droh (Eds.), *Music Medicine* (pp. 273–283). St. Louis MO: MMB Music.

Maranto, C. (1993). *Music Therapy: International Perspectives.* Pipersville PA: Jeffrey Books.

Maranto, C. (1995). A Cognitive Model of Music in Medicine. In R. Pratt & R. Sptinge (Eds.), *Music Medicine* (pp. 327–332). St. Louis, MO: MMB Music.

Maranto, C. (1996). Research in Music and Medicine: The State of the Art. In M. Froehlich (Ed.), *Music Therapy with Hospitalized Children* (pp. 39–66). Cherry Hill, NJ: Jeffrey Books.

Martin, J. (1991). Music Therapy at the End of a Life. In K. Bruscia (Ed.), *Case Studies in Music Therapy* (pp. 617–632). Gilsum, NH: Barcelona Publishers.

May, E. (Ed.) (1983). *Musics of Many Cultures: An Introduction.* Berkeley: University of California Press.

May, R. (1975). *The Courage to Create.* New York: W. W. Norton.

McClellan, R. (1988). *The Healing Forces of Music: History, Theory and Practice.* Warwick, NY: Amity House.

McDonnell, L. (1984). Music Therapy with Trauma Patients and their Families on a Pediatric Service. *Music Therapy: Journal of the American Association for Music Therapy, 4 (1)*, 55–63.

McIntosh, G., Thaut, M., & Rice, R. (1994). Rhythmic Auditory Stimulation as an Entrainment and Therapy Technique: Effects on Gait of Stroke and Parkinson's Patients. In R. Pratt and R. Spintge (Eds.), *Music Medicine* (Volume 2, pp. 145–152). St. Louis, MO: MMB Music.

McMaster, N. (1991). Reclaiming a Positive Identity: Music Therapy in the Aftermath of a Stroke. In K. Bruscia (Ed.), *Case Studies in Music Therapy* (pp. 547–560). Gilsum, NH: Barcelona Publishers.

McNiff, S. (1981). *The Arts and Psychotherapy.* Springfield, IL: Charles C Thomas.

McNiff, S. (1988). The Shaman Within. *The Arts in Psychotherapy, 15 (4)*, 285–291.

Merritt, S. (1996). *Mind, Music and Imagery: Unlocking the Treasures of Your Mind.* Santa Rosa CA: Aslan Publishing.

Mid-Atlantic Music Therapy Region (1988). *Music Therapy for Mental Health.* (Brochure). Washington, DC: National Association for Music Therapy, Inc.

Meyer, L. (1958). *Emotion and Meaning in Music.* Chicago: The University of Chicago Press.

Miller, L., & Schyb, M. (1989). Facilitation and Interference by Background Music. *Journal of Music Therapy, 26 (1)*, 42–54.

Mills, E., & Murphy, T. (Eds.) (1973). *The Suzuki Concept: An Introduction to a Successful Method for Early Music Education.* Berkeley: Diablo Press.

Monti, R. (1985). Music Therapy in a Therapeutic Nursery. *Music Therapy: Journal of the American Association for Music Therapy, 5 (1)*, 22–27.

Moreno, J. (1980). Musical Psychodrama: A New Direction in Music Therapy. *Journal of Music Therapy, 17 (1)*, 34–49.

Moreno, J. (1988). The Music Therapist: Creative Arts Therapist and Contemporary Shaman. *The Arts in Psychotherapy, 15 (4)*, 271–280.

Moreno, J. (1989). The Paiste Sound Creation Gongs in Music Therapy. *Music Therapy Perspectives, 7*, 77–80.

Munro, S. (1984). *Music Therapy in Palliative/hospice Care*. St. Louis, MO: MMB.

Munro, S., & Mount, B. (1978). Music Therapy in Palliative Care. *Canadian Medical Association Journal, 119*, 1029–1034.

Murphy, M. (1983). Music Therapy: A Self-help Group Experience for Substance Abuse Patients. *Music Therapy: Journal of the American Association for Music Therapy, 3 (1)*, 52–62.

Murphy, M. (1991). Group Music Therapy in Acute Psychiatric Care: The Treatment of a Depressed Woman Following Neurological Trauma. In K. Bruscia (Ed.), *Case Studies in Music Therapy* (pp. 465–478). Gilsum, NH: Barcelona Publishers.

Naitove, C. (1980). Creative Arts Therapists: Jack of All Trades or Master of One? *The Arts in Psychotherapy, 7 (4)*, 253–259.

Naitove, C. (1984). In Pursuit of Objectivity: The Development of a Multi-modal Evaluation Instrument. *The Arts in Psychotherapy, 11 (4)*, 249–259.

Natanson, T. (1984). Music Therapy Definition. In K. Bruscia (Ed.), *International Newsletter of Music Therapy* (Volume 2, p. 17). New York: American Association for Music Therapy.

National Association for Music Therapy (NAMT) (1960). A Career in Music Therapy (Pamphlet). Washington, DC: Author.

National Association for Music Therapy (NAMT) (1980). A Career in Music Therapy (Pamphlet). Washington, DC: Author.

National Association for Music Therapy (NAMT) (1983). Standards of Clinical Practice. *Music Therapy Perspectives, 1 (2)*, 13–16.

National Coalition of Arts Therapy Associations (1985). Association pamphlet. Washington, DC: Author.

New Zealand Society for Music Therapy. (1984). Music Therapy Definition. In K. Bruscia (Ed.), *International Newsletter of Music Therapy* (Volume 2, p. 16). New York: American Association for Music Therapy.

Nichols-Rothe, P. (1995). Singing Practices and States of Consciousness. In C. Kenny (Ed.), *Listening, Playing, Creating: Essays on the Power of Sound.* (pp. 151–158). Albany, NY: State University of New York.

Nishihata, H. (1993),. Music Therapy in Japan. In C. Maranto (Ed.), *Music Therapy: International Perspectives* (pp. 341–353). Pipersville PA: Jeffrey Books.

Nocera, S. (1979). *Reaching the Special Learner through Music.* Morristown, NJ: Silver-Burdett.

Nolan, P. (1983). Insight Therapy: Guided Imagery and Music in a Forensic Psychiatric Setting. *Music Therapy: Journal of the American Association for Music Therapy, 3 (1)*, 29–42.

Nolan, P. (1991). Group Improvisation Therapy for a Resistant Woman with Bipolar Disorder. In K. Bruscia (Ed.), *Case Studies in Music Therapy* (pp. 451–464). Gilsum, NH: Barcelona Publishers.

Nolan, P. (1992). Music Therapy with Bone Marrow Transplant Patients: Reaching Beyond the Symptoms. In R. Spintge & R. Droh (Eds.), *Music Medicine* (pp. 209–212). St. Louis, MO: MMB Music.

Nordoff, P., & Robbins, C. (1971). *Therapy in Music for Handicapped Children.* London: Gollancz.

Nordoff, P., & Robbins, C. (1977). *Creative Music Therapy.* New York: John Day.

Nordoff, P., & Robbins, C. (1982). *Music Therapy in Special Education* (Second edition). St. Louis, MO: MMB Music.

Nowicki, A., & Trevisan, L. (1978). Beyond the Sound: A Technical and Philosophical Approach to Music Therapy. Porterville, CA: Authors.

Odell, H. (1988). A Music Therapy Approach in Mental Health. *Psychology of Music, 16 (1)*, 52–61.

Oldfield, A. (1991). Preverbal Communication through Music to Overcome a Child's Language Disorder. In K. Bruscia (Ed.), *Case Studies in Music Therapy* (pp. 163–174). Gilsum, NH: Barcelona Publishers.

Oldfield, A. (1993). Music Therapy with Families. In M. Heal and T. Wigram (Eds.), *Music Therapy in Health and Education* (pp. 46–54). London: Jessica Kingsley Publishers.

O'Neill, C. (1995). Music Therapy as a Supportive Intervention for Professional Care Givers. In C. Lee (Ed.), *Lonely Waters: Proceedings of the International Conference on Music Therapy in Palliative Care, Oxford 1994* (pp. 23–30). Oxford, England: Sobell House.

Orff, G. (1974). *The Orff Music Therapy.* (English translation by Margaret Murray). New York: Schott Music Corporation.

Ostwald, P. (1968). The Music Lesson. In E. Gaston (Ed.), *Music in Therapy* (p. 317–325). New York: MacMillan Publishing.

Ostrander, S., & Schroeder, L. (1979). *Superlearning.* New York: Dell.

Paul, D. (1982). *Music Therapy for Handicapped Children: Emotionally Disturbed.* Washington, DC: National Association for Music Therapy.

Peters, J. S. (1987). *Music Therapy: An Introduction.* Springfield, IL: Charles C Thomas.

Pickett, E. (1991). Guided Imagery and Music (GIM) with a Dually Diagnosed Woman Having Multiple Addictions. In K. Bruscia (Ed.), *Case Studies in Music Therapy* (pp. 497–512). Gilsum, NH: Barcelona Publishers.

Plach, T. (1980). *The Creative Use of Music in Group Therapy*. Springfield, IL: Charles C Thomas Publishers.

Polit, V. (1993). Music Therapy in Mexico. In C. Maranto (Ed.), *Music Therapy: International Perspectives* (pp. 365–383). Pipersville PA: Jeffrey Books.

Priestley, M. (1975). Music Therapy in Action. London: Constable Press.

Priestley, M. (1980). The Herdecke Analytical Music Therapy Lectures (English translation from German). Stuttgart, West Germany: Klett-Cotta.

Priestley, M. (1994). *Essays on Analytical Music Therapy*. Gilsum NH: Barcelona Publishers.

Prinou, L. (1993). Music Therapy in Greece. In C. Maranto (Ed.), *Music Therapy: International Perspectives* (pp. 239–251). Pipersville PA: Jeffrey Books.

Pulliam, J., Somerville, P., Prebluda, J., & Warja-Danielsson, M. (1988). Three Heads are Better than One: The Expressive Arts Group Assessment. *The Arts in Psychotherapy, 15 (1)*, 71–78.

Purvis, J. & Samet, S. (1976). *Music in Developmental Therapy*. Baltimore: University Park Press.

Radocy, R., & Boyle, J. (1979). *Psychological Foundations of Musical Behavior*. Springfield, IL: Charles C Thomas.

Reber, A. S. (1985). *The Penguin Dictionary of Psychology*. New York: Viking Press.

Reimer, B. (1970). *A Philosophy of Music Education*. Englewood Cliffs, NJ: Prentice-Hall.

Rider, M. (1987). Music Therapy: Therapy for Debilitated Musicians. *Music Therapy Perspectives, 4*, 40–43.

Robbins, A. (1980). *Expressive Therapy: A Creative Arts Approach to Depth-oriented Treatment*. New York: Human Science Press.

Robbins, C. & Robbins, C. (1980). *Music for the Hearing Impaired and Other Special Groups*. St. Louis, MO: MMB Music.

Robbins, C., & Robbins, C. (1991). Self-communications in Creative Music Therapy. In K. Bruscia (Ed.), *Case Studies in Music Therapy* (pp. 55–72). Gilsum, NH: Barcelona Publishers.

Robbins, C. (1996, April). Creative Music Therapy and Psychotherapy in Music. *International Association of Nordoff-Robbins Music Therapists Newsletter* (pp. 13–15).

Robbins, C., & Forinash, M. (1991). A Time Paradigm: Time as a Multilayered Phenomenon in Music Therapy. *Music Therapy: Journal of the American Association for Music Therapy10 (1)*, 46–57.

Routhier, C. (1988). Statement: In a Song of Solidarity. *Music Therapy: Journal of the American Association for Music Therapy 7 (1),* 73–75.

Rudenberg, M. (1982). *Music Therapy for Handicapped Children: Orthopedically Handicapped.* Washington, DC: National Association for Music Therapy.

Rhudhyar, D. (1982). *The Magic of Tone and the Art of Music.* Boulder, CO: Shambhala Publications.

Rolla, G. (1993). *Your Inner Music: Creative Analysis and Music Memory.* Wilmette IL: Chiron Publications.

Rugenstein (1996). Wilber's Spectrum Model of Transpersonal Psychology and its Application to Music Therapy. *Music Therapy: Journal of the American Association for Music Therapy, 14 (1),* 9–28.

Ruud, E. (1980). *Music Therapy and its Relationship to Current Treatment Theories.* St. Louis, MO: MMB Music.

Ruud, E. (1988). Music Therapy: Health Profession or Cultural Movement? *Music Therapy: Journal of the American Association for Music Therapy 7 (1),* 34–37.

Ruud, E. (1998). *Music Therapy: Improvisation, Communication and Culture.* Gilsum NH: Barcelona Publishers.

Salas, J. (1990). Aesthetic Experience in Music Therapy. *Music Therapy: Journal of the American Association for Music Therapy 9 (1),* 1–15.

Salas, J., & Gonzalez, D. (1991). Like Singing with a Bird: Improvisational Music Therapy with a Blind Four Year-old. In K. Bruscia (Ed.), *Case Studies in Music Therapy* (pp. 17–28). Gilsum, NH: Barcelona Publishers.

Saperston, B. (1980). Music Listening versus Juice as a Reinforcement for Learning in Profoundly Mentally Retarded Individuals. *Journal of Music Therapy, 17 (4),* 174–184.

Scheiby, B. (1991). Mia's Fourteenth—The Symphony of Fate: Psychodynamic Improvisation Therapy with a Music Therapy Student in Training. In K. Bruscia (Ed.), *Case Studies in Music Therapy* (pp. 271–290). Gilsum, NH: Barcelona Publishers.

Schmolz, A. (1984). Music Therapy Definition. In K. Bruscia (Ed.), *International Newsletter of Music Therap* (Volume 2, p. 17). New York: American Association for Music Therapy.

Schomer, M. (1973). A Perceptual Development Program for the Music Therapist. *Journal of Music Therapy, 20 (2),* 95–109.

Schulberg, C. (1981). *The Music Therapy Sourcebook.* New York: Human Sciences Press.

Schwankovsky, L., & Guthrie, P. (1982). *Music Therapy for Handicapped Children: Other Health Impaired.* Washington, DC: National Association for Music Therapy.

Sears, W. (1968). Processes in Music Therapy. In E. Gaston (Ed.), *Music in Therapy* (pp. 30–46). New York: MacMillan.

Sekeles, C. (1985). Music Therapy Definition. In K. Bruscia (Ed.), *International Newsletter of Music Therapy*. (Volume 3, p. 10). Springfield NJ: American Association for Music Therapy.

Shields, A., & Robbins, A. (1980). Music in Expressive Therapy. In A. Robbins (Ed.), *Expressive Therapy: A Creative Arts Approach to Depth-oriented Treatment* (pp. 239–257). New York: Human Sciences Press.

Shoemark, H. (1991). The Use of Piano Improvisation in Developing Interaction and Participation in a Blind Boy with Behavioral Disturbances. In K. Bruscia (Ed.), *Case Studies in Music Therapy* (pp. 29–38). Gilsum, NH: Barcelona Publishers.

Skille, O. (1983). The Music Bath: Possible Use as an Anxiolytic. In R. Droh & R. Spintge (Eds.), *Angst, Schmerz, Musik in der Anästhesie* (pp. 11–14). Basel, Switzerland: Editiones "Roches."

Skille, O. (1989). VibroAcoustic Therapy. *Music Therapy: Journal of the American Association for Music Therapy 8 (1)*, 61–77.

Skille, O. & Wigram, T. (1995). The Effects of Music, Vocalisation and Vibration on Brain and Muscle Tissue: Studies in Vibroacoustic Therapy. In T. Wigram, B. Saperston, & R. West (Eds.), *The Art and Science of Music Therapy: A Handbook.* (pp. 23–57). Chur, Switzerland, Harwood Academic Publishers.

Slivka, H., & Magill, L. (1986). The Conjoint Use of Social Work and Music Therapy in Working with Children of Cancer Patients. *Music Therapy: Journal of the American Association for Music Therapy 6A (1)*, 30–40.

Smeijsters, H. (1993). Music Therapy and Psychotherapy. *The Arts in Psychotherapy, 10 (3)*, 223–230.

Smeijsters, H. (1997). *Multiple Perspectives: A Guide to Qualitative Research in Music Therapy*. Gilsum, NH: Barcelona Publishers.

Smith, G. (1991). The Song-writing Process: A Woman's Struggle against Depression and Suicide. In K. Bruscia (Ed.), *Case Studies in Music Therapy* (pp. 479–496). Gilsum, NH: Barcelona Publishers.

Somasonics, Inc. (No date). Somatron. (Pamphlet). Tampa FL: Author.

Sommer, D. T. (1961). Music Therapy without Music. *Bulletin of the National Association for Music Therapy, 10 (2)*, 3.

South African Institute of Music Therapy. (1984). Music Therapy Definition. In K. Bruscia (Ed.), *International Newsletter of Music Therapy* (Volume 2, p. 18). New York: American Association for Music Therapy.

Southeastern Pennsylvania Music Therapy Supervisors. (No date). Manual on Standards of Practice for Music Therapy. Unpublished manuscript.

Standley, J. (1986). Music Research in Medical/dental Treatment: Meta-analysis and Clinical Applications. *Journal of Music Therapy, 23 (2)*, 56–122.

Standley, J. (1991). *Music Techniques in Therapy, Counseling, and Special Education*. St. Louis, MO: MMB Music.

Standley, J. (1995). Music as a Therapeutic Intervention in Medical and Dental Treatment: Research and Clinical Applications. In T. Wigram, B. Saperston, & R. West (Eds.), *The Art and Science of Music Therapy: A Handbook*. (pp. 3–22). Chur, Switzerland, Harwood Academic Publishers.

Standley, J., & Hughes, J. (1997). Evaluation of an Early Intervention Music Curriculum for Enhancing Prereading/writing skills. *Music Therapy Perspectives, 15*, 79–85.

Steele, A. (1977). The Application of Behavioral Research Techniques to Community Music Therapy. *Journal of Music Therapy, 14 (3)*, 102–115.

Steele, A., Vaughan, M., & Dolan, C. (1976) The School Support Program: Music Therapy for Adjustment Problems in Elementary Schools. *Journal of Music Therapy, 13 (2)*, 87–100.

Stephens, G. (1983). The Use of Improvisation for Developing Relatedness in the Adult Client. *Music Therapy: Journal of the American Association for Music Therapy, 3 (1)*, 29–42.

Stephens, G. (1984). Group Supervision in Music Therapy. *Music Therapy: Journal of the American Association for Music Therapy, 4 (1)*, 29–38.

Stephens, G. (1987). The Experiential Music Therapy Group as a Method of Training and Supervision. In C. Maranto and K. Bruscia (Eds.) *Perspectives on Music Therapy Education and Training* (pp. 169–176). Philadelphia: Temple University, Esther Boyer College of Music.

Stige, B. (1993). Music Therapy as Cultural Engagement. Paper presented at the Seventh World Congress of Music Therapy, Vitoria-Gasteiz, Spain.

Summer, L. (1988). *Guided Imagery and Music in the Institutional Setting*. St. Louis, MO: MMB Music.

Summer, L. (1995). Melding Musical and Psychological Processes: The Therapeutic Musical Space. *Journal of the Association for Music and Imagery, 4*, 37–46.

Summer, L. (1996). *Music, The New Age Elixir*. Amherst NY: Prometheus Books.

Swedish Association for Music Therapy (SAMT). (1984). Music Therapy Definition. In K. Bruscia (Ed.), *International Newsletter of Music Therapy*. (Volume 2, p. 17). New York: American Association for Music Therapy.

Tomatis, A. (1996). *The Ear and Language*. Norval, Ontario: Moulin Publishing Company.

Tyson, F. (1981). *Psychiatric Music Therapy: Origins and Development*. New York: Creative Arts Rehabilitation Center.

Uruguayan Association for Music Therapy (UAMT). (1984). Music Therapy Definition. In K. Bruscia (Ed.), *International Newsletter of Music Therapy.* (Volume 2, p. 18). New York: American Association for Music Therapy.

Ventre, M., (1994). Healing the Wounds of Childhood Abuse: A Guided Imagery and Music Case Study. *Music Therapy Perspectives, 12(2)*, 98–103.

Warja, M. (1994). Sounds of Music through the Spiraling Path of Individuation: A Jungian Approach to Music Psychotherapy. *Music Therapy Perspectives, 12 (2)*, 75–83.

Watson, A., & Drury, N. (1987). *Healing Music: The Harmonic Path to Inner Wholeness.* Garden City Park, NY: Avery Publishing Group Inc.

Webster's New Collegiate Dictionary (1974). Springfield, MA: G. & C. Merriam Company.

West, T. (1994). Psychological Issues in Hospice Music Therapy. *Music Therapy Perspectives, 12*, 117–124.

Wheeler, B. (1981). The Relationship between Music Therapy and Theories of Psychotherapy. *Music Therapy: Journal of the American Association for Music Therapy, 1 (1)*, 9–16.

Wheeler, B. (1983). A Psychotherapeutic Classification of Music Therapy Practices. *Music Therapy Perspectives, 1 (2)*, 8–12.

Wheeler, B. (1995). *Music Therapy Research: Quantitative and Qualitative Perspectives.* Gilsum NH: Barcelona Publishers.

Whittall, J. (1991). Songs in Palliative Care: A Spouse's Last Gift. In K. Bruscia (Ed.), *Case Studies in Music Therapy* (pp. 603–610). Gilsum, NH: Barcelona Publishers.

Wigram, T. (1991). Music Therapy for a Girl with Rett's Syndrome: Balancing Structure and Freedom. In K. Bruscia (Ed.), *Case Studies in Music Therapy* (pp. 39–54). Gilsum, NH: Barcelona Publishers.

Wigram, T., & Dileo, C. (1997). *Music Vibration.* Cherry Hill NJ: Jeffrey Books.

Wilber, K. (1995). *Sex, Ecology, Spirituality.* Boston: Shambhala.

Wilber, K. (1996). *A Brief History of Everything.* Boston: Shambhala.

Winn, W., Crowe, B., & Moreno, J. (1989). Shamanism and Music Therapy: Ancient Healing Techniques in Modern Practice. *Music Therapy Perspectives, 7 (1)*, 67–71.

Winnicott, D. (1953). Transitional Objects and Transitional Phenomena. *International Journal of Psychoanalysis, 34*, 89–97.

Winslow, G. ((1986). Music Therapy in the Treatment of Anxiety in Hospitalized High-risk Mothers. *Music Therapy Perspectives, 3*, 29–33.

Witt, A. & Steele, A. (1984). Music Therapy for Infant and Parent: A Case Example. *Music Therapy Perspectives, 1 (4)*, 17–19.

Wolberg, L. R. (1967). *The Technique of Psychotherapy* (Part One). New York: Grune & Stratton.

Wolfe, D. (1980). The Effect of Automated Interrupted Music on Head Posturing of Cerebral Palsied Individuals. *Journal of Music Therapy, 17 (4),* 184–207.

Wolfe, D. (1982). The Effect of Interrupted and Continuous Music on Bodily Movement and Task Performance of Third Grade Students. *Journal of Music Therapy, 19 (2),* 74–86.

Wrangsjo, B. (1994). Psychoanalysis and Guided Imagery and Music: A Comparison. *Journal of the Association for Music and Imagery, 3,* 35–48.

Yamamatsu, T. (1984). Music Therapy Definition. In K. Bruscia (Ed.), *International Newsletter of Music Therapy* (Volume 2, p. 15). New York: American Association for Music Therapy.

Zinker, J. (1978). *Creative Process in Gestalt Therapy.* New York: Vintage Books.

Zwerling, I. (1984). Friday Morning Panel Discussion. In Hahnemann University, *Looking Ahead, Planning Together: The Creative arts in Therapy as an Integral part of Treatment for the 90's* (p. 15–54). Philadelphia: Hahnemann University.

OTHER BOOKS
BY
BARCELONA PUBLISHERS

Case Studies in Music Therapy. Edited by Kenneth Bruscia. Authors from around the globe present 42 case histories, each describing the process of music therapy with a broad spectrum of clients. ($40)

Essays on Analytical Music Therapy by Mary Priestley. A collection of the author's major writings on a psychodynamic approach to improvisational music therapy that she pioneered in England. ($30)

The Miracle of Music Therapy by Edith Hillman Boxill. The story of the author's life and work, with case studies and personal reminiscences—all pointing to her "Tao" as a music therapist. ($22)

The Music Within You by Shelly Katsh and Carol Merle-Fishman. In this second and expanded edition, the authors examine the natural and vital role that music plays in everyone's life, offering myriad ways for releasing the innate musical powers in each of us. ($28)

Music Therapy: Group Vignettes by Ronald Borczon. An experienced music therapist presents his approach to group work through transcripts of actual sessions along with frank discussions of his thoughts and feelings while leading each group. ($24)

The Dynamics of Music Psychotherapy. Edited by Kenneth Bruscia. In-depth analyses of transference and countertransference phenomena as manifested in various clinical approaches to improvisation, songs, and music imagery. ($45)

Snow White: A Practical Guide to Child-Centered Musical Theatre by Patricia Rickard-Lauri, Harriet Groeschel, Carol Robbins, Clive Robbins, Michelle Ritholz and Alan Turry. Designed to introduce children to the joys of creating musical theatre, this guide provides teachers and therapists with all the materials needed: the story with color illustrations, a play version, comprehensive production notes, and a complete musical score with CD. ($68)

Learning Through Music by Herbert and Gail Levin. Forty-two music activities for teachers and therapists to use with children of various ages, abilities and needs at the primary level. ($28)

Learning Through Songs by Herbert and Gail Levin. Sixteen easy-to-learn songs to help children develop educational skills and concepts at the primary level. ($16)

Paths of Development in Nordoff-Robbins Music Therapy by Kenneth Aigen. Eight case studies are presented, demonstrating the clinical work of Paul Nordoff and Clive Robbins and outlining the principles of Creative Music Therapy. Two CDs included. ($55).

Healing Heritage: Paul Nordoff Exploring the Tonal Language of Music. Edited by Clive Robbins and Carol Robbins. Complete transcripts of the famous lectures by Paul Nordoff, in which the late composer-pianist examines the clinical implications of each element of music in Creative Music Therapy. ($30)

Music Therapy: Improvisation, Communication & Culture by Even Ruud. An in-depth examination of fundamental questions about the nature of music therapy and its relation to quality of life. ($26)

Music Therapy Research: Quantitative & Qualitative Perspectives. Edited by Barbara L. Wheeler. The first and most comprehensive textbook on music therapy research, edited and written by eminent scholars in the field. Various quantitative and qualitative paradigms are presented with numerous examples from the literature. ($45)

Qualitative Music Therapy Research: Beginning Dialogues. Edited by Mechtild Langenberg, Kenneth Aigen and Jorg Frommer. A collection of monologues and dialogues by scholars from around the world, each on a quest to develop a qualitative research paradigm for music therapy. ($25)

Multiple Perspectives: A Guide to Qualitative Music Therapy Research by Henk Smeijsters. A survey of qualitative research paradigms used by music therapists in Europe and the USA, with insightful and sensitive commentary by the author. ($30)

Music for the Imagination. Ten CDs specially designed for use in Guided Imagery and Music by trained therapists. ($250)